ANDRÉ GIDE

JEAN HYTIER was born in Paris in 1899. While still a *lycéen,* he published his first collection of verse in 1916. After eighteen months of military service in the Rhineland and Alsace, he took his *license ès lettres,* started an avant-garde magazine that advocated a contemporary classicism, published a second volume of poems, his two doctoral theses (1923), a study of the novel (*les Romans de l'Individu*), an edition of Pascal in five volumes, and taught philosophy until 1928, when he was offered a position as Professor of French Literature at the University of Teheran. He remained there until 1937, when the French government appointed him to the Faculty of Letters in Algiers. Mobilized twice during World War II, he combined with his military service his professorship, several positions with the Service Général de l'Information in Algeria, and the Direction of Fine Arts in the Provisional Government. From 1945 to 1947 he directed the Service des Lettres in the Ministry of National Education in Paris, sat on many committees and was a member of the French Delegation to the General Assembly of UNESCO. Since 1947 he has taught French literature at the graduate school of Columbia University. He was made Chevalier of the Legion of Honor in 1945, Officer in 1959.

Jean Hytier is known for his works of literary criticism and aesthetics. He has edited the definitive edition of the works of Paul Valéry for the Bibliothèque de la Pléiade. His *The Poetics of Valéry,* for which he was made Laureate of the Académie Française, received the Académie's Le Métais-Larivière Prize in 1953.

Jean Hytier

ANDRÉ GIDE

Translated by Richard Howard

The aesthetic point of view is
the only sound one to take in
discussing my work.

ANDRÉ GIDE

FREDERICK UNGAR PUBLISHING CO.
NEW YORK

Copyright © 1962 by Jean Hytier

Republished 1967 by arrangement with
Doubleday & Company, Inc.

Printed in the United States of America

Library of Congress Catalog Card Number: 62-10462

CONTENTS

1. Lyrical Prose (i)   7
2. Lyrical Prose (ii)   35
3. Ironic Works (i. The *Soties*)   67
4. Ironic Works (ii. *les Caves du Vatican*)   91
5. *Récits*   120
6. Plays   148
7. *Les Faux Monnayeurs* and the Art of the
   Novel (i)   180
8. *Les Faux Monnayeurs* and the Art of the
   Novel (ii)   206

The pages that follow are the text of eight public lectures given at the Faculté des Lettres of the University of Algiers, from February to May, 1938.

1. Lyrical Prose (i)

As epigraph for the following chapters, I have taken a sentence from the author to whom they are devoted. André Gide, dissatisfied with the studies of his work by even such dedicated disciples of his art as the sensitive Jacques Rivière, wrote in his *Journal* for April 25, 1918: "The aesthetic point of view is the only sound one to take in discussing my work." I should gladly apply this formula to the study of all literature and, with the slightest encouragement, even make it the basis of all criticism.

In any case, an attempt to speak impartially of a great contemporary writer would seem impossible if I were not first to forswear discussing his person and his life. We are so accustomed to the biographical method *à la* Sainte-Beuve that we find it difficult to separate the author from the work, and so eagerly do we turn toward the author that we no longer notice it is the work that is turned toward us. A great creative work must have its own life apart from its creator's, and if we admire it, it must be for reasons independent of our psychological curiosity or of our weakness for hypothetically reconstructing the circumstances in which it was produced. It is such motives for valuing the work of André Gide that I wish to elucidate here. But things have reached a point where one seems to advance a paradox when one claims to study a work for itself, so completely has the study of literature become a fief of history. I could, like others, collect a series of anecdotes about the author of *Si le Grain ne meurt* . . . and deal with Gide as indiscreetly as he has dealt with himself; but I have not construed his example, motivated by reasons more serious than mine would be, as an authorization. Let us abandon to scholars of the future the task of explaining what, in Gide, *is not* his work, or at least not its beauty: having classified the documents time has not destroyed, and criticized the testimony the author is no longer with us to deny, they will draw a portrait of Gide after their fashion and trace a graph of his destiny which will astonish only the poet's last survivors. Is this not what we often call making literary history?

Since we intend to make a study in applied aesthetics of André Gide's work, it is worth pointing out that aesthetic criticism is not, as one sometimes supposes, the realm of subjective impressionism. It has its methods and its language. It also has its independence—and that is why I ask the reader not to be startled if he discovers no mention of either chronology or development, of *milieux* or movements, or of anything that smacks of personal history. It is only the separation of realms that may permit, on one side as on the other, a real advance in the two chief techniques at our disposal for studying works of art.

Works of literature are divided into several groups, according to the nature of the genre to which they belong. I shall therefore distinguish in Gide's production the lyric works from the ironic works (which form the series of *soties*, or satirical farces), the narrative works

8

to which Gide has refused the title of novels, reserving for them the name *récits*, or tales, the dramatic works and, lastly, the single novel Gide has composed. I shall reserve for a further study all his activity in the realm of criticism in the largest sense of the term (literary, artistic, moral, social), and particularly what is perhaps Gide's most important work: André Gide himself; for some writers, the creation of their eternal countenance, or at least of their countenance *sub specie aeternitatis,* constitutes their decisive work, and its study has virtually nothing to do with their inner lives, insofar as we may know them, but relates to the ideal personality they have chosen to manifest, and therefore constitutes a new chapter of aesthetics which I propose to call the aesthetics of personality.

André Gide's lyrical works, which are the object of our first study, present themselves in various, even somewhat heterogeneous guises. We sense that, for Gide, lyricism is not linked to a particular form of expression. If there is an entire range, and an extremely important one, of his work from which poetry is not only absent but even excluded, it nonetheless appears in strong doses in many works where it has no avowed purpose—for instance, in the confessions or memoirs of *Si le Grain ne meurt* . . . or in certain pages of the *Journal;* it affects certain works where it does not form the essential design, but to which it adds an aureole, as in the *récit l'Immoraliste,* or a fringe, as in the drama of *le Roi Candaule.* But even in the books where poetry flowers explicitly, it occurs and appears only through masks and veneers. The exceptions are the rare poems in verse (moreover, in verse of a rather irregular form), the early poems such as *les Poésies d'André Walter, les Mois,* the seven stanzas in the *Journal* at the end of 1914, the poem entitled *Traversée,* the *Quatre Chansons* reprinted in *les Nouvelles Nourritures,* and the

9

pieces scattered through the poetic works in prose, where they constitute grace notes or ornaments, like the *Envoi* to *le Voyage d'Urien* and the many *Rondes* in *les Nourritures terrestres.*

But when Gide wants to reveal himself most profoundly as a poet, not only does he by preference turn to prose, but he encloses his emotion in a particular form—whether journal or notebook, what he calls a *traité* or treatise, or the travel narrative; we find something of all three methods combined in several of his briefer lyric works.

Les Cahiers d'André Walter, les Nourritures terrestres, les Nouvelles Nourritures have the diffuse aspect of irregularly kept notebooks. Among the *Voyages,* the only really poetic ones have been collected in *Amyntas: Mopsus, Feuilles de Route, De Biskra à Touggourt;* while *la Marche Turque* and, even more, *le Voyage au Congo* belong to a more objective literature. They still partake, if only by their lacunae, of the nature of notebooks, but are more closely related to the treatises by a more uniform composition. *Le Renoncement au voyage,* moreover, bears in its title the intent of a treatise. The transition might be furnished by the entirely imaginary *Voyage d'Urien* (sometimes written *Voyage du rien*) which is a treatise while at the same time it is presented as a *récit,* or tale, and anticipates the series of *soties,* or satirical farces, by its third section, in which Gide's preposterous comedy makes its first appearance.

The brief treatises are an original attempt to discuss moral questions under a symbolic aspect. The *Traité du Narcisse,* moreover, bears the subtitle *théorie du symbole. La Tentative amoureuse ou le Traité du vain désir, El Hadj ou le Traité du faux prophète* are confined within a fictional frame, while *Philoctète ou le Traité des trois morales* and *Bethsabé* affect the manner of brief dramas. The most beautiful of these treatises, *le Retour de l'enfant prodigue*, harmoniously combines the starkest narrative with dialogues of an intense severity. It is possible to consider *les Nourritures terrestres*, and perhaps even all of Gide's works, as so many more treatises by this man who has declared that he wished to write only to inflame or to instruct. This genre, renewed with such ingenious subtlety and even, one may say, invented in this form by André Gide, has constantly attracted his pen. He has given us only a fragment of the promised *Traité des Dioscures*, in the drier form of his *Considérations sur la Mythologie Grecque*, and he has only projected an *Entretien avec Nicodème*, a mystical treatise which was to have supplemented *l'Enfant prodigue*. But we find in the appendix to the *Journal des Faux Monnayeurs* the draft of a promising *Traité de la non-existence du Diable*, and we shall not regret the *Essai de bien mourir* when we recall that it inspired the touching conclusion of *la Porte étroite*.

In this group—less voluminous than it appears in this résumé, for most of these works are brief—not everything is entirely poetic. If we defer until our study of Gide's critical works the theory of the symbol proposed by the *Traité du Narcisse*, as well as the scattered declarations in the *Cahiers* or the *Nourritures* which anticipate the aesthetic theories peculiar to André Gide; if we postpone until we draw his spiritual portrait the moral problems, the struggles and victories which have inspired the passionate thought of these works; if finally we must return, apropos of the plays or the *récits*, to this or that aspect of some one of them, there still remains the somewhat precious poetic essence that gives Gide's subtlest works their original flavor and which, purified, perhaps more powerful, in the great works which it will imbue less deliberately, will never altogether cease reminding us, even in the works that aim at the highest degree of objectivity, such as the *Voyage au Congo* or the *Retour de l'URSS,* of the vow of the young author of *André Walter:* "It is a poet that I wish to be; it is a poet that I am."

Poetry, certainly, is a metaphysic of the heart, an imaginative creation intended to satisfy our deepest emotions in ideal terms. These emotions, either those of the poet more or less consciously possessed by them and expressing them more or less indirectly, or those of the reader sympathetically discovering his own secrets echoed in the poet's words—these profound emotions I call *themes.* The occasions by which the theme is satisfied I call *pretexts.* The role of the poetic imagination is, in fact, to adapt these pretexts to these themes and, so to speak, to *orchestrate* the theme around the pretext. Poetic originality therefore consists first of all in a particular sensibility and, since the number of profound emotions is relatively limited, in experiencing these not only with special intensity, but with whatever individuality the personality as a whole can add to them: it is the theme's original *nuance* that will give the poem its affective and unforgettable *timbre.*

Gide's poetic production is articulated almost exclusively around the theme of desire. It is chiefly characterized by exhibiting every nuance of *fervor,* a word that ceaselessly recurs in the Gidean vocabulary. Consequently it seems to me that rather than constituting a specifically poetic *oeuvre,* Gide's poetic works are actually lyrical—if, at least, one accepts the notion that what constitutes lyricism is less its poetic content than the ardor with which that content is conveyed. Moreover, as we shall see, it is this emotion in the voice—which Gide never altogether abandons, even when he has deliberately turned his back on lyricism—that gives his sentences so disturbing, so engaging a resonance, and that in any consideration of his poetry makes a study of the Gidean *tone* so essential.

12

We discover how desire, or rather desires, to specify what is necessarily vague about this broad term if it is not given objects, can be indulged by the storytelling that symbolizes their gratification, either direct or inverted. This is still a pleasure of *reverie*, whether pleasure in the pure sense or the bitter pleasure of suffering. If we occasionally find Gidean themes characterized by a certain mournfulness, these remain exceptional: in this author, everything aspires toward happiness, and in sadness itself he has chosen to see only *fervor relapsed*. His whole being is an assent to life, with neither slackness nor sloth—only a furious energy of appetite, which accounts for the inevitable grafting of the heroic theme of the need for self-transcendence upon the basic theme of the desire for gratification.

This thirst for pleasure was at first only a simple longing, full of misgiving and anxiety, struggling against a religious, mystical, Protestant conscience which rejected it as impure; it sought indirect satisfactions in Platonic love, subject to sudden lapses into solitary, remorse-breeding aberrations of the flesh. The reader will recognize the subject of *les Cahiers d'André Walter*, which might be subtitled "The Treatise of Unavailing Chastity." At a bolder though still diffident stage, desire takes the form of a temptation timidly nursed and indulged; it is gratified in terms of a fiction, a work of imagination which the apprehension of reality or the fear of life keeps from being carried out. "You will never know the effort it has cost us to interest ourselves in life." Books then appear to the poet as "postponed temptations"; this is the case with *la Tentative amoureuse* and also with the imaginary *Voyage d'Urien*, in which irony already promises liberation. In his *Journal*, Gide has outlined a theory of this liberation from desire, which is a curious one considering its date: 1892. Much later, Gide was to refer to Freud as "an imbecile of genius." "I wanted to show, in this *Tentative*

13

amoureuse, the influence of the book on its writer, and
during the very act of writing . . . In this case, I was
miserable because a dream of unrealizeable joy tormented me. I relate the dream and make that joy my
own, isolating it from the dream; my dream has broken
the spell and I am full of joy . . . No action upon an
object without retroaction of that object upon the subject that acts . . . ; the subject that acts is oneself;
the object that retroacts is an imagined subject. Consequently it is an indirect method of acting upon oneself that I have presented here; and it is also, quite
simply, a tale. . . . Luc and Rachel want to gratify
their desire too; but while I satisfied mine, in an ideal
sense, by writing it down, they, dreaming of that park
they saw only from the outside, want to enter it physically: doing so gives them no joy at all."

The book of Gide's in which instinctual impulses are
no longer shackled, where in fact the cure of a nervous
illness resulting largely from the repression of desires
is accomplished, and where the obsession with death
and the brevity of life serve those desires as a springboard, is of course that famous manual of pleasure *les
Nourritures terrestres,* a fiery work actually dangerous
for the reader who fails to observe the author's last
exhortation: "Nathanaël, throw away my book . . ."
Through the sort of Paradise Regained which a pantheist atheism reconstructs out of perfect fragments of
pure pleasure courses a frenzy of voluptuous enjoyment
virtually unprecedented in literature. It is a continuous
—and continuously renewed—excitation of all the senses,
in which supremacy is accorded to the most sensual of
all: the sense of touch, which stands for the rest just
as thirst symbolizes the other desires. This intensifica-
tion of pleasure to the point of exacerbation leads to
an odd hygiene of desire, intended to keep it perpetually
awake and refreshed, and whose most poetic *fiat* is the
recommendation of inconstancy, of perpetual flight, the

tireless escape from desire by taking refuge in forever new desires. Yet this progression into desire concludes, strangely enough, by purifying and stripping it. Hence Gide proceeds from oasis to oasis, each more beautiful than the last: "The next day, I loved only the desert."

Such pleasure is sought in pain itself: the love of life is extended to even its disturbing or repugnant forms; the keen edge of pleasure, honed in the quest for its own refinement, lacerates to the point of suffering. "And sometimes I sought, beyond the pleasure of the flesh, a second, more secret pleasure." The goal of this search is to transcend gratification by abandoning the objects of desire for the sake of desire itself: to prefer thirst to any drink, provocation to any pleasure.

At this point, where hedonism is transformed into a voluptuous asceticism, the soul has been inured to renunciation. The disgust with possessions has been prepared by a flight from desire to desire; and renunciation itself facilitated by a perpetual escape.

A principal theme in the *Nourritures* was a search for the immanence of pleasure, which is succeeded by its transcendence. The kind of heroic joy Philoctetes achieves when he voluntarily abandons to young Neoptolemus the bow which is his only possession, and which Ulysses has treacherously tried to steal from him, has its root in a need to transcend the self by purification, reaching its climax in a marvelous limpidity of one's entire being: "I would have my actions . . . still firmer, finer; true, pure, crystalline, lovely—lovely, Ulysses, like those crystals of clear frost which reveal the sun, when it appears, undistorted. I would not obstruct even one of Zeus' rays; let them pass through me, Ulysses, like a prism, and let his light make my actions divine. I long for utter transparence, for abolition of my opacity until, watching me in action, you yourself would see the light . . ."

Thus André Walter's mystical spirit has at last triumphed over every obstacle of material joy; it has fused so fiercely with the sensual life that it has transfigured it, culminating in the purification of desire and in the evangelical impoverishment of being, nurturing the complete oblivion of self and the gift of that self to others: "What we desire, Nathanaël, is not possession but love."

After these variations on the same theme—the essential theme of Gide's direct poetry, the exaltation of joy—comes the minor theme, infinitely diversified, of the sadness of disappointed desire, which has its *raison d'être* only in the first theme but which, by the self-consciousness to which it compels the soul, enchants it with an even more penetrating charm. First, all joys—especially all pleasures—are necessarily incomplete, ephemeral, and deceptive. "And you, objects of our desires, are like those perishable concretions which, once they are touched by fingers, leave only ash behind." Then, with time, desires grow dull: "What I want is to be hungry enough, some day, to desire these chick-peas—a handful that the vendor would skim from the top of the pan and pour into a cone of straw-colored paper spotted with brine— . . . be thirsty enough to drink from the spigot of the leather bottle that this woman whose face I cannot see holds on her hip and would tip toward my warm lips . . ." But the primordial coolness cannot be recovered, and repeated experiments bring no more than half satisfactions, when they are not complete disappointments: "Nothing equals the first contact."

Le Renoncement au voyage is filled with these melancholies, where the present itself has already the bitterness of the past and anticipates a nostalgia still to come: "You will never see again, I told myself, thrusting my hands into it, you will never see again, and yet here it is, this fountain where you come to sit in the night." Any change observed in the order of beloved objects seems to denature their recollection and, however slight, to displace a harmony that could be perfect only in its first form: "That is why, on these paths, the clay, after the rain, is no longer so soft underfoot; dry, it is no longer so pink, nor, once the sun has saturated it, covered with such fine crackling." When nothing seems to have changed, it is man who is no longer the same. "I revert to the heart of my youth. I walk in my own footsteps. Here is the charming countryside of the path I used to take, that first day when, weak still, having escaped the horror of my own death, I sobbed, drunk with the simple astonishment of existence, with the ecstasy of being alive: how soothing to my still-weary eyes was the shadow of the palms! Sweetness of the pale shadows, murmur of the gardens, perfumes, I recognize everything, trees, things . . . only I am unrecognizable."

These disillusionments lead to the powerful theme of regret; the lost opportunities are dramatized in memory and leave us inconsolable, particularly upon the approach of age. It is this regret that at times pierces the vigorous optimism of the *Nouvelles Nourritures,* but, under the mask of a perfect prose, the expression, it must be confessed, is less that of a poet than of a moralist; wisdom has come, anxiety gone, and with it that communicative *frisson.* "Regret for the *temporis acti* is the most futile of an old man's occupations. I assure myself of this; yet I yield to it . . . For it is at the age when the soul and the body are readiest for love, worthiest to love, to be loved, when the embrace is most powerful, curiosity liveliest and most instructive, pleasure keenest, it is at this age that the soul and the body both find most strength to resist the solicitations of love.

"What you called, what I too called: temptations, are what I regret; and if I repent today, it is not that I yielded to some of them, it is that I resisted so many

17

others which I pursued later on, when they were already less charming, and of less value to my thought.

"I repent having clouded my youth, having preferred the imaginary to the real, having turned away from life."

Yet if there is one theme which Gide has never developed, despite these words, it is the theme of repentance. This warrior has always emerged victorious from his battles, even when he has chosen defeats for his victories. Regrets and nostalgia have never had a plaintive accent in his work; this virile admirer of Browning has never lacked courage in his perplexities and oscillations. If he greatly admired Hugo's profound, almost Baudelairean line:

> *Comme le souvenir est voisin du remords!*
> (How close memory is to remorse!)

he has never made it into a maxim for his personal use. When he wants to celebrate the intense theme of remorse and the futility of ill-gotten joys, he puts his words in the mouth of King David, in the poignant little drama *Bethsabé:*

> I ask of God: what shall a man do
> If behind each of his desires God is hidden? . . .
> If he has taken the sheep which was the poor man's
>   only possession,
> And even this is not what his roving desire would
>   have. . . .
> Only see! I have restored his Bathsheba to him,
> I do not desire her save in the shade of her garden.
> What I desired was Uriah's peace, among these
>   things
> That are so simple, and that in my service he aban-
>   doned. . . .

It is, in fact, because remorse is the condemnation of fervor. And Gide, far from ever renouncing fervor, will even flatter its simulation when it has gone. This is the meaning of the *Traité du faux prophète*, in which El Hadj, who lost his faith at the very moment he became a prophet, is obliged to feign it, and bears at the same time the burden of its disenchanted lucidity and dejected nostalgia: "For I know now that there are prophets, by day concealing from those they lead the anxiety, alas! and the bewilderment of their soul, simulating their past fervor to dissimulate its death—who sob when the night has come, when they are alone again—and are enlightened no longer save by the countless stars and perhaps by the too distant Idea,—in which they have yet ceased to believe." Gide will always retain this regret for the mystic fervor which animated the struggles of André Walter and exiled him so far from life, and which the *Nourritures terrestres* seemed to have routed, although, by a singular compromise which can be explained only as a kind of stubbornness, Gide has never ceased referring to all the objects of his desire as God. "Even today," he wrote late in life, "I suffer a kind of nostalgia for that mystical and fiery climate that once exalted my being; I have never recovered the fervor of my adolescence. And the sensual ardor in which I later delighted is only a mocking imitation of it. At least so it appears to me, now that my senses are aging. How easy it would be for me, even today, to write in pathetic tones about this subject— phrases which my reason, tomorrow, would deny. Nothing is easier than to be stirring once you no longer discipline yourself against writing extravagantly. What permits the lyricism of childhood is illusion." In this passage, which implies so severe and so unjust a condemnation of the *Nourritures terrestres*, we see on the other hand how right Gide was to emphasize, in the preface he added to the book in 1927, that salient feature of his personality: fidelity, countering the reproaches of inconstancy which have often been made against his ethic. Even in its most scandalous flights, the source of this poetry has always been of puritan inspiration, and its debauchery has never been more than a heady compensation; this disturbing poetry has always, in fact, attempted by some obliquity to return to the divine and to transfigure or transcend itself—and ultimately Gide abandons poetry itself for moral activities no doubt more urgent in our troubled age . . . If Gide could jokingly write in his *Journal:* "I am only a little boy who is having fun, combined with a Protestant minister who bores him," it is ultimately the Protestant minister who gets the upper hand; except that he has been converted by the little boy; and then the little boy died . . .

Whereas the apparent themes are sustained in these works with occasionally too rich an insistence, there is a *hidden theme* which appears only clandestinely. This constraint—according to Gide, the vital condition of art, which dies from excessive freedom—gives the expression of this furtive theme an allusive reserve, maintaining for secret delectation the poetic mystery which it would certainly have lost, at least for most readers, if this theme of private pleasure had been treated overtly. "I have made myself a prowler so I can be near all that prowls: I have grown fond of whatever has no place to warm itself, and I have passionately loved anything that wanders." Gide has replaced the *bad habits* of childhood with *bad company*. Reading Valery Larbaud's delightful poems makes him regret that he was not more cynical in his *Nourritures*. A moralist's regret, one might say, but what a mistake from the poetic point of view! Such discretion, on the contrary, has made acceptable what would not have been tolerated. It has preserved the equivocal charm of a Virgilian effervescence which any crudity of tone would have crushed at once.

We have just seen how a theme gains in suggestion

by being treated clandestinely. To discover how a theme
is denatured, transformed by the metamorphosis of a
feeling, we must read, in *le Renoncement au voyage*
(where an "objective" prose already pre-empts two
thirds of the subject), those pages where the soul reacts
in astonishment at no longer experiencing in the beloved sites the same emotions as in the past; yet since
the soul remembers them, it generates—by momentary
and still vivid returns, a reprise in a minor key—triumphant motifs. It is not yet the impoverished mono-
chrome of old age, but the disillusionment of maturity,
which begins with fragile second crops. "Perhaps the
recollection of that time is a little vague in places, for I
have a bad memory, but the bouquets of sensations I
have brought back from this first trip still exhale an
odor so strong that sometimes it keeps me from savoring
the present moment. Yet I forbid myself to compare;
but I do worse: six times I turn back, seeking the past
in the present, extenuating my emotion, demanding of
it that same freshness it once owed to its novelty, and
from year to year finding in my aging desires recom-
penses that are always less vivid . . ." The theme has
not only developed, it has lost some of its power: nothing could equal the fierce surge of the primitive impulse, nothing save a despair of an equal intensity,
which Gide, grown wiser and committed to happiness,
has not known.

The poetic weakening of the themes is proportional
to their rationalization. In the *Nouvelles Nourritures,*
whatever poetry subsists is due almost exclusively to
the poet's somewhat complacent resumption of themes
he has already handled; the only one that remains
really vivid and alive is the regret for pleasures, sharp-
ened by the sense of advancing age. The language here
is no less skillful, the thought is even more generous—
more fraternal, one might say—but the poetic themes
are replaced by reasoned convictions of a rather peda-

gogic eloquence which cannot substitute for the accents of passion: "It is not only the world that must be changed, but man himself. And where is this new man to come from? Not from outside. Comrade, you must discover him in yourself, and as a pure metal without dross is extracted from ore, you must demand this looked-for man of yourself. He is not cheaply found. In each being there are admirable possibilities. Be convinced of your strength and your youth. You must ceaselessly remind yourself: 'It is up to me alone.'"

In Gide's *Journal* we find a curious page where, beginning to describe a moonrise over the sea in poetic terms, the writer, as though exasperated, chides himself and harshly breaks off his overwrought sentence with "that will do." And yet this was prose, a language which Gide has always valued far above verse. Without being actually hampered by versified forms, one can certainly say that in them Gide has achieved only moderate successes; their elegance is always somewhat fragile. He has quite naturally reserved for prose his most vigorous lyric inspirations, and the poetic weakness of his things in verse, like the *Poésies d'André Walter* or the *Calendrier*, derives precisely from the innate weakness of their themes. They are not significant enough even for the delicate and already reduced means which they call into play; the theme is still too meager, too evanescent in proportion to the uncertain pretexts beneath which it is concealed.

THE PARK

When we saw that the little gate was closed,
We sat weeping a long time;
When we knew that there was nothing to do,
We slowly walked back down the path.
All day we followed the garden wall,
Behind which we could sometimes hear voices,
    laughter;

We thought there might have been picnics on the
grass,
And that thought made us sad.
The sun toward evening reddened the walls;
We didn't know what was happening inside, for we
saw
Only the branches that stirred over the top of the
wall
Letting a few leaves fall now and then.

All these themes require for their expression an occasion, a frame, a detail, an object. This is the pretext.
The pretext in itself has nothing poetic about it, but any
pretext can become poetic if it is made capable of affording the theme satisfaction. Yet there are pretexts
which by nature are more likely to be made into
poetry, for they contain possibilities of *reverie*. Everything, strictly speaking, can be a pretext, and the originality of some poets has consisted less in the affective
nuance of the themes they treat than in their aptitude
for discovering hitherto unexploited pretexts in banal
or bizarre objects. Gide's pretexts have nothing rare
about them; they are borrowed mostly from nature,
occasionally from the inner life, almost never from art.

Here we must clear up a misunderstanding. Critics
sometimes use the word "theme" in fact without much
precision and rather as a synonym for "subject" or "general idea"; hence one speaks of the theme of the sea in
the work of Victor Hugo, or the theme of factories in
the work of Verhaeren. I scarcely need remark that for
me, these so-called themes are only pretexts, and that
I regard as themes only the major directions of the
deepest affectivity, such as an aspiration to eternity, or
the need for brotherhood.

One may take as an example of a pretext half elaborated, already suited for poetic treatment, yet in which
there still remain certain impure elements, this exquisite

page of Gide's *Journal* where the longing for oblivion, oblivion of self and of the world, is related to a motif which at first glance does not seem particularly likely to satisfy it: the little stall of a Biskra merchant. Incidentally, with this theme of escape by absorption into the duration of the present is entangled, in attenuated form, the secret theme we have already referred to: "I used to spend [all my evenings] in a low, dim stall that by day was used for a scanty henna commerce, and where in the evening gathered Bachir, Mohammed, Larbi, Bachir's brother and a few other friends of theirs. They played cards. Bachir made coffee. The little kief pipe passed from mouth to mouth. I delighted Athman by calling this dismal spot the 'little casino.' Yet I spent every evening there. What did I do? I wonder today. I neither smoked nor played cards with the others, and I was not really in love with any—no, but with that atmosphere itself, with that darkness, that silence, with their society that I could not do without. Each of them was if not handsome at least lithe and graceful; I have spoken of them in another place. I know that today, more restless, alas! deeper in debauchery, I could not remain in contemplation as I did then. Not a single evening of the two months I frequented the place did I focus my desires upon any one of them. And it was this which allowed me to prolong my pleasure so interminably. The time passed; never, since, have I so completely lost the sense of time, of age, and of the hour. The kief would have added nothing."

And here, prepared for an analogous theme—but cast in the future because expressed in the mood of hope— here, after the complete elimination of *prose*, taken as a form of thought disengaged from all *reverie*, is a pretext completely transformed into poetry. Gide is evoking a little garden surrounded with clay walls, in El Kantara. "Walls of earth! Hated Walls! my incessant desire assails you; I shall certainly enter at the last.

"Deep within the clay wall is hidden a little wooden door.

"We shall come to this little low door, and a child shall have the key; we shall bend our heads; we shall become as a child to enter. . . . Oh! we shall say, Oh! here is a quiet place. Oh, we did not know one could be so still, find a place on earth so calm. . . . Bring us flutes and milk—we shall stay here until evening. —A breath of wind escapes into the palms; the shadow wavers; the sun laughs; under the huge apricot trees, the ditches of yellowish water turn blue; the fig trees grovel; but what delights us most is the grace of the oleanders.

"Stir no more; let time close over us like a pool, like a pool into which you throw a pebble; the confusion we made coming in withdraws like the ripple on the pool; let time's smooth surface close over this world."

The pretexts are of course innumerable, and since, on the one hand, they are of interest only for their adaptation to the themes and, on the other, the same pretext can serve several themes, their systematic classification does not offer any real advantage to aesthetic analysis. I shall indicate a few, in order not to appear to be avoiding my responsibility. But let us note from the start that the phenomenology of their classification could derive from physics or from psychology, depending on whether one preferred to start with the universe, or with perception. Moreover the *Nourritures terrestres*, by the multitude of natural phenomena evoked or the variety of pleasures of which these phenomena are the source, gives the impression—always delightful, sometimes excessive—of a textbook of poetic physics or of a catalogue of sensations. "In my sun-steeped body, I seemed to taste some chimerical benefit; I forgot . . . torment, constraint, solicitude, and while every intention evaporated, I let sensations, in a self as porous as a hive, secretly distill that honey which flowed in my

Nourritures." Major categories like space, time, change, or movement . . . permit us to establish in this chaotic nature a number of orderly pathways, as in a French garden. We have on one side, carefully bordered and defined, landscapes, gardens, cities, the desert, the Moorish or Italian cafés, even barbershops . . . or springs, streams, fruits, flowers, or perfumes, aromatic herbs, pastry shops, things to drink, preserves . . . On the other, we have moments, time's distortions, occasions of oblivion and of remembrance . . . Lastly we have roads, the oases, caravans . . . and the seasons, climates, variations in light . . . Redefine all these by a line that connects objects to intermediate forms (behavior and attitude) whereby the desires attain them: vision, contact, walks, bathing; waiting, departures, journeys; intoxication, debauchery; escapes, vagrancy, pursuit; rest, sleep, exhaustion; privation, ascesis, annihilation, ecstasy . . .

There remains the most curious form of pretext: the inspiring emotion, no longer seeking its satisfaction in the external world, tries to apprehend *itself;* in this inner pursuit, it is the theme which takes itself as a pretext. This is what happens in Gide when the exaltation of some particular desire and of its object is succeeded by the intoxication of the quest for desire in the pure state, the desire for desire, hunger preferred to nourishment, thirst to drink, love to any embrace . . . He will recall it in the *Nouvelles Nourritures:* "Possession seemed to me less precious than pursuit, and I came more and more to prefer thirst itself to the quenching of thirst, valuing above pleasure its promise, seeking beyond satisfaction the endless release of love."

The art of furnishing pretexts for themes and of nourishing the latter by enriching the former, the art of incarnating feeling in a universe of perception created or re-created by the poet, derives from an aesthetic of the poetic imagination altogether different from the aesthetic of the novelistic or dramatic imagination. Analysis is difficult because the poetic imagination almost always mingles with the other forms, so that it becomes difficult to separate, in fiction or drama, what is poetic from what is merely picturesque, touching, or eloquent, particularly since there is nothing in the powers of the mind—not even the most lucid intelligence, as we see so clearly in Valéry's example—that is incapable of being made into poetry. The poetic imagination circulates among the other forms, including the ideological imagination. It may also function in an isolated, almost completely pure state.

In any case its methods of composition are quite peculiar to itself. They recall Pascal's "art of pleasing," and this kind of seduction is not easily reduced to formulas. The architecture of a novel or a play is, in spite of everything, easier to discern than the secret structure of a poem, or of an often brief fragment whose magic inevitably functions by invisible modes. It nevertheless seems to me that the law of poetic treatment lies in the *intimate harmony of details with the themes,* while the law of aesthetic composition is found in the *hierarchy of elements.* From this double point of view, the *Cahiers d'André Walter* suffer from a great irresolution. Gide tells us that he wanted to nourish them "on all his inner argument, all his anxieties, all his perplexities, above all on his love, which formed, strictly speaking, the axis of the book around which all the rest was to gravitate." However touching the young man's laceration by contrary tendencies, this struggle was too inward to provide substance for a drama, and it was more appropriately contained within a narrative where the anxieties and uncertainties would be duly unfolded in the intricacies of analysis. As for poetry, it does not adapt itself to such conflicts, though the contrary is occasionally assumed; its spell requires monotony, insistence, and something of the immobility of pure feeling. The *Cahiers d'André Walter* reveal another defect difficult to endure in a work of art: instead of an organic composition, they betray a confused dispersion of substance, and I allude to this defect only because it becomes almost a virtue in the *Nourritures terrestres*. It is easy to see why: on this later occasion a textual diffusion was in accord with the sporadic nature of the philosophy of individual moments, preached by a disseminated, nomadic, and vagabond hedonism.

I hesitate to use the term *orchestration* here to indicate this steeping of the theme in its pretexts, with the co-operation of all the resources of the sensual imagination, though it seems to suggest quite nicely the instrumental and luxuriant side, without which poetry never gives us quite the impression of being incarnate in a living creation. The tact of Gidean poetry forbids so ambitious a denomination. One might better seek an analogy from the technique of the piano. Gide is content to accompany his theme quite sparingly, to harmonize his melody with frugal elegance. The theme functions all the more effectively for being hidden, expressed less in the form of an idea than seeming to exhale something of a vague perfume: "Deep in this forsaken oasis there is a disturbing spot. I want to go there. Here every path vanishes; one's foot sinks in the moment it leaves a tuft of grass; but a few steps farther, the rotten earth, I know, sends up reeds. . . . Here they are! Now is the moment when the sun silvers them most gracefully. To bend their stalks, a bird resting there is enough. Out of a tangled thicket of oleanders, they spring up, high, very high; their volley gleams in the blue air.

"I wanted to gather some of them, yet as soon as they were in my hand, they were nothing more than a harsh spindle, blurred at the tip by a hemp-gray calking, without beauty." Elsewhere in the *Nourritures* the theme is occasionally developed and varied with a kind of triumphant insolence, as in the famous *Ronde de la Grenade*:

> You would still be seeking long
> For the impossible joy of the spirit.
> Joys of the flesh and joys of the senses
> Let others, if they choose, condemn you,
> Bitter joys of the flesh and the senses . . .
>
> Yes, sweet is the fog, in the sun rising over the plains
>
> And sweet the sun;
> Sweet the moist earth to our bare feet
> And the sand moistened by the sea,
> Sweet to bathe in was the spring water;
> To kiss, the unknown lips my lips touched in the
>   shadows . . .
> But the fruits—the fruits, Nathanaël, what shall I say
>   of them?
>
> Oh, that you have not known them,
> Nathanaël, that is my despair.
> Their pulp was delicate and juicy,
> Luscious as bleeding flesh
> Red as blood from a wound.

The satisfaction of a need as simple as thirst, a theme as uncomplicated as possible, has nevertheless inspired Gide to write a luxuriant poem. All its richness is in the feverish succession of pretexts, each occasion affording him a promise of sensuality. Remarkable in this procession, where wine is merely alluded to, is the precedence of water, undoubtedly a Protestant drink.

RONDE DE MES SOIFS ÉTANCHÉES

. . . .

> The greatest joy of my senses
> Has been the slaking of my thirsts . . .

. . . .

I have drunk from glasses so slender
That I feared my mouth would break them
Even before my teeth had touched them;
And what I drank tasted sweeter in them,
For almost nothing separated them from my lips.
I have drunk from soft goblets
That I pressed between my hands
To make the wine rise to my lips.

I have drunk heavy sirups in the thick mugs of inns
On the evenings of days when I had walked in the
     sun;
And sometimes the cold water of wells
Made the later evening's shadow deeper.
I have drunk water kept in leather bottles
That smelled of tarry goatskin . . .

. . . .

The shepherds drank the water in their hands;
I taught them to suck it up with straws.
Certain days, I walked under the full sun,
In summer, during the hottest hours,
Seeking great thirsts I might slake.

And do you remember, my friend, how one night,
during our terrible journey, we got up from our beds,
sweating, to drink from the earthenware pitcher the
water it had made icy?

To incarnate a theme in a pretext, the imagination
possesses, among a host of other resources, an indirect
method: symbolism. Gide has used this technique very
discreetly, much more sparingly than his contemporaries. He merely tolerated Symbolism as a movement,
and it has left relatively few traces in his work. We
recall the counsels of escape given to Nathanaël: "Once
a place has come to resemble you, or once you have
come to resemble a place, it is no longer of profit to

you. You must leave it. Nothing is more dangerous to you than your family, your room, your past . . ." The concierge of a Marseilles hotel, not suspecting that she was summing up an entire existence, once said to Edmond Jaloux: "Monsieur Gide does nothing but come in and go out." Yet in the *Nourritures* there is a full development of the daydream inspired by a superb Normandy farm, in which a great part is played by those magnificent objects so likely to transform themselves into symbols: *the Doors*. The poet has opened, one after the other, the doors to the barns, the granaries, the milk sheds, the stable, the fruit bins, the wine press, the distillery, the coach house, and one after the other he celebrates what these interiors suggest by way of exalting visions; and remarkably enough almost all—and particularly those suggested by the pretext of the carriages stored in the sheds—wrench the mind from these enclosures to send it wandering, a vagrant, out of doors. The poet reaches the last door, which symbolizes all departures, and he lets the suggestion form in the reader's mind by suspending all evocation of the infinite possibilities:

"The last door opened onto the plain . . ."

We rarely find in Gide an anthropomorphic tendency to attribute our ways of feeling to natural objects. He grants them some share of foreboding, of anticipation: "I have seen the sky tremble, waiting for the dawn . . . I have seen the night's expectation . . ."; but this kind of emotional transposition is exceptional in his work. I suspect that his intelligence has found it factitious. On the other hand, one can discern an aspiration—much less artificial, much more sincere—to dissolve himself in the object, to participate in nature, to experience its forms and activities. This aspiration recalls the Romantics' pantheism or the symbolists' identification with the outside world, the *Einfühlung* of the German aestheticians.

It is an attempt to infuse the theme into the pretext as directly as possible—and its possible failure lies in the reader's refusal to accept those participations that seem peculiar or bizarre to him. Hence, perhaps, the occasional disappointments of the original and imperfect *Ronde de tous mes Désirs:*

> I do not know what I could have dreamed that night.
> When I awakened all my desires were thirsty.
> It seemed that in my sleep they had crossed deserts.
>
> . . . .
>
> Our desires have already crossed many worlds;
> They are never surfeited.
> And all nature suffers
> Between a thirst for rest, a thirst for pleasure.
>
> We have groaned with agony
> In empty rooms
> We have climbed towers
> Where we saw nothing but the night;
>
> Bitches, we have howled with grief
> Along the shriveled beaches
> Lionesses, we have roared in the Aurès—and we have
> grazed, camels, on the gray kelp of the salt
> ponds, sucked the juice of hollow stems—for
> water is rare in the desert.
>
> We have crossed, swallows,
> Vast seas without sustenance;
> Grasshoppers, we have had to devastate all to feed
> ourselves.
> Algae, we have been storm-tossed;
> Flakes, the winds have taken us.

Gide's power of sympathy, which has made him, like his Ménalque, "indistinctly through all things des-

perately adore," is equaled only by his capacity to
withdraw, to refuse himself. The latter has given his
criticism its independence; the former has afforded his
poetry that ardent familiarity with the universe which
restores it to us with more savor than when we had left
it. This, in my opinion, is what gives Gide's exoticism an
aspect that is so unprovocative, even so unpicturesque,
or rather it is what forbids us to invoke exoticism at all
in dealing with a writer who has sought to communicate
with all of nature's variations. Already the *Traité du
faux prophète* had suggested the relativity of exoticism
by showing us in the countries of the North a definite
affinity for the Southern peoples, and the *Traité des
trois morales* curiously united inverted exoticism and
symbolism by putting Philoctetes, abandoned by his
companions, on an island covered with snow and ice, in
which his purification seeks models. But Gide has
above all renewed exoticism by eliminating it, by a
wholehearted adherence without prudery, without dis-
criminations that re-establish "foreignness," with, in
fact, an eagerness—or rather a gift—not to remain alien.
Algeria was essential to his success.

Even in Naples, the singing reminds him of the
Orient, and he analyzes it with that loving curiosity
which in small details, as in great impulses, constitutes
Gide's most spontaneous intellectual contribution: "How
peculiar that Oriental chant, beginning on too shrill a
note which strangely descends to the tonic in two parallel phrases, trilled as though between the notes, accented spasmodically and stopping with a gasp." Here
we have an obvious intention to reduce the alien quality by comprehending it in its essence. What we get is
the achieved, completed, affirmative adherence in the
Feuille de Route: "My love for the desert is limitless.
The first year, I feared it a little because of its wind
and its sand, then in its purposelessness one didn't know
where to stop any more, and I exhausted myself so

quickly. I used to prefer the shady paths under the palm trees, the gardens of Ouardi, the villages. But last year, I took tremendous walks. I had no other goal than to be out of sight of the oasis, I walked until I felt myself, at last, immensely alone on the plain. Then I began to look around me. The sands had a certain bloom in the shadow of the dunes, where traces of insects remained; gourds withered here, tiger-beetles ran about; there were wonderful caresses in each breeze, and because of the great silence, the faintest sound could be heard. Sometimes an eagle soared over the great dunes. Every day this monotonous space seemed more plausible in its variety."

It is this admirable sympathy, I think, combining as much lucidity as love, which, extended later to include the social structure as well, earlier permitted Gide not only to paint with penetration the beautiful portraits we find in his psychological works, but to give so authentic an accent to his voice, even when he borrows his subjects from the exoticism of the past—when he speaks Greek out of the mouth of Philoctetes, when he tells the parable of the prodigal son in tones of biblical simplicity.

Which takes us from this notion of *tone,* of imaginative orchestration of themes, to the poetic *formulation.* We shall attempt to discover in the next chapter how the metaphysics of feeling is expressed by means of a verbal music, and how, in Gide's lyric works, the "musicalization" of language resorts by choice to prose.

2. Lyrical Prose (ii)

In the last chapter I attempted to demonstrate that poetry is a metaphysic of the heart, and that Gide's poetry is a metaphysic of *desire*, which attempts to transcend itself in a metaphysic of *ascesis*, of love and of renunciation. We have seen how Gide's imagination orchestrated in its characteristic way the affective themes around pretexts *"d'une diverse monotonie."* I should now like to show that this aesthetic of poetic treatment, of poetization, does not necessarily demand any particular literary genre for its expression, not a predetermined instrument, prose or verse, nor even literature in general; the incarnation of all these themes we have discussed could perfectly well be the result of techniques alien to the arts of language, such as music, painting, or an art as rich in possibilities of poetic suggestion as the cinema. The pretexts might have altered, partially at least, but at least there would be pretexts, and the poetic treatment might have varied in its methods, but not in its fundamental operation. What would have been transformed is the mode of expression, which gives the work its recognizable aspect and which pertains to what I shall call the aesthetic of formulation. So that if we consider a particular mode, such as the painting, the statue, the symphony, or the poem, we must be careful to distinguish in it, on the one hand, what makes it a painting, a statue, a symphony, a text in verse (or lyric prose), and on the other what constitutes the charm of the *Embarquement pour Cythère,* the majesty of the *Venus of Milo,* the grace of the *Pastoral Symphony,* the melancholy of the *Tristesse d'Olympio;* which comes down to saying that there is not one aesthetic, but two: an aesthetic of the beautiful, and an aesthetic of the poetic.

The formulation may be beautiful, and it may be poetic. In literary works in which poetry constitutes the principal design, the metaphysic of the heart seeks expression by means of a verbal music. But the poetic formulation is not only a musical formulation, for there are musical verses which are not poetry, a harmonious or sonorous, eloquent or cadenced prose which is not poetry; the poetic formulation is, moreover, an intentional one in which poetry seeks to realize its function in the choice and elimination of methods having to do with expression, vocabulary, syntax, images, and figures. What particularly characterizes the poetic formulation is a certain tone.

I propose to define tone as an affective choice of language by an attitude of consciousness. From the limitless realm of expression, poetic consciousness chooses only what it regards as congeneric; what, as Baudelaire says, speaks "to the soul, in secret, the gentle language of its birth"—everything that flatters and reflects its disposition of the moment. Or, at least, if the poetic treatment of language is not carried this far, to this degree of purity and density, it avoids those aspects of the language which would jar by their prosaic quality and prepares, by neutral passages, the imminent impulses of inspiration. If not everything is poetic, nothing, at least, will be anti-poetic.

Tone, consequently, poses the crucial problem of the work of art. As a matter of fact, tone is that intermediary temper which links inspiration to expression, which proceeds from one to the other and participates in both. So one might say that tone is at once the style of inspiration, and the inspiration of style. The poetic tone, which is a tone unto itself, quite different from the picturesque or the eloquent—the poetic tone must therefore transmit the theme's color into language, and it is in this way that language echoes the timbre of the personality and the individual emotion that makes it resonant.

Naturally the tonality of a poem is not uniform. The tone changes to indicate the inflections of the feeling. Under this tonal variety subsists a common, a fundamental tone, which constitutes the poem's unity, just as the permanent sentiment that concerns the spirit provokes the series of secondary sentiments that modify the poem. What makes it possible to discern the fundamental sentiment under the multiplicity of secondary sentiments is the direction of energy and the fulcrum of the will, the object of desire, whether achieved or lost.

Let us try to show in a brief passage how the tone is achieved. I shall choose the beginning of Scene II of *Bethsabé*. King David is telling Joab—and seeing it again in telling it—about his reception in the house of Uriah, his loyal and modest general, where he has been invited after having glimpsed, one morning, from a terrace of his palace, Uriah's wife bathing in the fountain. He had imagined that he desired Bathsheba, but the object of his desire, whose flickering anxiety is admirably rendered later on, is precisely this irreproachable happiness which the powerful can no longer possess and which is found only in purity of heart and poverty of life. "I thirst for that happiness of Uriah's," he will say, too late, when he has come to full awareness of his desire, "and that it should be made of nothing great."

We may say, then, that in the fragment we are considering, this poetic theme is—rather than jealousy, rather than envy even—the desire for another man's happiness by which one is dazzled. Let us disregard the adaptation of this theme to the pretext—remarkably chosen though this is—of the frugal reception in a pastoral atmosphere. And let us attend only to the tone, which reflects in the language the inspiring emotion and its modulations. David speaks:

> He lives in a little garden . . .
> The table where the meal was laid for me under the
>   trellis was white.
> 'Look,' he said to me, 'at my vines and the shade
>   they cast.'
> And the shade upon the table was charming;
> 'What little wine I have comes from them;
> Here, King David, it is sweet, taste of it.'
> And his wife having come out
> (It is Bathsheba that she is called),
> Bending, filled my cup.
> I had not recognized her.
> And at first I did not even recognize the garden.
> Dressed in that fashion, she seemed much more beau-
>   tiful to me.
> The dim torrent of her hair
> Seemed to palpitate about her.
> Her unknown face was smiling . . .
> But the garden, Joab, the garden! What shall I say
>   of it?
> It was not like that of the morning,
> Filled with mists:
> It was a secret place . . . I drank that cup of wine.
> I have drunk many wines, Joab, but that wine
> I had thirsted for, I think, long beforehand;
> It sank within me like a deep happiness;
> It filled my heart like the fulfillment of prayers.

I felt the strength of my loins revived.
Bathsheba was smiling; the garden filled with light.
Everything shone with love and the happiness of
 Uriah.

Aside from Uriah's few courteous words, eager without servility and shaded with modest contentment, the tone is set by David. It is the tone of amazement. He enjoys not only the peace of this quiet place, but the charm of the whole and of the details, and is affected by the secret of a happiness that depends on so little and seems so miraculous. It is this amazement that inspires the omnipotent king with the tyrannical sentiment that such happiness is his due. Too obviously above using physical force, David will try to appropriate it secretly, like a thief in the night.

This tone is first of all fixed by the choice of words. There are words in which an affective charge has been accumulated, particularly when they are quite commonplace, like the adjectives *little, deep, charming*. "He lives in a little garden"; "And the shade upon the table was charming"; "It sank within me like a deep happiness." There are verbs full of spiritual resonance: "It *filled* my heart"; "Everything *shone* with love"; "her hair seemed to *palpitate* . . ." And I have not quoted the whole series of simple substantives evoking, by their very simplicity, the notion of an indivisible happiness. There is no need to insist on the rustic vocabulary: *garden, vines, trellis, wine;* nor on the abstract words, so old and so young: *love, happiness;* nor on words ennobled by certain associations: *shade, cup, mist . . .* Let us note, however, the deep, energetic, almost harsh notes that reveal the violence of criminal desire: *thirst, strength, loins . . .*

Certain words are somehow sensitized by their location, such as these ordinary adjectives, rendered so suggestive, so mysterious: "It was a *secret* place," "her *unknown* face was smiling," "the *dim torrent* of her hair."

But the tone is accentuated more strongly by the suggestive, entirely affective turn of speech (poets avoid constructions whose logic is too rigorously stressed): "But the garden, Joab, the garden! What shall I say of it?" a line in which a sense of the ineffable is rendered by exclamation, insistence, and interrogation without response.

The tone imbues the entire language and the entire style. It is even expressed—it is expressed particularly here—by an admirable absence of effects. Simplicity is expressed by simplicity. The easy, relaxed sobriety, the perfect and unadorned naturalness of the beginning suit these delighted impressions of the guest:

> The table where the meal was laid for me under the
> trellis was white . . .
> And his wife having come out
> (It is Bathsheba that she is called),
> Bending, filled my cup.
> I had not recognized her.
> And at first I did not even recognize the garden.

But it is by an accent, on the contrary, that the distentions of emotion are betrayed:

> The dim torrent of her hair
> Seemed to *palpitate* about her.

And the birth of a desire indissolubly linked to its object, to the climate of its object, will be expressed by the magnificent fullness of conviction, the intensity of affirmation, the very luster of the language, the invention of the formula under the irrepressible impulse of emotion:

> I have drunk many wines, Joab, but that wine
> I had thirsted for, I think, long beforehand.

Still halfway between the observer's disinterestedness
and the rage of lust, the spell turns naturally to a hymn
of praise:

It sank within me like a deep happiness;
It filled my heart like the fulfillment of prayers.
I felt the strength of my loins revived.
Bathsheba was smiling; the garden filled with light.
Everything shone with love and the happiness of
Uriah.

We could attempt a converse test: depoetize a page
of Gide, translate it, so to speak, into prose (prose in the
sense of *uninspired language*), then repoetize it by sub-
stituting the Gidean expressions for the familiar forms
and words. The experiment would reveal to what degree the emotion is the creator; exalted, it seeks expression: it is the animal's cry, the savage's feverish agitation or, despite the ritual clichés attached to the
circumstances, the colloquial invention of admirable expressions of passion, and finally, in the poet, the miracle
of a new language.

If we applied the same method of analysis to other
poetic passages by André Gide, we should easily manage to determine all the kinds of tones, all their varieties,
and we could classify them neither more nor less than in
botany or zoology. The interest of such a classification,
however, would be as limited as that of the catalogue of
pretexts we sketched in the last chapter. This is because
aesthetic effects are of interest only when connected
either to a theory that tries to account for them or to
specific texts which indicate, demonstrate their value.
Scholars, for example, have frequently drawn up tables of methods used by writers or established lists of
images employed by poets; these undertakings, for all
their experimental façade, are unusable, for they sys-
tematically put on the same level those effects which
succeed and those which do not come off, and fail to

take into account specific cases and differences in value. In aesthetics, taste is part of method.

We might observe this rule: if a theme is capable of being *named,* a tone which characterizes it in its expression must be *distinguishable.* The nuances of the theme produce the nuances of the tone, as it is natural that the emotion, undergoing various attitudes, should employ various languages. Love will assume a tender, voluptuous, urgent tone, etc.; passion a vehement tone; jealousy a tone either plaintive or reproachful. Since the theme of desire runs through Gide's poetic work, we have no need of a minute abstract of the passages where it is expressed or a count of the moments of pleasure in which it is satisfied to be certain that the dominant tone of Gidean poetry will be a tone of *fervor.* The texts we have quoted adequately manifest this ardor and its nuances of exaltation, of delight, of dissatisfaction, or of lapse.

Gide has not always fully succeeded here. Yet for the most part *accuracy (justesse)* of tone is one of his most eminent qualities, and one of the most French. But he has not achieved this without difficulties. There is still a good deal of affectation in certain overagitated phrases of the first brief treatises, whereas the propriety of tone is perfect in *le Retour de l'Enfant Prodigue.* To express the effect created by the perfect adaptation of the tones peculiar to each of the characters, and the subordination of all to a more general tone—grave, religious, biblical—I should not hesitate to call this dramatic parable, in somewhat barbarous terms, a *symphony of tones.* Consider the dialogue of the prodigal son, embarrassed, reticent, dissatisfied, with his older brother, severe, narrow-minded, rational—or his tender, vanquished, abandoned confidence in his mother, herself kind, anxious, questioning—or his serious discussion with his understanding father—and above all his dialogue with the younger son, where the theme of the double longing for escape and adventure is admirably transposed from one tone to another in the same character—the prodigal son—who shifts from the discouragement he feels to the encouragement he gives, handing on his disappointed hopes to his braver younger brother—and at the end a resolution, in the musical sense of the term, that dissolves the sentiments of the two brothers, the generous victim and the intrepid novice, in the harmony of a marvelous complicity.

The prodigal inclines his head and hides his face in his hands.

"But first?"

"I had walked a long time over the great untamed earth."

"The desert?"

"It was not always the desert."

"What were you seeking there?"

"I no longer understand what it was myself."

"Get up from my bed. Look, on the table beside my pillow, here, near this torn book."

"I see a cleft pomegranate."

"It is the swineherd who brought it to me the other evening, after he had been away for three days."

"Yes, it is a wild pomegranate."

"I know it; it is so bitter it is almost hideous; yet I feel that if I were thirsty enough, I should bite into it."

"Oh, I can tell you now; it is such a thirst as that I was seeking in the desert."

"A thirst which only this sugarless fruit can slake . . ."

"No; but you must love such thirst."

"Do you know where to pick them?"

"It is a little abandoned orchard, which you can reach before evening. No wall separates it from the desert any more. A stream used to flow there; a few half-ripe fruits were hanging from the branches."

"What fruits?"

"The same as those in our garden; but wild. It had been very hot all day long."

"Listen; do you know why I was waiting for you this evening? I am leaving before the night is done. This night; this night, once it fades . . . I have girded my loins, I have kept on my sandals this night."

"Oh! What I have not been able to do, you will do?"

"You have shown me the way, and the thought of you will sustain me."

"To admire you is my task; yours is to forget me, instead. What will you take with you?"

"You know that I am the younger son and have no share in the patrimony. I shall leave without anything."

"That is better."

"What are you looking at from the window?"

"The garden where our dead family is lying. . . ."

"My brother . . ." [and the child who has risen from the bed puts his arm, which becomes as gentle as his voice, around the prodigal's neck] "come with me."

"Leave me alone! Leave me! I am staying behind to console our mother. Without me you will be bolder. It is time now. The sky is paling. Leave without making any noise. Go now! Embrace me, my young brother: you take with you all my hopes. Be strong; forget us; forget me. May you not return . . . Go downstairs softly. I shall hold the lamp . . ."

"Oh, give me your hand as far as the door."

"Be careful of the steps at the threshold . . ."

How far Gide was from this mastery when he was writing the *Cahiers d'André Walter!* However interesting they may be for anyone who wants to study the formation of Gide's personality, it must be admitted that, compared with the works of his maturity or even of his youth, they are vastly inferior. The reader may recall that Gide, regretting his adolescence, once claimed to see in the sensual ardor that inspired the *Nourritures terrestres* only a caricature of mystical fervor. Yet from the aesthetic point of view, it is the contrary which is true. If there is a caricature of mysticism, it is in the *Cahiers d'André Walter* that we find it, but it is a caricature which is unconscious of itself, for the author is its victim. We find the true portrait of mysticism in *la Porte étroite*, without victimization of author or reader. André Walter's tone is forced, grandiloquent, and full of that juvenile sincerity which finds in itself a justification exceeding all other virtues. Instead of the *Nourritures terrestres* being a sensual distortion of André Walter's spirituality, it is the *Cahiers* that are a confused and clumsy draft of an impulse that will affirm itself as it gains in self-awareness and self-clarification. Moreover Gide has not deceived himself about this matter and has judged this early work severely. He has specified its defects with an irritated perspicacity: "When I reopen my *Cahiers d'André Walter* today, their jaculatory tone exasperates me. I affected at the time the kind of words which leave the imagination full licence, such as *uncertain, infinite, unspeakable*—to which I appealed, as Albert had recourse to mist to conceal the parts of his model he had difficulty drawing. Words of this kind, which abound in the German language, gave it a particularly poetic character in my eyes. I understood only much later that the character proper to the French language was a tendency toward precision. Aside from the evidence that these *Cahiers* bring to bear upon the anxious mysticism of my youth, there are very few passages of this book I should desire to preserve."

If the *Nourritures* are rich in nuances of fervor, and the *Enfant prodigue* dominated by a simple majesty worthy of the Scriptures, *El Hadj* is perhaps the most curious of those works composed in a serious tonality. Imagine a tale by Voltaire, remembering that narratives like *Candide* and *Zadig* are animated by the secret and ever-present idea of continual disappointment, and suppose that instead of being improvised in the rapid tone of pessimistic gaiety, it had been declaimed in the lingering tone of exalted bitterness. Even the curious length of the sentences, prolonged linearly from clause to clause, avoiding burdensome subordinations, contributes to the effect of an inner and somehow ruminative eloquence in the rancorous speeches which the false prophet, obliged to feign faith when he speaks in public, and with no refuge for his sincerity save in these intimately agonized monologues, addresses to himself in the secrecy of his tormented spirit.

With the detached tone, we appear to leave the poetic tone for the realm of the ironic, as we find it, for example, in *Paludes*. But actually, in works like the *Tentative amoureuse* and the *Voyage d'Urien*, what we discover instead is a delightful, disturbing, and flippant mélange of attachment and detachment, with all the surprise effects that can be provoked by the unexpected transition from one to the other. We are here faced with one of the peculiarities of André Gide's nature; this man is endowed to the highest degree with the faculty of correcting himself; capable of giving himself with enthusiasm, this critical spirit withdraws at the crucial moment, and even in his style, even in his syntax, occasionally even in the turn of his phrases, he persists in this behavior, which he rarely abandons in the manipulation of ideas, where it underlies a variegated thought, and by which it is likely he has given his life an unforgettable physiognomy. "I remember days when repeating to myself that two and two were

46

still four was enough to fill me with a definite beatitude
—and the mere sight of my fist on the table . . .

". . . and other days when such things were quite
indifferent to me."

But if we wish to grasp this movement at first hand,
we must consider how it intervenes to change the orientation of the narrative in a characteristic passage of
the *Tentative amoureuse:* "Luc longed for love, yet
feared carnal possession like a murderous thing . . .
Yet no! Luc was not like this; for it is an absurd ec-
centricity to make one's inventions always like oneself.
Consequently Luc possessed this woman." In the *Tentative amoureuse,* that delayed, postponed temptation,
there is a perpetual oscillation between abandonment
and refusal, between relative adherence and half with-
drawal, which gives this little work a half-poetic, half-
coquettish quality of *marivaudage.* Underneath it all
there is a playing with fire that manages to ennoble a
caprice in danger of falling into mere prettiness. Given
this fear of life, irony serves only to mask a lack of
self-confidence; it constitutes the rather thin and acid
charm of the *Poésies d'André Walter.* Already more
self-assured, the self-conscious irony of the *Voyage
d'Urien* anticipates the social and moral irony of *Paludes,* the metaphysical irony of *le Prométhée mal enchaîné.* This irony functions, moreover, in settings which
are in no way ironic but on the contrary treated with
a loving respect for a decorative and sumptuous nature,
where one is not surprised to find taken quite seriously
figures and episodes apparently straight out of legend.
We see that here too there is room for a play of tones,
subtle, graceful, and not without a certain preciosity.
Thus the charm of evocations into which one lets oneself be lured is intertwined with the implicit and im-
manent mockery which effects a release from one's own
romanticism, a subject that has become classic with
Don Quixote and *Madame Bovary.*

47

Irony can mask a latent poetry, to the degree that it represents the defense and the modesty of a sensitive emotion with which we sympathize. Irony is then a paradoxical poetry turned against the very adversaries of poetry. The ironist is then a poet who makes himself an *homme d'esprit* in order to oppose *la raison bourgeoise*. There is another irony, not aerial but heavy, which is the irony of *la raison bourgeoise* against poetic illusion. But the prettiest form of irony is that which is practiced, by a delicate kind of decency, toward what one loves, and it is with this kind of irony that the young Gide protects himself against the emotions of his still-tender sensibility. This is why a great deal of poetry still remains in the false bottom of a satire like *Paludes*. In the *Voyage d'Urien*, the caustic pungency of irony appears only occasionally, to provide a comic relief on this journey down the long course of an ever-meandering fancy.

A final observation: when this irony is humanized, we may remark traces of familiarity in the tone. It appears that Gide was encouraged in this path by the vogue of Jules Laforgue. We know in any case that he admired the *Moralités légendaires*, but it is the Laforgue of the *Complaintes* that seems to have influenced him, though only at rare moments. Laforgue's originality has perhaps been only to introduce into the language of the gods the tone of triviality; at most he has been able to give Gide an instrument; to lend him a suitable cadence. A few of Gide's things in verse have passages whose flippancy recalls the Laforguian tone:

> But you exclaimed: "Enough
> Of this abstract dogmatism!
> This reading all the time
> Has given me a headache!"

And here is even a Laforguian pretext:

The moon, oh! the moon
Will not rise very high tonight.
If the moon importunes you,
We'd be better off sitting down.

Here is the vocabulary: the metempsychoses, the
sound of the horn, the *automne* that rhymes with *monotone*, the characteristic tics of language, the predilection for the adverb *lors*, the substantive expressions "a
farewell, like a 'good-by,'" and the notation by apostro-
phes of the elisions of a relaxed diction:

> *M'amour, ne t'mets donc pas en peine:*
> *Dans six ou sept jours je m'amène . . .*
> *J'ai dit six; ce c'sra p't'êtr' que quatre:*
> *Faut pourtant pas t'laisser abattre.*

Fortunately the tone of popular irony represents only
an accident in Gide's work. It *jars*.

There is a well-known device in poetry which is quite
difficult to place. It can be taken for an ornament, and
it is often the essential part of the poem. It is neither
theme nor pretext, though inspired like the former, pictorial and concrete like the latter. It is relatively independent of form, for it can be expressed in several
ways, and it is related to form by the distinctness of its
contour. It is related to thought because it manifests a
relation, and to language because it is at the root of
most words. One could not say it constitutes a tone
in itself, and yet by the way it is chosen it contributes
to the nature of the tone. It is not a style, but it is in
style, and serves to qualify it. The reader has recognized *the image*.

The image can assume many forms, and it is at the
basis of many figures, swift metaphor or developed
comparison. But it is particularly important to separate
the poetic image from other kinds. Its function is dif-

ferent. The poetic image is a vigorous and voluptuous satisfaction of the theme. Other images are merely pictorial or explanatory. The distinction between poetic images and the rest is almost always easy to make, provided one feels spontaneously, although some cases may lend themselves to argument, as is natural, given the diversity of sensibilities and the subjectivity of poetic pleasure. Images are relatively rare in Gide, and this despite the abundant examples one could cite. We know, first of all, that it is impossible to write without them, or at least without metaphors, since all language is metaphorical, and it is certain that one would have no difficulty finding more illustrations in one of Gide's contemporaries like Claudel. This rarification in Gide is both natural and deliberate. Heredia having remarked of the *Cahiers d'André Walter* that "they suffered from a certain dearth of images," Gide replied that "he still found too many." Elsewhere Gide ridicules those literary men who could not see an object without its immediately reminding them of another. Apparently he had just reread Jules Renard.

Besides, Gide is perhaps the author who has most reduced the interval between the image in the psychological acceptation of the term and the image taken poetically. This is understandable, if we note that Gide, being rather lacking in imagination and not inclined to impose upon reality an analogical faculty he does not possess, always brings his entire attention to bear on his immediate perception. It is in order to refine this perception, to improve it, that he is impelled by the intensity of his representation to transcend language itself, despite what his exquisite knowledge of it enables him to discover by way of resources, in order to conclude with the metaphor adhering most closely to the idea. In Gide, metaphor paints. It will show us riverbanks *"blooming* with pink flamingos," a delightful extension of meaning which is miraculously justified. He will use a verb that adds a dramatic sense to the impression of movement in order to make visible the diminution of "a narrow stretch of shade that the sun was gradually *strangling*."

One might almost say that in Gide metaphor is anterior to expression and interior to perception. This is what one feels in comparing passages like these, which illustrate a complete transposition of the sense organs: "And for a long time the inquiring eye listens to how a blue tone changes to pink, then from pink to rust, to red-gold." "Through all my exhausted and flayed senses, I drank in . . ." "My eye which, in the absence of sunlight was fasting these last few days, wakens to the sun, wanders and stares with appetite." If this playful series comes off without being really poetic, here is one that does not, at least to our Western eyes; yet it might please Orientals, who are less timid about the incoherence of images: "Oh!" exclaims El Hadj, "if the wind were to carry me off on its wings, to the other end of the blazing sea.

"Oh! let it be where the bleeding moon, shepherd of the sky, will bathe before returning to pasture!" A few pages later these incompatibilities are reassimilated in a semisuccess where only one detail, the shepherd, still comes as a shock:

I speak to him of the great trees of the north
And of the cold ponds where the moon,
Shepherd of the sky, like a mistress, will go to bathe.

And despite his fondness for the Persian poets, Gide manages the Oriental tone less well than the biblical. We know from his *Journal* that one of the books he envied most was Meredith's *Shaving of Shagpat*.

It has often been remarked that poets compare one object to several others; it has been insufficiently noted that the same term of comparison often attracts them enough to subjugate the quite diverse objects of their experience to it. We may call such returns of an image *motifs*. The motif is an excellent index of sensibility. What would be a favorite motif for a lover of pleasure who has drained it to the dregs? The image of ash, the final product of combustion, is in order. This motif is hardly original, but Gide has renewed it by accentuating its material qualities, by closely associating it with other metaphors—wind, burning—thereby combining with the modalities of sensation experiences not directly in the realm of the senses, such as time, memory . . . and finally juxtaposing the metaphor with the representation of its real prototype, the ash of the hearth, beside the ash of time. Take the following three examples from the *Tentative amoureuse:* "O you objects of our desires, you are even as those perishable substances which, once our fingers grasp them, leave nothing more than ash.

"Rise then, winds of my thought—that will scatter this ash."

From the *Renoncement au voyage:* "O, had the night been more resonant still, the vaporous air even clearer, the perfumes more intoxicating, what would be left me, this morning, but a little ashen memory that gathers in the hollow of my heart, that a little wind will scatter, leaving where it was only a charred place." And finally, from the same work: "I waited and followed, motionless, the slow disintegration of the hours; there remained, toward the end of the day, an ash of subtle time, bitter to the taste, soft to the touch, in looks quite like the ashes of this hearth, between the little columns, here, near the mysterious cellar, to the left: where sometimes, pushing away the ashes, the attendant revives a half-extinguished coal under the heap . . ."

We have remarked that Gide's poetic treatment was pantheist and sympathetic rather than anthropomorphic. The metaphors that animate the inanimate are rare in his work. He describes the mirage as a dream the desert might have: "Beneath the unshaded sunlight, the mirage grows now. Flowing water, deep gardens, palaces, it is the impotent desert that dreams, before the nonexistent reality, like a destitute poet." Elsewhere, "the startled oasis trembles, tries to live." And with a happy choice of words Gide paints "the staggering sand of the desert"—this last, quite objective example comparable with another quite subjective one, in which the personal impression is somehow transferred to the thing that has produced it: "I have drunk many wines since, but none gave, I know, that vertigo of fasting, that vacillation of the plain in broad daylight, before I fell asleep, the sun risen, in the hollow of a haystack."

Gide's metaphor can appear as an attenuated comparison: "Here, touching the dune, at ground level, a deeper crimson line in the distance, a cloud bloody and streaming, even as a scorch upon the sky"; or turn to explicit comparison: "An uncertain sun tries to smile at the desert, and like a cosmetic on a corpse, crumbs of salt turn silver." Gide especially favors wide-ranging metaphors and comparisons, like the transparence of Philoctetes, which tends toward the symbolic. They are often psychological:

> But desire, Joab! desire enters the soul
> like a hungry stranger . . .

and:

> The sky was so pure that you heard the springs murmur.
> And the darkness seemed, around Uriah,
> a calm deepening of his happiness . . .

Or, again, this admission of the poet's discouragement:

"Today I reread my travel notes. For whom should I publish them?—They will be like those resinous secretions which yield their perfume only when warmed by

the hand holding them." But Gide is sparing of these
lyrical extensions. He is shy of emphasis, and his images
tend to be reabsorbed in the rarity of the expression
itself. Consequently one no longer knows whether there
is a metaphor or a perfect verbal adequacy when he
describes for us, in the desert night of El Hadj, the
moon *decomposing* in silence. But Gide even renounces
—and this was the greatest test of his art—the *search*
for expression, and one might quote certain phrases
where the metaphors are made deliberately banal until
they reveal the nakedness of the thought: "My heart,
drained of everything, *fills* with love. *At the price* of all
my goods, I had *bought* fervor." Here the images re-
side more in the words' relations than in their quality.

Fundamentally Gide prefers to paint or draw rather
than to compare. He is not mistaken. Comparison is not
an end in itself; it is only a means of expressing a vision
that resists words or of prolonging a sentiment that
would otherwise cease. Instead Gide will give us exemplary scenes that harmonize many specific details, without conflicts or disparities, to produce the effect of unity:
"Hail, morning full of smiles . . .

"The sea, leveled by the sun, stands straight before
me like a wall of light, a pane of pearly iridescence
that the fine, faint line of the mist-softened, spongy-
looking hills frames and separates from the sky. In the
still-foggy harbor, invaded by the smoke of enormous
ships, a trembling flight of sailboats scatters, rises to the
gleaming open sea and, oars occasionally outstretched,
glides and seems to soar as though in liquid light. And
opposite the sun, upon the earth, between the trembling
quays and the sky, the city laughs." And he will ex-
quisitely prolong the fleeting moment: "Now is the
time, I was thinking, when the blue smoke rises from
El Kantara and steals away the oasis. Bou Saada is not
so beautiful, but the *ksar*, filling now with murmurs,
seems, at the moment it enters the night, to grow sud-

denly excited like the African sparrows in the branches
before sleep touches them."

If the comparison is only an accessory, though a
choice one, in Gide's poetic formulation, it is because
he is much less a dreamer than an observer. There is a
crucial passage in the *Renoncement au voyage* where
he himself explains as much. Describing what he can
see of Rome from the Pincio, he adds: "Leaning over
the balustrade, resting on my elbows like Polyhymnia,
in the posture that makes the passer-by say: 'he is a
dreamer,' I do not dream at all; I look . . . No, I am
not dreaming. And what would I dream about? Why,
before this reality, should I close my eyes in order to
dream?" His poetry does not turn away from reality;
nor does it accept it only to transfigure it; quite simply,
Gide's poetry is born of reality. And that is why
Gide's pretexts have a more urgent necessity than those
of other authors. They are not so much chosen as accepted and, so to speak, submitted to.

We now come to the poetic formulation itself. Gide's
prose, from the first, was already firm, if a little forced;
it was always to remain studied. He tells us, apropos
of the first pages of his *Journal* that nourished the
Cahiers d'André Walter and the narrative of *Un Voyage
en Bretagne:* "Everything I might have expressed easily
seemed commonplace to me, without interest." His first
works are too well written. Yet young Athman, whom
he met in Algeria, found his *Tentative amoureuse* badly
written; he preferred Hérold's *Joie de Maguelonne;* he
told Gide, "You use the word 'grass' too often." But from
this time on, we shall find Gide carefully inventing a
prose which faithfully reproduces the contours of his
thought. When Valéry asked him, at this period, to express in a phrase, a metaphor, the movements of a
swimmer holding his clothes out of the water with one
arm, Gide replied that he wouldn't want to "express

this movement otherwise than by the movement of the sentence . . . Nonsense; but then, we were scarcely over twenty." We find in Gide, less than in other authors however, some of the verbal mannerisms and period phraseology which have given a dated look to many works of the symbolist school. He borrows from its precious vocabulary, but already with the discretion imposed by his sharp sense of the ridiculous. The charm of the early treatises is a little faded today, as is the rather Maeterlinckian tinge of the names of the dim characters who slip through the *Voyage d'Urien,* bearing patronymics whose strangeness, sometimes turns to mystery, sometimes to a kind of familiarity: Urien, Nathanaël, Mélian, Agloval, Cabilor, Paride, Pargain, Alfasar, Axel, Aguisel; or Tradelineau, Ydier, Lambègue, Odinel, Clarion, Hélain, not to mention the women, who are rare in this book—the beautiful and perfumed Queen Haiatalnefus, and the charming Ellis who waited for fourteen days on the lawn, sitting under an apple tree, with her polka-dot dress, her cerise parasol, a plaid shawl over her arm, eating an endive salad while reading the *Prolegomena to any future Metaphysics.*

Gide will long retain a predilection for the rare word, or rather for the rare use of a word, and for the neologism, or rather for the re-creation of a term: he will call a vision *miragineux,* refer to the *monomorphie* of palm trees, the *ternissures* of heat, and describe the property of memories as *immédiatité;* he will use an infinitive like *emboire,* an adjective like *prévespéral.* On the other hand, he will hazard the adverb *clémentement,* coin a verbal adjective like *surodorant,* create a whole series of privative verbs: *dépondérer, désennoblir, déséprendre.* He will even affect archaic turns of phrase, like the imperfect subjunctive to indicate volition:—*"Ah! que m'emportât une lame assez forte."* He will transform a pronoun into a substantive: *"le quelconque de sa banalisation";* present participles into verbal adjectives, and overuse this mannerism: *"les attendantes réponses."*

The preference for rendering the concrete by the abstract will lead him to use the substantive in the adjective's place. This too is a symbolist characteristic. We recall in Henri de Régnier:

> *La forêt résonnante où se dresse*
> *La multiplicité verticale des troncs.*

Instead of referring to the desert as *"diversement monotone,"* Gide will describe it as *"d'une diverse monotonie,"* adding a recherché turn of phrase to the abstraction.

Like every great writer, and in an entirely classical fashion that recalls Racine, Gide will combine words to establish a relation among them both striking and natural. This was the case of the preceding example (*diverse monotonie*), as well as when he describes a handsome old cadi whose poverty *"garde une dignité discrète."* As well as these combinations based on contrast, there are hidden analogies which satisfy the imagination, such as those carriage wheels which, on entering the sand, *"crissaient soyeusement."* Elsewhere an eloquent adaptation gives his adjectives a value all the greater in that the neutral substantive is touched by a strange accent, as when Gide is astonished to cross *"un pays rauque."* Consider too, by an effect analogous to the energetic qualification of the substantive, the generous form assumed by the adverb when joined to the verb, of which it forms a kind of adjective: *"Peut-être irrite-t-il les dieux par sa pensée et cesse-t-il* horriblement *de nous souhaiter la victoire."*

We have seen that, despite his metaphors, Gide's style avoids metaphor. We might also say that despite his stylistic efforts, Gide's style avoids effects. His preferences are for sparingness, sobriety, purity, almost to the

point of dryness. In one of his *Feuillets* he has judged
the matter perfectly: "H. C. accused me one day of
coquetry in the arrangement of my sentences; nothing
could be more mistaken. Only the strict, the stripped
pleases me. When I began to write my *Nourritures*, I
realized that the very subject of my book was to exile
every metaphor from it. There is not one movement of
my sentences that does not correspond to a need for
order. The writer's eloquence must be the eloquence of
the soul itself, of thought; artificial elegance is a burden
and an object of contempt to me. As is any secondhand
poetry." This naked prose, without academicism or
bizarrerie, is in the tradition of the finest French prose,
in the line that descends from Rousseau and Chateaubriand. It will be of incomparable service to the author
of the *récits* and the autobiographer of *Si le Grain ne
meurt* . . . We must admire this exact art, so lightly
moved yet of an enchanting sensitivity in this impeccable page: "We are in sight of Touggourt. The sinking
sun deepens in color. The sky is uniquely blue, a blue
gilded around the edges. The approaches to Touggourt
surpass all my memories. On the horizon to the left, the
fine line of the oasis that continues from M'garine seems
a coast, and the sandy sea on which we sail comes to
meet it. To the right, nothing; the gold sand that meets
the tremulous gold of the sky. In front of us, imposing
Touggourt.

"Haven delayed! Far away still, one sees on the slope,
almost beyond the oasis, only two strange minarets silhouetted like lighthouses, black against the sky.

"Yet the sun is vanishing. In the east, the sand, pink
and green for an instant, immediately turns livid, its
pallor exquisite beneath the pink and lilac sky . . ."

Gide's prose is especially remarkable for the originality of its syntax. His sentence is sometimes wrought to
the point where it apparently breaks under the strain:
"*Je me soutenais par orgueil, mais regrettais alors*

Hilaire qui me départissait l'an d'avant de ce que mon humeur avait sinon de trop farouche."

Gide likes to restore the tone of an adjective by placing it before the substantive. He will say *"une préalable torpeur," "les distantes crêtes," "nulle retorse méthode."* He frames a quite simple substantive with two adjectives heavily charged with meaning: *"une suffocante eau transparente."* He makes almost an abuse of inversions. The sentences are countless in which the subject is shifted to follow the verb: *"Sous une grelottante rosée, la plane Mitidja s'irisait; il semblait que coulât vers elle, émanant du flanc des montagnes, l'azur."*

There are examples of this kind of thing on almost every page of the *Renoncement au voyage.* Here is an extremely odd one where the subject follows two propositions which it controls: *"J'admire, instrument léger, quelle diversité je goûte en ta monotonie, suivant qu'in-siste en en précipitant le cours, ou que l'endort sous son souffle charmant l'enfant musicien aux doigts souples."* Similarly he inverts the verb after the complement: *"Devant moi, sur l'autre versant, croissait l'ombre; et, quand elle atteignit les troupeaux, ceux-ci, brusquement dévalant, vers le repos du soir s'acheminèrent."* By the significance of the word set at the end of the proposition, and which he separates from the element to which it refers, Gide obtains an effect of relief, and produces in prose an effect analogous to that of the run-on line in verse. He is fond, too, of constructions in which inversion is obligatory or customary. Since he does not hesitate to place these sentences beside direct constructions, the two types complement each other, as surprise and repose. Notice, moreover, all the beginnings of sentences in a page of Gide's: save for the case of intentional repetitions, they are of an extreme diversity. On each occasion the mind is struck or captured by a different *pace.*

The linking elements of the clauses are no less singular. *El Hadj,* particularly, musters all the means of making a sentence progress from one relative clause to another. It uses the conjunction *and* in a particular way to co-ordinate divergent grammatical elements that are without parallelism. Speaking of a eucalyptus branch, Gide will say: *"branche heureuse, et dont la lumière, aujourd'hui, mieux que l'ondée d'hier, lave les feuilles."*

But where Gide has been boldest is in the *disarticulation* of the sentence. He disjoints his phrases not to break them but to make them more supple, as one might train young acrobats. Supposing one wanted to make the remark, one might say that it is necessary, if rosebushes are to produce splendid blooms, that they do not flower all year round: *"Oui, pensai-je, c'est ainsi que, seuls, les rosiers soumis à l'engourdissement de l'hiver produisent les roses les plus belles."*—and that would already be a rather "wrought" sentence. Gide will say: *"Oui, c'est ainsi, pensai-je, que produisent les roses les plus belles les seuls rosiers soumis à l'engourdissement de l'hiver."* Gide would not say with Monsieur Jourdain's teacher: *"Belle marquise, vos beaux yeux me font mourir d'amour";* he would say: *"Vos yeux beaux, belle marquise, d'amour mourir me font."* Gide is a poet and rearranges all the logical elements of a sentence in an order that speaks to the heart. This arrangement is apparent in a brief passage like the following, which might have adopted a rational order: *"Mais le regret de ce jardin, le soir—de ce jardin de nuit où j'allais tous les soirs . . . ah! comment le supporterai-je?"*

There is also, in this modulation of the laws of harmony, a resultant gain in suppleness. Suppose that you wished to indicate that at a certain period of your life the little town of Blida was perfumed by the odor of kief, you might say—poetically enough: "What shall I tell you? there was a time when all Blida was scented with its narcotic odor." Gide says: *"Il fut un temps, que vous dirai-je? où de sa narcotique odeur Blida toute était embaumée."* Notice the placing of the adjective before the substantive: "narcotique *odeur*"; the shifting of the subject to follow the complement: *"de sa narcotique odeur* Blida," the first giving the second its atmosphere, particularly since it is immediately linked to it by juxtaposition; the isolation of *toute*: "Blida toute," which seems to extend the effluvia of perfume even more; and above all, the two chief accents of the sentence's close, which fall on two words with parallel effects: *odeur* and *embaumée*, creating between these two notions a *rhyme of ideas.*

This subtle disarticulation of syntax causes the normally constructed sentences to seem finer, more assured, and to produce an effect of noble simplicity. Extended, they no longer seem to assume the inner rhythm the poet meant to impose upon things, but to conform suitably to their natural structure . . .

The other characteristic of Gide's syntax is *condensation.* He prefers constructions which permit him to omit words. As in the locutions inherited from old French, he gladly omits the article: *"La racine . . . s'épaississait alors,* formait tigelle, *puis* tronc *nouveau."* He prefers economical particles, the relative *quoi,* on which he confers a kind of neutrality: *"Petite flûte à quatre trous, par quoi l'ennui du désert se raconte."* He abbreviates the forms of negation: *"N'ayant goût de fixer rien de mortel."* He writes *non voir* rather than *ne pas voir, non doutant* rather than *ne doutant pas.* He prefers the present or past participles that eliminate all superfluity and replace a longer subordinate clause. Nothing is more curious than the structure, at first glance too juxtaposed, of an aerated phrase like the following one, where an adjective and a past participle each stand for a whole proposition: *"Les vastes terres qu'au mois dernier, sèches, je vis roussâtres et vides, à présent, attendries, verdissent."* He chooses, for their brevity rather than for their rarity, rather uncommon turns like the interrogative form of the first person of the present indicative: *"me trompé-je!"* He derives a comic effect from it in *Paludes*—the famous and ludicrous *"gémis-je?"*

But Gide's prose is particularly rich in ellipses. Ellipsis of the verb: *"Quand la nuit eût été plus sonore, quand l'air plus vaporeux, quand plus amoureux les parfums."* Ellipsis of the auxiliary: *"l'éclosion de l'amour et l'étreinte seront mêlées de fièvre, la volupté, à peine naissante, pâmée . . ."* There is a kind of slight rest before the second past participle. The most felicitous result of these ellipses is poetic density. Gide has been able to combine this with amplitude, as in this sentence, which closes on a condensation of phrase mixed with repetitions: *"Comment rentrer, comment dormir, sachant qu'au dehors, dans l'air doux, cette claire lueur continue, et, sachant que la lune, avant mon départ de ces lieux n'éclairera pour moi la ville, chaque nuit qu'un peu plus tardive et chaque nuit qu'un peu décrue?"*

The poetic formulation finds its completion in a verbal music.

The reader has already anticipated, when we characterized Gide's syntax by *disarticulation* and *condensation,* how much the breaks and cesuras of the sentence count in the rhythmical intentions of his work. One might say the same of the successions of elements that serve as much for prolonging a cadence as for evocative purposes. This is the case when a series of circumstantial objects of the verb each adds a tiny touch and a measure to a musical *tableau:* "In the third café, a very old Arab wearing glasses was reading a story to a whole motionless crowd. And, for fear of breaking the thread of it, I refused to go in but stood outside, at the door, on a bench, in the dark, for a long time . . ." I ventured to use the expression *rhyme of ideas* apropos of a sinuous sentence on the perfume of kief in Blida; this rhyme of ideas was accentuated by the quality of the two rhythmic elements, two octosyllabic lines:

Où de sa narcotique odeur
Blida toute était embaumée.

It would be puerile to consider all the types of rhythm of which so harmonious an *oeuvre* furnishes examples. First of all, there are probably no exceptions to be found. (This is the danger of enumerations ready-made in advance.) I should prefer to point out that Gide's punctuation frequently functions as musical bars for measures: "*Voici le vieux Hamman; près duquel un café; . . .*" or in "*on était bien; on était aise; on étouffait.*" Notice the equality of the elements (two measures of six, three measures of four).

Even in the most muted passages, the emotion of the voice is apparent. It is the pressure of this secret force which, slightly constrained and gently liberated, impels Gide to punctuate with brief exclamations the sinuosity of phrases that model themselves after the form of desire and flatter its solicitations. Gide's exclamatory sentence is never more remarkable than when it sets the exclamation in an unaccustomed place within the clause it syncopates, and it is in this sense interval that there appears, with sudden aspiring intensity, a sigh releasing an ardent, concentrated poetry, a bird-cry punctuating the melody's continuity. Consider the end of the advice to Nathanaël: "*et crée de toi, impatiemment ou patiemment, ah! le plus irremplaçable des êtres.*" This method, which could so easily have degenerated into a mannerism, has been a happy innovation in the interrupted or suspended expression of hope or desire. Gide also employs the usual methods which place the exclamation of desire and pleasure at the beginning of the clause: "*Que souhaiter encore, coeur exigeant, coeur inlassable? . . . Par ces chaudes journées, je songe à l'essor des nomades; ah! pouvoir à la fois demeurer ici, fuir ailleurs! Ah! s'évaporer, se défaire, et qu'un souffle d'azur, où je serais dissous, voyageât . . . !*"

Note how another exclamation, the admiring *Oh!*, worn though it is, is filled with splendid passion at the end of this musing evocation: *"Dans l'automne de Normandie je rêve au printemps du désert . . . La rafale du Nord bat ma vitre. Il pleut depuis trois jours.— Oh! que les caravanes étaient belles, quand, le soir, à Touggourt, le soleil se couchait dans le sel."* By doubling the exclamation, Gide sometimes manages to paint the extreme excitation of desire or the crisis of pleasure. But in these cases the effect borders on failure; it risks making us smile.

I shall not linger over the play of alliterations and assonances, the expressive combinations of sounds which rely both on meaning and on rhythm. In a page where Gide, evoking the desert by the analogy of a little flute, gives us a kind of *ars poetica*, and a highly developed example of it, let us note simply the initiatory attack of the "t's" at the start, then, in what follows, the lightness of the vowels sustained by several splendid sonorities, either low-pitched or veiled by nasals:

> *"Petite flûte à quatre trous, par quoi l'ennui du désert se raconte, je te compare à ce pays, et reste à t'écouter t'ébruiter sans arrêt dans le soir. Ah! de combien peu d'éléments est fait ici notre bruit et notre silence! le moindre changement y paraît. —Eau, ciel, terre et palmiers . . . j'admire, instrument léger, quelle diversité subtile je goûte en ta monotonie, suivant qu'insiste en en précipitant le cours, ou que l'endort sous son souffle charmant l'enfant musicien aux doigts souples.*
>
> *"Je voudrais que, de page en page, évoquant quatre tons mouvants, les phrases que j'écris ici soient pour toi ce qu'était pour moi cette flûte, ce que fut pour moi le désert—de diverse monotonie."*

It would be unfair not to remark that Gide's poetry in verse, without being of the same value as his prose,

has its own relaxed and delicate form. He has even succeeded, in the four songs of 1911 reprinted in the
Nouvelles Nourritures, in modulating with naïve suavity
a pure, aerial song that at moments achieves the crystal
of Valéry and at times the touching simplicity of Marceline Desbordes-Valmore:

> *La brise vagabonde*
> *A caressé les fleurs.*
> *Je t'écoute de tout mon coeur,*
> *Chant du premier matin du monde.*

The poems of the *Nourritures terrestres* are quite different, heavy with substance. When he wrote the *Ronde
de la Grenade* ("without preconceived notions"), Gide
had no intention other than a "more subtle obedience
to the interior rhythm." But is this not an illusion shared
by many symbolists and writers of *vers libre?* Like the
psychological melody, the interior rhythm seems to be a
metaphor, a simple *façon de parler.* Rhythm comes only
from varied repetition, and consequently from breaks in
the continuum. It is only at the moment when the interior life yields to language that it becomes conscious
of itself; only by expressing itself does it assume a
rhythm, though that rhythm is first of all an interior
one. Whatever the case, the poems of the *Nouvelles
Nourritures* are of an extremely irregular form, exhibiting the charm of verse alternating with the delights of
a more or less freely rhythmed prose. It should be noted,
moreover, that quite often, after a more or less strict
beginning, these pieces run out into pure prose. Occasionally we get a cadence of versicles whose accents
have a decisive pace. The multiplicity and the anarchy
of forms, moreover, fit together well and contribute flavor
to the general design of this rich and diffuse work.

Gide's real music is in his prose. However unobtrusive
it may be there, it is no less essential. It depends less
on sonorities than on a complex ensemble difficult to

isolate, on the continuity or, occasionally, on the discontinuity of a slightly accented but supple song, preferring slight intervals to violent leaps, uniting originality of rhythm to exquisiteness of melody, as is clearly indicated by Gide's favorite word in speaking of his prose: its *number,* a term which implies many constituent elements. But we cannot exaggerate its importance, as this declaration of Gide's in his *Journal* for 1923 proves: "The exigence of my ear, until recent years, was such that I would have subjugated the significance of a phrase to its number." Add to this another admission in which Gide decides that the writer must let himself be guided by words, as the musician by sounds, and we understand why, between the two mental families which he distinguishes—the poets and the artists—and which he has placed under the double sign of the Dioscuri, Castor and Pollux, Gide should, here too, have put himself in the *extreme center.* Gide is, in fact, as we have seen, a poet and an artist in his lyric prose. But is he the same distance from the two poles of creation? As in politics there is a center where we can still discern a left and a right, we see that Gide seems rather right of center—that is, though certainly both poet and artist, he is notably closer to art than to poetry.

3. Ironic Works (i. The *Soties*)

Irony is the contrary of fervor, yet irony frequently presumes fervor. It proceeds from it, being fervor *inverted*. It was therefore almost inevitable that the poet of *André Walter* and *les Nourritures* should be counterbalanced by the satirist of *Paludes* and *le Prométhée mal enchaîné*. If we add to these two disturbing little books the adventure story entitled *les Caves du Vatican*, we have the only three works Gide has baptized with the curious subtitle *soties*—reviving an old word from the theatrical vocabulary of the late Middle Ages. Naturally dramatic form has nothing to do with the works in question here. Gide's *soties* are tales in which wisdom is dissimulated beneath folly, as his *récits* disclose folly under the simulacra of wisdom. A tale like *Isabelle* would be a good example of a point where the two series intersect. But we might wonder if, in a sense, all of Gide's works are not *soties*. In all of them, even *les Nourritures*, in the plays *Saül* and *le Roi Candaule*, in *les Faux Monnayeurs*, the critical spirit is present.

Gide's ironic works include, in any case, the three *récits*, so frequently misconstrued, which preceded the publication of *les Caves du Vatican: l'Immoraliste, la*

Porte étroite, Isabelle, and no doubt also those which were to follow it: *la Symphonie pastorale,* and the trilogy: *l'École des Femmes, Robert, Geneviève.* Gide has denied the name of novel to all these works, although *les Caves* had been announced as a *roman d'aventures* and both *l'Immoraliste* and *la Porte étroite,* in spite of their author's wishes, have been published as novels. In the dedicatory letter to Jacques Copeau in *les Caves du Vatican,* which, moreover, was suppressed by Gide just as the book was going to press, the author declares: "Why do I call this book a *sotie?* Why call the three which precede it *récits?* To make clear that they are not, strictly speaking, novels. Still, it matters little to me if they are taken for such, provided I am not later accused of *not* fulfilling the rules of the "genre"; and of failing by reason of chaos and confusion. —*Récits, soties*—it seems to me that I have written up until today only ironic or, if you prefer, only critical works."

We shall deal first with the *soties.*

These *soties* are enigmatic satires. *Les Caves,* actually, thanks to its novelistic procedures, seems more explicit, but *Paludes* and *le Prométhée mal enchaîné,* enveloped and even lost in the meanders of a burlesque whimsicality, might pass for obscure works. But the fate of obscure works is to become clearer, until posterity is astonished at the incomprehension manifested by their contemporaries. It is true that the same applies to works that have been regarded as clear from the first, and whose obscurity we are then obliged to discover. Like other works by Gide, the *soties* require the reader's collaboration. Their very mysteriousness has a specific purpose. A work must make us work—make an effort; it must not leave us as we were when we began it, it must instruct us, "broach" us, as Gide says, and in order to do this is not the best way to disturb us? "A splendid function to assume; that of disturber," he writes in the *Nouvelle Pages de Journal.* Then too, a

mysterious book grows even deeper upon rereading; it
develops its implications, and (assuming, of course, that
the interpretation remains faithful to the spirit of the
book) it is not impossible that the author's thought
may then be followed—correctly, according to its course
—even beyond his own awareness. We know how much
Gide has always feared sacrificing possibilities by making a choice. In *Paludes* he did not intend to lose that
surplus of intentions which the book might include even
without his knowledge. "Before explaining my book to
others, I expect others to explain it to me. To attempt
to explain it first is immediately to limit its meaning;
for, if we know what we wanted to say, we do not
know if we were saying only that. —One always says
more than THAT. —And what particularly interests me
is what I have put in without knowing it—that unconscious share which I should like to call God's share
[Gide will later call this the Devil's share]. —Let us
await the revelation of things from all sides; from the
public, the revelation of our works."

In any satire there is a negative share and a positive.
The negative portion is more amusing, the positive more
serious and instructive. The former concerns what one
attacks; the latter, what one defends, and the two are
indissolubly linked, like the real and the ideal. If we are
to deal with a satire properly, discerning its true meaning, we had best try to distinguish, through the objects
of its ridicule, its moral affirmations, for every satire has
a moral intention. That is what we shall do apropos of
Paludes and *le Prométhée mal enchaîné*.

What complicates the analysis of the refusals fundamental to a work like *Paludes* is that it is, on the one
hand, a satire more hinted at than worked out, and on
the other so generalized that the author can ask in the
dedication: "For my friend Eugène Rouart, I wrote this
satire on what?"

Satire on what? was doubtless what Gide's readers must have asked for a long time too, rare as they were in 1895 when he published, amid general indifference ("a dismal flop"), this opusculum that was still innocent for being so little handled, but which has since continued to exercise upon young minds its function of disturbing.

Paludes has been called a satire on the commonplace, and also a satire on moral stagnation as symbolized by the story of Tityre surrounded by marshlands, whose civil status Gide has borrowed from Virgil and whose story the nameless hero of *Paludes* proposes to write under this same title, but (judging from the extracts of it we are shown) in a poetic and serious guise —while Gide's *Paludes* includes and transcends the *Paludes* of his mouthpiece in a deliberately comic presentation. Here as elsewhere, we measure the extent of the distance between Gide and the representative characters he puts before the public; he does not intend to endow any of them with full responsibility. Yet even more than a satire on banality or on sloth, *Paludes* is a satire on resignation. And, in fact, one cannot long satirize things, or the state of things, or of manners, without attacking that human disposition morally responsible for them. Which is why any satire supposes freedom and always indicts the misuse of our freedom.

The indictment is conducted in an insidious manner which is one of the charms of *Paludes*. The problem is constantly concealed and constantly reappears in a new form, like an obsession that is discreet in its aspect and insistent in its repetition and polymorphism. This is what gives its unity to this little notebook kept from day to day (for a little less than a week) by the simultaneously stubborn and whimsical, anguished and ludicrous writer, in whom Gide has entertained himself by seeing the author of a *Paludes* which is and yet is not his own.

In his relations with the dim, absurd beings of his acquaintance, this author vainly tries to make them share his anguish and to understand the subject of *Paludes* (which is the same thing). And, quite judiciously, he adapts the subject to the personality of each of his interlocutors (if they may be said to possess anything so distinct) or to the circumstances which regularly provoke the avowal of their preoccupations.

We consequently have—already!—a whole series of interpretations of *Paludes* anterior to *Paludes* itself, and these gradually rough out its meaning and finally etch the identity of the thought beneath the diversity of the symbols. "*Paludes* is the story of a bachelor in a tower surrounded by marshlands . . . He watches the bogs." —"*Paludes* is the story of a man who, possessing the field of Tityre, does not try to leave it, but on the contrary is content to stay there." —"*Paludes* is in particular the story of a man who can't travel." —"*Paludes* is the story of the neutral terrain that belongs to everybody—better still, it's about the normal man, the one each of us begins with; the story of the third person, the *one* one talks about—who lives in each of us and doesn't die when we die—In Virgil, he's named Tityrus—and we are expressly told that he is lying down—'*Tityre recubans*. —*Paludes* is the story of the man who lies down.' —'Really,' said Patras—'I thought it was the story of a marsh.' —'Monsieur,' I said, 'opinions differ—the essence remains. —But please understand that the only way of telling everyone the same thing is to change its form according to each new mind. —At this moment, *Paludes* is the story of Angèle's salon.' —'*Paludes?* It's the story of certain animals that live in dark caves and lose their sight by not using their eyes.'"

And when the particularity of his subject is stupidly criticized, the writer attests, with the artistic sense of which he also gives proof in *Paludes* (for *Paludes* also contains an *ars poetica*), the "possibility of generaliza-

tion; generalization is up to the reader, the critic."
"'Monsieur,'" someone objects, "'you make your task
singularly easy.' 'If I didn't I would do away with yours
altogether.'" Which is once again the subject of *Paludes*
on the aesthetic level, where the stagnation of taste and
the lethargy of stock responses can also be indicted;
there is an aesthetic sloth which is as irritating as the
moral variety.

The state of mind of *Paludes'* hero is explained, with
regard to its causes, by his own declaration:

"'What I want to express is the emotion my life has
given me: the boredom, the emptiness, the monotony.
—Myself, I couldn't care less, because I'm writing *Paludes*—but Tityre's life is nothing; and our lives, I assure you, Angèle, are even more colorless and mediocre.'
'But I don't think so,'" Angèle says. "'That's because
you haven't thought about it. That's just what my book
is about. Tityre isn't discontented with his life . . .'"

His explanation is still better if we consider this passage a stylized projection, distorted to the point of caricature, of the state in which Gide found himself on his
return from Algeria, cured of his adolescent mysticism
and in possession of his truth (or, if one prefers, of his
vital lie). He had the feeling of bringing back "a
drowned man's secret"; falling once more into a Pari-
sian milieu where nothing that interested him seemed
to be understood, opposing the members of his milieu,
he nevertheless hoped to persuade them and, as he said,
"deliver his message to them": "such a state of *estrange-
ment* (from which I suffered particularly among my
own family) soon would have driven me to suicide,
had it not been for the escape I found by describing it
ironically in *Paludes*." The book was "nourished" by his
"anguish," and enough of the latter has gone into it, for
all its mannerisms, to touch us by the accents of its
hero, whom he will define so felicitously, later on, as
an "agitated agitator." Like his Prometheus, he will be

convincing because he is convinced—or, if one prefers, like the Pascal about whom the kindly schoolteacher in Gide's recollections prompted his students' answers, he is "disturbing because he is dis? . . . dis? . . . disturbed!"

Another evidence of the bitterness of his attitude is a letter to Francis Jammes, written after *Paludes* but indicative of the intellectual aspect of this struggle: "Why don't you understand that I loathe my thought. I wear myself out fighting against it, but I can only deny it by means of itself, the way you drive out a demon by means of Beelzebub, prince of demons (what else was I trying to show in *Paludes*?), and this very procedure strengthens it."

In fact *Paludes* has this strong point, that the object of its satire inevitably reappears not only externally, in all the forms of life, but internally, in all the manifestations of consciousness. How can one escape habit? Routine? Even the most valiant, even the most original suffer fatigue and relapse. The marshes are always forming again. "It seems to me that I always carry *Paludes* with me—*Paludes* will bore no one so much as myself . . . —'If you left it behind . . .' she tells me. —Angèle! Angèle! You don't understand! I leave it here, find it again there; I find it everywhere; the sight of people obsesses me with it, and this little trip will not have delivered me from it."

The hero of *Paludes* inveighs incessantly against a way of life so utterly mechanized: "What monotony! . . . Not one event! We must try to stir up our existence a little. But you can't invent your passions. —Besides I don't know anyone except Angèle; she and I have never loved each other in a very decisive way: what I shall tell her tonight, I could have said just as well the night before; there's no progress . . ." "What an intolerable existence! . . . It's enough that it could be different and that it isn't . . . All our actions are so

familiar that a substitute could perform them and by
repeating our words of yesterday, form our phrases of
tomorrow . . ." "There are things that you begin again
every day, simply because you have nothing better to
do; this means neither progress nor even keeping up."

But the satire advances when it shifts from dissatisfaction with a state of things to an attack on those who
tolerate, accept it, or are even satisfied with it. Here
Gide has touched, with a cruel hand, on an attitude
which constitutes the relative repose of society and in
which he then saw not so much a virtue as a form of
cowardice: "Virtue of the humble—acceptance." Consider the portrait of Richard and his family: all the
virtues they manifest in a necessarily mediocre way of
life Gide pitilessly mocks, belittling them or (to be
fair) dreadfully accentuating their pettiness, without
sparing their misfortunes or their joys. "'All careers
without profit to the self are dreadful—those which
earn only money—and so little that one must constantly
begin all over again. What stagnations! At the moment
of their death, what will they have accomplished?'
'They will have filled their place.' 'I should think so!
They've taken one as small as themselves.'" "Myself, I
couldn't care less, because I'm writing *Paludes*, but
otherwise I'd judge myself as I judge them." "And to
think that all of them do exactly the same thing every
day! . . . Every day it's the same pathetic second-bests,
the substitutes for all the first-rate things in the
world . . ."

Forty years later Gide, without disowning *Paludes*,
but having shifted from the moral to the social plane,
resumes this complaint against men's apathy: " . . . But
the great majority of men accommodate themselves
quite well to their misery, don't suffer from it, don't
even notice it. The man who tries to rouse them, to
disgust them with their sordid apathy risks playing the
futile game of the agitated agitator in *Paludes*. By trans-

posing the dissatisfaction in this book from the moral
to the social level, I think I would only have diminished
it. But it is easy to perform this transposition imagina-
tively . . . In this world that is so imperfect, and which
could be so beautiful, shame on the man who is content! His *so be it*, as soon as it favors unconcern, is
impious."

Compare the *disturber's* formula to that of the *agitator* and we shall understand how, with time, Gide's
thought, while remaining faithful to itself, has become
applicable to the political terrain from which it seemed
furthest at the outset of his literary life. This is one
of the implications of *Paludes*, one of the least apparent,
since the disdain for Richard's cowardice produces a
false notion of Gide's aristocratic attitudes; but if Richard were to let himself be convinced, he would find in
the artisan of his awakening a mainstay of his cause.

"What are you complaining about?" the hero of *Paludes* is asked, and he answers: "About the fact that no
one complains! Acceptance of an evil aggravates it . . .
the fact that one looks as if one is having a good dinner when one is eating garbage . . . the fact that no
one rebels . . . *inside*. It's not distribution I'm complaining about . . . ; it's about ourselves, about the way we
live."

Gide's evolution has consisted in fact of reaching the
point of protesting against *distribution,* after having realized that responsibility for stagnation is not entirely
Richard's, or Tityre's, but also of the marshlands by
which he is surrounded. For Richard *is* Tityre, although
married and the father of four children—they are six instead of one. "I have made Tityre alone, to concentrate
this monotony. It's an artistic method" and "Tityre is
myself and also not myself; —Tityre is an ineffectual; he
is me, you, all of us."

Tityre's mistake is to be content, to accept. "It is because Tityre is content that I myself desire to be so no

longer. One must be outraged instead. I am going to make Tityre contemptible by his very resignation."

The attitude of the hero of *Paludes* is of course not understood by his entourage. His proselytism and his propaganda meet with utter failure. He attempts to persuade Angèle, to the scandal of his great friend Hubert, who doesn't see why one should persuade people they're not so happy as they think they are: " 'Myself, I couldn't care less, since I'm writing *Paludes*—but what is unendurable to me is that she doesn't understand this state *Paludes.*' Hubert, at the end, grew excited: 'Now why do you want to disturb her, if she's happy the way she is?' 'But she's not happy, my dear friend; she thinks she is because she isn't conscious of her condition; can't you see that when mediocrity is added to blindness, it's even worse.' 'And when you open her eyes, what else will you have done except to make her unhappy?' 'That would already be much more interesting; at least she wouldn't be content any more—she'd be searching.' " Finally he will rejoice at having brought her a little closer to his ideas: "Can it be that I have at last put a certain bitterness in your smile?"

As a matter of fact, *Paludes* remains on an egoistic level, despite the hero's good will. He fails to rouse his friends, and he scarcely succeeds in rousing himself. But at least he finds a solution for the artist. Through the work of art, one escapes from life's monotony and frees oneself from anxiety. The effort of persuading others is disinterested, if not fruitful; it is, however, not altruistic. Hence the *leitmotiv* which recurs so amusingly: " 'Myself, I couldn't care less, because I'm writing *Paludes.*' 'But when you come down to it, what is it you want?' 'Myself, what I want, personally speaking, is to finish *Paludes.*' " Yet the artist escapes less than he supposes, at least the artist who has only one idea. He relapses into inertia under the very semblance of movement. After *Paludes*, he writes *Polders*. Gide did *not*

write *Polders* after *Paludes;* he wrote something altogether different: *les Nourritures terrestres,* the eulogy
of escape after the satire on captivity.

The reader will have noticed in *Paludes* the role
played by windows and the variations sounded on the
verb *sortir*—to depart, emerge, leave, exit, etc.—by the
hero sitting on the bench on Angèle's landing, while
Martin, on the bench of the landing on the floor above,
is writing parallel and contradictory commentaries on
blindness and the bliss of not seeing clearly. Recall too
the little weekend trip with Angèle, a journey *manqué*
whose sadness is adequately rendered by the word
aristolochia (birthwort) and which, reduced to certain
poetic moments, fills only two pages of the narrator's
notebook. All this indicates the failure of the attempts
to escape, and the disappointment of the traveler who
has set out with the best intentions: "I am leaving, leaving on a journey. . . . Where? I don't know . . . If I
knew where I were going, and what I were going to
do when I got there, I wouldn't escape my troubles. I
am leaving merely to leave; surprise itself is my purpose
—the unexpected . . ." and whose return is so painful
because it merely reinforces the impression of habitual
captivity: "I sense more clearly all that I would have
liked to leave behind, now that I see all that I come
back to." The fact is that one does not escape. The same
oppression is encountered everywhere, allows no respite,
no loophole: "When we built on the plain some roof to
shelter ourselves, that roof followed us . . ." Hence this
heart-rending complaint: "One must carry to the last
whatever ideas one picks up . . ."

We know the success enjoyed, after World War I,
by ideologies of escape and adventure, the results, both
dangerous and extreme, that were claimed for them,
and the failure to which they actually led; for our ad-
venturers either never left, soon returned, or—the best
among them—went into service (I mean the service of

77

humanity; no other is justified). They had heeded the
bold counsel given, for all its modest appearance, in
Paludes. Roland refuses to set off on a journey: "'Too
many responsibilities hold me back. . . .' 'But the
whole point is to give them the slip. . . . Do you intend to be enslaved by them forever?'" And how many
things will be given the slip in order to obey such
splendid injunctions of desire: "Let everything go,"
Breton will say at Dada's height, in a fulminating article
(collected in *Pas perdus*), compared to which his sur-
realism looks like an obedient child. But consider the
rest of the conversation with Roland: "Myself, I couldn't
care less, you understand; I'm leaving on another journey . . .", in which we may see a more secret counsel:
another journey, one that will be not the abandonment
of his duties, but the fulfillment of his destiny.

It is this resignation, this apathy which accounts for
the poverty of our actions. We find in *Paludes* the
caricature of action in all its forms, first of the radical
incapacity for action, then the appearances of action,
false action, sterile activity, *illusions* of action: consider
the hero who fills his schedule with resolutions that are
either futile, or that he will not carry out, or that are
only the echo of easy habits: "In my diary there are
two sections: on one sheet I write what I shall do, and on
the opposite page, each night, I write what I have done.
Afterwards I compare; I subtract, and what I haven't
done, the deficit, becomes what I should have done
. . . Thus this morning, opposite the note: try to get
up at six, I wrote: got up at seven—then, in parentheses:
negative contingency." Finally action itself has its hypocrisies: "In the diary, once I was up I could read:
try to get up at six. It was eight; I took my pen; I
crossed out the line and wrote instead: Get up at eleven.
—And I went back to bed, without reading the rest."

What characterizes true action is that it cannot be
crossed out; it is carved out of living rock; it is painted

while it is still wet, and it cannot be retouched: what's done is done. We shall return to this problem apropos of the character of Lafcadio in *les Caves du Vatican*. But the hero of *Paludes* bestirs himself without acting effectively on his own account; he achieves a half-success, the illusion of action, when Angèle, moved by his ravings, argues with him: "'We have never been more alive,' said Angèle. 'Could anyone, tell me truly, be more alive? What gave you the feeling of any greater exuberance? Who told you such a thing was possible?—Hubert?—is he any more alive because he's always on the move?' 'Angèle! Angèle! Look how I'm sobbing now! Can it be that you've begun to understand my anguish? . . . I believe you're crying now—Wonderful. I'm happy. I'm in action—I'm going away to finish *Paludes*.'"

Such diminished action is already a success without a future, for the hero himself is quite prepared to relapse into the mechanical repetition of his occupations; he is in despair like anyone else at the notion of the slightest change in his habits: "If Hubert leaves, who will come to see me at six?" For better or worse, everything starts over in another form: "At six, in came my great friend Gaspard. He was on his way back from fencing. He said: 'Well! You're working?' I answered: 'I'm writing *Polders* . . .'," the last lines of *Paludes* reproducing the first, with only a slight variation.

But the action over which this character rejoices when he sees Angèle cry is a very special action indeed. It is not the action one performs oneself, but the action of causation: it is the capacity to make others act; in its definitive form, it is *thought*. Inciting thought does not require of the self that it be engaged in life; it leaves the self much more virtual, and in this sense it is not too paradoxical to claim that thought is true action—on condition that it does not remain mere theory, that others execute it, realize it, carry it to its conclusion.

Yet it is inevitable that they shape it after their own fashion. Thought inspires actions which simultaneously realize and betray it. "I prefer to make others act than to act myself," Gide writes later, and his readers know the importance the notion of *influence* assumes throughout his life.

Paludes also affords a charming comedy of influence. The hero of *Paludes* had vainly advised Roland to take a trip to Biskra; the latter had objected that he had too many responsibilities. But now Hubert declares: "'I am leaving for Biskra in two days;—I have persuaded Roland to come with me.' Suddenly I grew furious: 'Presumptuous Hubert—I am the one who persuaded him to go. We were leaving Abel's, both of us—I remember, when I told him he should take that trip.' Hubert burst out laughing; he said: —'You? but my poor friend, just remember how much trouble you had getting as far as Montmorency! How could you pretend . . . ? —Besides, maybe it was you who mentioned it to him first; but what good is it, I ask you, putting ideas in people's heads? Do you think that's what makes them take action?'" In order to be influenced, one must be predisposed. Here too action, already reduced to thought, finds itself diminished still further.

The point is made more strongly. Is it good to influence others? Doesn't it diminish their responsibility, detach them, so to speak, from their actions? This is what Barnabé, the moralist, declares to the hero of *Paludes:* "You want to force people to act because you have a horror of stagnation—force them to act without considering that the more you intervene in their actions, the less these actions depend on them. Your responsibility is thereby increased; theirs is accordingly reduced. Yet the responsibility for actions is the only thing that makes them important for each man—their appearance is nothing. You can never teach people how to will . . . you merely influence them; what good will it be if all you finally succeed in doing is to procreate a few worthless actions!" To which our disturber replies, pertinently enough, that Barnabé increases not responsibilities but scruples—the fear of action; and he informs him that he encourages the fatal stagnation he should be exposing to others: "It's not action I want to generate, it's freedom I want to disengage . . ."

The problem of action necessarily leads to the problem of freedom. The reader knows the importance which the notion of the free act assumes for Gide; we shall come back to it apropos of the *gratuitous act,* which plays a certain role in *Prométhée,* but is especially important in the composition of *les Caves du Vatican. Paludes* affords us only a sketch of it.

The effort of liberation preached by the hero of *Paludes* is not metaphysical; nor is it social, as we have seen, save by ricochet; it is exclusively moral, individualistic, personal. Each man is reproached for not making it in his heart of hearts. "I prefer to walk today on my hands rather than on my feet—the way I did *yesterday* . . ." If such an effort endangers our liberty, subjects us to being shut up like madmen, what annoys Gide is that "the external world—its laws, numbers, even its sidewalks may look as though they were deciding our relapses and assuming our monotony—when, actually, everything agrees so well with our love of repetition." He indicts not society, but the individual.

The last lesson of *Paludes* is that the individual must be a *self,* must be made manifest in his acts, instead of allowing his acts to conceal, to bury him. "What burdens us is the necessity of repeating them." These actions must be original. ". . . Our personality is no longer distinguished from the way in which we act . . . Who is Bernard? He is the person seen Thursdays at Octave's. —Who is Octave? The person who receives Bernard on Thursdays. —But beyond that? He is the person who goes to Bernard's on Mondays . . . Who are we all, gentlemen? We are the ones who go to Angèle's every Friday."

The problem of action led to the problem of freedom; the problem of freedom leads to the problem of *personality*.

Personality is somewhat the contrary of that "third person" referred to in *Paludes*. There is, in this little book, a text which affords a good transition between *Paludes* and *le Prométhée mal enchaîné*, and this is the declaration made in favor of the hero of *Paludes*, who is delighted to find himself thus supported, by the famous Valentin Knox, who regards the normal man as uninteresting, dispensable. This is an idea Gide will return to, in his *Dostoevsky*, for instance. "We are worth something only to the degree that we distinguish ourselves from others; idiosyncrasy is our disease of value."

Paludes focusses especially on shaking the personality free from its chains. *Le Prométhée mal enchaîné* is entirely dedicated to the determination of the nature of that personality, inquiring what constitutes its value and its destiny. It too is a moral work, but it is more psychological, and above all it is a work of metaphysics.

Its morality is less individualistic; it concerns *relations between persons*: the waiter in the café, who plays a *louche* and pandering role, brings personalities into relation with one another "at little tables for three": he "relates," they endure the relation and don't know it; he gains an awareness of their personalities, observes them—a little like God himself, with whom he is connected, moreover, and whom Gide introduces as a banker named Zeus, whom he also calls the Miglionnaire (pronouncing the gl like lyə, as in the name of the Ducs de Broglie and of the Baraglioul family in *les Caves du Vatican*). *Prométhée* is less individualistic a work than *Paludes* because it is humanity as a whole which is the object of the hero's concern, and as a hero

Prométhée is a much larger figure than the minor writer of *Paludes*. The work is more psychological, because the study of the characters' moral functioning is more detached from consequences and envisaged independently and from outside, treated with a draftsman's clarity of design. It is, above all, metaphysical, because in it are posed the relations of human behavior with the transcendence of our aspirations and with the existence of God.

If Angèle's little salon was suitable as a setting for the satire on everyday resignation, it was not a bad idea to displace both mythological and legendary personages in order to bring them together in a fable whose scope is concealed by the ridiculousness of this outrageous anachronism, established once and for all (Gide derives no continuous effects from it in the manner of *la Belle Hélène*, for instance), though still retaining something grand in its extravagant whimsey. I am certain that there was a similar intention in having Prométhée's eagle fly down between the Madeleine and the Opéra and break the restaurant window where Coclès, Damoclès, and Prométhée happen to be sitting together, thanks to the waiter. Indeed, this meeting is the result of one of Zeus' gratuitous acts: he has decided to drop his handkerchief on the boulevard, to ask the first passer-by who picks it up (Coclès) to write someone's name (Damoclès) on an envelope containing a five-hundred-franc note, and to slap him on the cheek in thanks, after which he slips away. He has nothing more to do but observe the play of events.

There is no need to describe the psychological reactions through which the story of the characters' transformation by the Miglionnaire's act leads to Prométhée's lecture, to Damoclès' death, and to the funeral banquet. We need only remark that the whimsey of the narrative prevents a direct satire; everything is transposed to an abstract level. The effect of the gratuitous act has been to confer personalities upon Damoclès and upon Coclès. Damoclès has been "original for the last thirty days"; previously he had attempted to be ordinary (which is, moreover, impossible); he was banal, but free; now he is determined . . . "I was anyone; I am someone." Note this curious feature concerning commonplace freedom, as opposed to predetermined originality. One might reverse the terms and posit freedom in originality, determinism in banality. But Gide has always seen something restrictive in choice, which excludes all other possibilities. "What arrogance in choice!" says the hero of *Paludes*. To choose is to deprive oneself, impoverish oneself. As for Coclès, he had walked out into the street seeking an external determination: "I thought my destiny would depend on the first thing that happened to me . . ." He picks up the handkerchief and consents to write the address: "I had no desire to withdraw myself from exterior motivation." But "everything is complicated instead of explicated . . . Between your gain and my pain, there's a relation; I don't know what it is—but there's a relation." He realizes that he has been right not to slap Damoclès back: "You would have thought you had to give me that banknote, and . . . it doesn't belong to me." As for Damoclès, who is a man of duty, he will die of not being able to discharge himself of his obligations; his entire life is oriented by accident. Coclès, on the other hand, although one of his eyes was put out by the wingtip of Prométhée's eagle, always manages to survive; he forgets the slap and finds a way to pride himself on his glass eye. He knows how to benefit by circumstances, even disagreeable ones.

Compared with these two characters—so meagerly and yet so intensely constituted, and who remind us of a caricature of the concept of personality, for they escape the commonplace only by the relief which an accident of their existence assumes, and thus have only an accidental, adventitious originality—Prométhée is granted an idiosyncrasy that is powerful in another way, so powerful that it is externalized in the magnificent symbol of the eagle. Coclès says to him: "'Show your distinctive characteristic: what do you have that no one else has?' 'What do I have, Messieurs, what do I personally have?—ah yes, it's an eagle!'" If I understand this correctly, then, what constitutes the personality's essence is what gives it a reason for living—its ideal, to which it sacrifices itself.

And this is not only the personality's originality, but also the source of its value. Prométhée tries to spread this notion with a touching clumsiness which recalls the labors of the propagandist in *Paludes*, but with more pathos in the comedy. He gives a lecture of which the first two points (he has not prepared the third, and counts on inspiration) are:

first: "One must have an eagle."

second: "We all have one anyway" (whether it is a vice or a passion, or simply a conscience).

The first point begs the question; that is, according to Prométhée, it conceals an affirmation of temperament. "I don't love men; I love what devours them" is his formula—a beautiful one, moreover, if somewhat inhuman. "Now what devours man? His eagle. Therefore, Messieurs, one must have an eagle."

Prométhée's eagle is born of his concern for men, and he has also given *them* an eagle, belief in progress:

"I invented several kinds of fire for them; and that was when my eagle began." "I have loved men passionately, desperately, and deplorably. —And I have done so much for them that one might say I have made them into themselves; . . . like a fire to illuminate them, Messieurs, I made this consciousness out of all my love for them . . ." "I brought into being the devouring belief in progress . . . it was their eagle. Our eagle is our reason for existing, Messieurs. . . . The history of man-

kind is the history of eagles, Messieurs." Gide returns
to these ideas of progress later. In 1929 he writes to
Montgomery Belgion: "We have a tendency to set the
exchange value of humanity much too high"; "man
is not . . . worthy of being venerated for himself . . . ;
what incites humanity to progress . . . is . . . not to
consider itself as an end—neither its comfort nor its
repose satisfies—but instead as a means by which . . .
something transcending it can be realized."

It seems, then, that despite the book's end, where
the eagle is killed, cooked, and eaten, this *sotie* is not a
unilateral condemnation of the fervor that excites and
arouses Prométhée. It does not appear as entirely er-
roneous, ridiculous. It remains as a useful example. It
is up to each of us to weigh what he owes, or does
not owe, to his eagle.

How is Prométhée induced to renounce his ideal? I
see three reasons for this:

1) The ideal does not bear its own justification
within itself. This is why Prométhée wishes to force his
eagle to explain itself in public: " 'And now I approach
the grave question:—why the eagle? . . . Let him speak
for himself. . . . Eagle! Will you answer now?' The
eagle . . . remained silent. 'Who sent you?—Why have
you chosen me? Where do you come from? Where are
you going? Speak: what is your nature?' "

2) What might justify the sacrifice of self to the ideal
—that is, God—does not answer either. Gide has treated
the Miglionnaire in a manner which, if it is not entirely
equivalent to outright atheism (which is not found for-
mulated anywhere in Gide), is not worth much more.
The portrait is a disrespectful and blasphemous one.
" 'And the Miglionnaire?—He's a tricky one!' the waiter
said. 'If you think that all this bothers him . . . he observes.' " When Damoclès, infected by his scruples, is
about to die, the Miglionnaire refuses to concern himself. "He wishes to maintain his incognito." "Damoclès

would recover . . . if he knew his benefactor . . . it's not Damoclès but rather his disease that interests him."

In the curious interview with the Miglionnaire, the latter explains the gratuitousness of his actions, and his passion for gambling. This is a theodicy much more Diabolic than Voltairean. Prométhée interrupts, begging the Miglionnaire to reveal himself to Damoclès. " 'Monsieur, let us say no more about it,' Zeus said; 'I am not accustomed to taking advice from anyone.' " And before he leaves: " 'Forgive an indiscreet request. Oh! Show it, I beg you!' 'Show what?' 'Your eagle!' 'But I have no eagle, Monsieur! . . . As for eagles, it's I who give them to others.' " In other words there must be eagles for the elite, as there must be religion for masses. But God himself, not so stupid as all that, has no eagle. He is therefore set beneath man with regard to the idea. Pride and wickedness, total contempt for men. When Prométhée returns to his argument, the Miglionnaire carries egoism to the point of fatuity, and to a kind of shabby prudence which completes his degradation: "I understand why you are killing Damoclès, since it gives you pleasure, but at least let him know who is killing him—so he can die in peace." The Miglionnaire answers: "I don't wish to lose my prestige."

3) One incurs a terrible responsibility when, in preaching an ideal, one precipitates other people into ruin.

Coclès escapes quite well from his misadventures. "He sees better since he only sees out of one eye now. He shows everyone his glass eye and prides himself on the fact that people feel sorry for him . . . He has grown rich . . . A charity subscription has been taken up for him . . . He's a crafty one . . . He's thinking of opening an asylum . . . just for one-eyed men. He has appointed himself its director."

But Damoclès will die . . . "of a stricture of the

column." The effect of Prométhée's lecture on him has been overwhelming. Prométhée had made direct hints to Coclès and Damoclès: "I also wanted to say that you must love your eagle . . . because then it will become beautiful"; "These are not words spoken out of interest, these are words of devotion. You must devote yourself to your eagle." "The secret of the life of Coclès and of Damoclès is in their devotion to their debt; you, Coclès, have your slap; you, Damoclès, your banknote . . ." "That is your own eagle, there are others; there are more glorious ones. But I tell you this: the eagle devours us in any case, vice or virtue, duty or passion; cease to be just anyone, and you will not escape it." Coclès has been influenced favorably: "he no longer speaks of anything except devoting himself and spends all his time looking through the streets for a new slap which will be worth money to some new Damoclès. He turns the other cheek in vain." But Damoclès has taken everything seriously, tragically. His mind wanders, recalling his misfortunes: "He has been at death's door ever since the day he tried to slip five hundred francs into the interstices of events," by surreptitiously paying for the restaurant bill the day when Prométhée, Coclès, and Damoclès lunched together and when Prométhée's eagle broke the window and put out Coclès' eye with its wingtip. "I have tried, in my cowardly way, to rid myself of my debt, but I have not succeeded." "Duty, gentlemen, is a horrible thing; I have decided to die of it." "But how much more horrible is this remorse for having tried to discharge oneself of a duty . . . upon someone else, upon Coclès . . . Then help me to understand myself, for pity's sake!" Damoclès comes to an edifying end; he has this sublime and touching last word: "I hope at least it won't have left him short . . . The One who gave me . . . something."

Prométhée considers his death horrible, agonized as he is that his lecture should have been the cause of his disease. He would no longer say the same thing today: "'Aren't you convinced any more then?' 'Damoclès was too convinced. I have other ideas about my eagle.'"

He will express these ideas in a speech at Damoclès' funeral. He takes as his text: "Let the dead bury the dead," and tells an anecdote, the story of Tityre, his goat, Angèle and Ménalque: after having lived to care for his goat, a source of prosperity and embarrassment, occupations, responsibilities and scruples, and after having torn himself from it in order to leave with Angèle and the cashbox for Paris, Tityre discovers that Angèle has eloped with Ménalque to Rome (*"Eo Romam, urbem quam dicunt Romam"*) leaving him alone, completely surrounded by marshes, as at the start of the anecdote . . . "Let's say that I've said nothing"—a phrase that emphasizes the vanity of his efforts and of his escape. —"Since Damoclès' death, I've found the secret of laughter," Prométhée confides, and at the same restaurant he pays for Coclès' and the waiter's lunch. Prométhée has killed his eagle. This is why he is so fat and dares to laugh. "He ate me long enough; I decided it was my turn."

"The meal was more hilarious than it is permissible to relate here, and the eagle was pronounced delicious. 'So it served no purpose at all?' they asked. 'Don't say that, Coclès! His flesh has nourished us. —When I questioned it, it answered nothing . . . But I eat it without rancor: if it had made me suffer less, it wouldn't have been so plump; if it had been less plump it would have been less delectable.'" That is the moral conclusion. "'What remains of his former beauty?' 'I have kept all his feathers. It is with a pen made of one of them that I am writing this little book.'" That is the aesthetic conclusion.

But the metaphysical conclusion, more deeply hidden, is in the epilogue. The reader will recall the legend of Pasiphaë and the bull. Gide attributes to Pasiphaë these words, which she addresses to Tyndare: "There's nothing to be done. I just don't care for men," which comically recalls Prométhée's preference for what devours them. In writing *Paludes*, Gide looked for what he called "God's share"; similarly Pasiphaë declares about her bull: "I hoped a God was concealed inside. If Zeus had had anything to do with it, I would have given birth to Dioscurus; thanks to this animal, all I brought into the world was a calf." —A modest conclusion for an artist "to try to make the reader believe that if this book is what it is, it isn't the author's fault." "One doesn't write the books one wishes," says the *Journal* of the Goncourt brothers, quoted as an epigraph to this conclusion. It is not Gide's responsibility to make the Miglionnaire reveal himself, to make the eagle speak, and it is not his fault if the book concludes—less lofty but more discreet—in the sense of another book where he says "that one must not spoil one's life for any goal."

Le Prométhée mal enchaîné in a sense concentrates into a single story *André Walter* and *Les Nourritures*, mystical asceticism and surrender to life; it also has a parallel with *la Porte étroite*, for it asserts the futility of the spirit of sacrifice only after having elaborately shown its pathetic beauty.

The reader can see that he must read the *Prométhée* backward. So eloquent is the eagle's lesson that we are convinced by it, ready to devote ourselves to whatever —incomprehensibly—transcends us, before we are told that we will have been *dupes*—which is dreadfully sad, at least if we set heroism higher than wisdom.

4. Ironic Works
(ii. les Caves du Vatican)

If, as we have seen, *Paludes* and *le Prométhée mal enchaîné* could pass for obscure books, they nonetheless revealed a meaning, upon examination, that was quite explicit: this is because they were constructed around basically clear ideas. In the case of *les Caves du Vatican*, precisely the opposite is true. Considered externally, it is the clearest of adventure stories; but its significance is evanescent, for it must be related to an idea—from which the whole book proceeds—that is extremely obscure: the idea of *gratuitous action*. Let us therefore attempt first to be certain what Gide means by this.

The reader will recall the reproach the moralist Barnabé addresses to the author of *Paludes;* the latter, by attempting to force people to act, diminishes their responsibility for their actions: "You can never teach people to will: *velle non discitur;* you merely influence them; what good will it be if all you finally succeed in doing is to procreate a few worthless actions!" To which the hero of *Paludes* retorts that Barnabé himself, by claiming to increase responsibility, merely enlarges scruples and diminishes freedom: "'The truly responsible act is the free act; our acts are no longer free . . . It's freedom I want to disengage . . .' [Barnabé] then smiled subtly to give point to what he was about to say, and this was: '—Well then—if I understand you properly, Monsieur, you want to constrain people to freedom.'"

Some pages before, Alexandre the philosopher, whom the hero of *Paludes* always mistrusts, never answering him whatever he says, had discussed his interlocutor's conception in his own fashion: "It seems to me, Monsieur, that what you call a free act would be, according to you, an act dependent on nothing;—you follow me: detachable;—note my train of thought: omissible,—and my conclusion: worthless . . . Attach yourself to everything, Monsieur," Alexandre continues, "and don't ask for contingency; first of all, you won't get it—and then, what good would it do you?" To which the hero of *Paludes* finds nothing to reply: "I said nothing, as usual; when a philosopher answers you, you never understand what it was you had asked him anyway."

Hitherto nothing but the *free act* is in question. But not the *gratuitous act*, as yet. It is in the *Prométhée* that the two expressions are made synonymous.

The waiter in the café, it will be recalled, likes to establish relationships between people. Why? "You will ask me: what does all this bring me in? Oh! Nothing at all. It's my hobby to create relationships . . . Oh! not for myself . . . it's what you might call a gratuitous act" (in other words: an act performed without advantage, without personal interest, out of preference, out of pleasure).

"A gratuitous act! Does that mean anything to you? To me it seems extraordinary. For a long time I've believed it was gratuitous action that distinguished man from the animals. I used to call man: the animal capable of a gratuitous act. And then I thought the contrary: that man was the only being incapable of acting gratuitously. Gratuitously! just think: without reason—

yes, I know what you're thinking—let's say: without motive; he's incapable of it! Then it began to bother me. I said to myself: why is he doing this? why is he doing that? . . . Not that I'm a determinist . . ." Consider the waiter's dilemma; it is not peculiar to him. Gide is attacking a notion that is extremely equivocal, one that will render the meaning of *les Caves* so ambiguous, so necessarily vague.

Naturally Gide succeeds no better than any metaphysician in resolving the conflict of freedom and determinism which has lasted for centuries without in the least preventing us from acting; but we find him trimming his definition of an act as gratuitous insofar as it in no way benefits its author. The Miglionnaire, who is intelligent, says to himself: "A gratuitous act? How's it done? [Note that God himself is embarrassed by the problem of freedom.] And you understand that it doesn't mean an action which brings nothing in, for otherwise . . ." And, in fact, it is conceivable that an action performed without seeking advantage could, in spite of everything, become profitable, just as it could become harmful; the point is, the consequence must not be anticipated, it is accidental. Nonetheless the Miglionnaire here corrects the waiter and, in advance, the Lafcadio of *les Caves*, both of whom regard the absence of advantage as a condition of the *acte gratuit:* "an act which is motivated by nothing. Do you understand? Neither interest nor passion, nothing. The disinterested act: selfborn; an act without purpose either; consequently, without a master; the free act [here we reach the synonymy of the free and gratuitous act], the autochthonous act."

The obscurity of the notion is apparent: we must first of all conceive of an act to which nothing which could be called a motive impels us (that is, no emotion, and perhaps no idea); then we must consider the act as selfsufficient, without connection between the moment just past and the moment to come, somehow self-generated, like a true absolute, a kind of metaphysical *coup d'état*, like God's spontaneous creation of himself. It is an act that is unthinkable, save in theory.

It was quite obvious that such an act, combining omnipotence with absurdity, should be committed by the Miglionnaire.

It was much more to be expected than on the part of the waiter. I do not know whether the reader regards the hobby of contriving relationships as a gratuitous act, as the waiter prefers to think; there are houses where one does nothing else, and Gide long thought of writing a play which would revive the character of the go-between by presenting him as disinterested.

The free, gratuitous act which Zeus commits is also the instigation of a relationship; and it is double. "Do you understand? Two gratuitous acts at once: a five-hundred-franc note to an address he [the Miglionnaire] hasn't chosen and a slap for someone who himself has chosen to pick up the handkerchief. Could anything be more gratuitous than that? And the relationship! I bet you aren't examining the relationship closely enough. For since the act is gratuitous, it's what we call here: reversible. One gets five-hundred francs for a slap, the other gets a slap for five-hundred francs . . . and then you can't tell any more . . . you lose track. —Just think! a gratuitous act! There's nothing more demoralizing." One must not search this charmingly preposterous passage too deeply. Is the act reversible because it is gratuitous, as the waiter claims? This is all the less arguable since the relationship itself is incorrectly posited. For, after all, the "one who gets the five-hundred francs for a slap" is Damoclès, but if he has received the five-hundred francs, he has not received the slap, and "the other [who] gets a slap for five-hundred francs" is Coclès, but if he has received the slap he has not received the five-hundred francs. It is understandable that the waiter loses track. He is not a good logician.

Are there *two* gratuitous acts? When God descended to the boulevard, he had a plan, which he discusses in the interview with Prométhée: "I went down into the street, looking for a way of making someone suffer from the gift I was about to make to someone else; to make this other person profit by the suffering I was going to cause the first. A slap and a five-hundred franc note were all I needed. For one the slap, for the other the note. Is that clear? What is less clear, is the way to give them." God is a better logician than the waiter, and he establishes his system of equations perfectly; I am certain, in fact, that one of the logistics experts of the Couturat or Péano schools could pose the problem according to the best rules of logical algebra, since they have apparently succeeded in reducing a page of the *Odyssey* to mathematical formulae. If Prométhée had not interrupted Zeus, the latter would certainly have told us that this *way of giving* he was about to mention (it is more important than *what* he gives) is the initiation of a relationship by dropping the handkerchief and asking a passer-by to write an address. We are presented a complex technique which scarcely recalls the simplicity of the impenetrable ways of the author of the *fiat lux,* but whose ensemble of arrangements instead suggests a single act rather than two.

But what is more surprising is the Machiavellianism of the act, the repercussions caused, the dosage of good and evil to be provoked one by the other. Where is the gratuitousness here? It is not in the machination itself; is it in its author? He has just presented himself as impelled by "the love of the game; not of the gain, you understand—of the game; what could I gain that I don't already have? . . . Yes! I have a passion for gambling . . ." Yet we recall that the Miglionnaire had previously defined the gratuitous act as committed *without passion* ("motivated by nothing. Do you understand? Neither interest nor passion, nothing"). Just like the waiter, Zeus gets confused in his own explanations, and his perpetual "you understand" is an obvious sign of this. We shall see that Gide has contradicted himself just as much. —As a matter of fact, the Miglionnaire is impelled by a complex tendency which we shall meet again in Lafcadio; there is in both a mixture of the love of gambling, a taste for the unexpected, and a spirit of curiosity which includes a certain scientific appetite and a certain secretiveness; all God lacks is the passion for risk, the lure of danger—but God risks nothing, by definition. They also have in common *the contempt for humanity:* "I gamble by lending to men. —I lend, but only in play; I lend, but with sunken capital; I lend, but it looks as if I'm giving. —I like people not to know I'm lending. I play, but I conceal my hand; I experiment; I gamble the way a Dutchman sows, the way he plants his secret bulb. I amuse myself by watching what I lend men, what I plant in men. Otherwise men would be so empty!" It seems to me that Zeus's modes of action—not so much divine as diabolical, the result of a perverse demiurge—are in no way gratuitous. On the other hand I do find gratuitousness in the chance distribution of his goods, for the note and the slap, instead of falling to Coclès and Damoclès, might just as well have gone to Calliclès and Agathoclès . . . Hence there is gratuitousness neither in the act (which treats man, whatever his condition, as an amusing toy), nor antecedent to the act (whose motive is curiosity in experimentation), but only perhaps in the contingency of the act's point of contact with reality. And even here we might claim that divine prescience should have warned Zeus of the result. If we cannot posit freedom in God, there is no use attempting to conceive it in man.

In *les Caves du Vatican* the theory of the free act is not altered, but it is applied to a particular kind of act: the wicked act, the crime.

The passages which illuminate it are for the most part put in the mouths of the characters in the novel, but since they express the same ideological position there is no need, for the moment, to take into account their personalities or the fashion in which these ideas develop in them or the influences they have undergone. For instance the academic novelist Julius de Baraglioul explains to his brother-in-law Amédée Fleurissoire that "'Ever since La Rochefoucauld we've been blinded by his *Maximes* . . . interest is not always what motivates man; there are disinterested actions . . . By disinterested, I mean: gratuitous. And evil, or what is called evil, may be as gratuitous as good.' 'But in that case, why do it?' 'Precisely! As a luxury, out of a need to spend, to gamble. Now I claim that the most disinterested souls are not necessarily the best in the Catholic sense of the word. . . . On the contrary, from this Catholic point of view, the best-disciplined soul is the one that keeps its accounts best.'" Since "contempt for what is useful . . . is a sign of a certain spiritual aristocracy," Julius has imagined a character whose soul "escapes the catechism, escapes complacency, escapes calculations . . . keeps no accounts at all." And he has realized that since the gratuitous act could not be understood, its author would be above suspicion: "For the cause, the motive of the crime [note this new synonymy, which identifies cause and motive] is the handle by which the criminal is generally seized. Indeed the judge's maxim is: *Is fecit cui prodest*." [The action's author is its beneficiary.]

On the whole, the concept of the free act is not metaphysical in Gide, it is *psychological,* by its connection with the idea of disinterestedness, by its rejection of motivation by interest alone, and it is *juridical* by the connection between the crime's incomprehensibility and the criminal's being above suspicion. For Gide, a free act, whether a crime or not, is an act accomplished in such a way that other men do not see why a particular man should have committed it and consequently do not assert him to be its author.

Yet the act has been committed by a particular man. For it to be the *product* of this man, Gide finds himself obliged to obey two contradictory conditions: 1) to maintain the act's absurd aspect in the individual by stripping it of all those motivations, like vengeance, rage, jealousy, cupidity, which would permit its rationale to be grasped; 2) to make us feel how *this* individual could have committed *this* action which would not have been committed by any other man, which could have been committed only by this man: that is, *to link this surprising action to a particular human nature,* which comes down to an explanation by personality. The free act is the act of a *certain* personality. It is upon this personality that Gide will focus all his effort of explanation; he will determine it as much as he can, he will particularize it to the point of singularity—so that its incomprehensible action will not seem improbable to us.

This is a difficult challenge, for it means creating an exceptional being whose nature could explain how he might commit an exceptional action, yet without the latter's being explicable to himself. This attempt at *squaring the circle* is indicated by the formula: "I don't want any motive for the crime, it is enough for me to motivate the criminal" employed by Julius de Baraglioul in a conversation with Lafcadio. "Yes, I want to make him commit the crime gratuitously; I want him to try to commit a perfectly unmotivated crime." There follows the strange dialogue in which Julius and Lafcadio give themselves up to an astounding intellectual leapfrog, but whose entire significance is in creating for the imagined criminal, the prototype of whom Julius does not suspect is his interlocutor (hence the zest of the scene), *a personality which might produce such an action:* acting in play—preferring pleasure to interest—taking pleasure in

self-discipline to the point of dissimulation—loving risks
—heeding the demon of curiosity; Julius sketches his
criminal's beginnings as a *free man:* minor thefts, and
rare ones, for they are committed only if they require
skill and cunning, and only if they reveal him somewhat;
—more of a juggler than a crook;—encouraged, but also
exasperated by his impunity;—finally driving himself on
to greater dangers, he will act all the more adroitly
for having a cool head. "Just think: a crime motivated
by neither passion nor need. His reason for committing
it is precisely to commit it without having a reason."
But here Lacadio makes a crucial remark: "It's you who
are reasoning his crime for him; he merely commits it."

The gratuitous crime by definition has no reason, but
this absence of reason is not reasoned; the crime is
spontaneous; it is the fruit of a personality in which
spontaneity is the distinctive characteristic, although
Gide, to my amazement, never uses this word apropos
of Lafcadio. The difficulty of reconciling spontaneity
with the lack of impulsiveness, with *sang-froid,* is precisely what makes the criminal of *les Caves* so exceptional; one would have to speak of a spontaneity *à froid.*
Is such a thing possible? Is it conceivable? We are still
in a state of utter contradiction.

"To motivate the criminal and remove all motive from
the crime" is possible only by a paradox that consists
of making *non-motivation,* gratuitousness, the *psychological law* of such an individual. As Barnabé said, he must
be constrained to freedom—an untenable position. Gide
has made his Lafcadio into "a creature of inconsistency,"
but inconsistency can only be exceptional. Even in the
most capricious person, actions can be established only
in sequences. Logic always succeeds in asserting itself
among them. And this is what Julius declares to
Amédée: ". . . no doubt this apparent inconsistency
conceals a subtler and more secret consistency . . ."
We need not suspect Gide of irony here, for like his

Julius, he himself ended by establishing determinism at the heart of the gratuitous act. In the *Préface* to the first volume of the *Ne Jugez pas* series, *L'Affaire Redureau,* he frankly asserts: "Of course no human action is strictly unmotivated; no act is gratuitous save in appearance." As I was saying, ultimately the gratuitous act is merely the act witnesses find inexplicable, or even, still more simply, merely the act as yet unexplained. Then how was Gide led to construct an entire novel on a notion which, by his own admission, vanishes upon examination? . . . It is, I believe, in his lectures on Dostoevsky that we find the clearest answer to this question. He admires the great Russian's capacity for discovering *abysses* (as Jacques Rivière called them) in his characters; by this token he is opposed to Balzac —not that the latter was incapable of discovering them, but, in conformity with the logical spirit of the French, he tries "to achieve consistent characters . . . On the contrary, it seems to be inconsistency that most interests Dostoevsky. Far from concealing it, he constantly makes it apparent; he illuminates it"; and Gide explains it, in Dostoevsky's characters, by the "cohabitation of contradictory feelings." A very judicious explanation, one that Freud restates under the label *emotional ambivalence*—yet we cannot help noticing that it does not at all apply to Lafcadio, and that Gide makes no use of it to explain his hero.

In 1910 Gide reproached La Rochefoucauld for letting "everything contradictory in the human soul" escape. In his *Dostoevsky* he insists on this point: "There is in man much that is unexplained, granted that there is not much that is inexplicable." Which is why, from our ignorance of the "unexplored regions" of the human heart, from its *terrae incognitae,* he will derive excellent counsels of prudence in the exercise of human justice, of which he himself had been, briefly, one of the most conscientious representatives, as a juror in the Rouen

Cour d'Assises (see his *Souvenirs de la Cour d'Assises*).
Justice, in applying its logic: *Is fecit cui prodest,* risks
"letting itself be swept into the worst errors."

Dostoevsky suggests a further example, one described
by Gide himself as an "absolutely gratuitous action"—
Kirilov's suicide in *The Possessed;* impelled by a mystical idea, Kirilov kills himself to assert his unbelief, "for
if God exists, everything depends on him, and I can do
nothing external to his will." He will be the first man
to kill himself "without any motive and solely to testify
to his independence." Gide's comment on this case is
very explicit; by gratuitous act he means "that its motivation is not external," and further: "this act, if it is
gratuitous, is still not unmotivated." Gide frankly abandons defining *gratuitous* as without motive.

Consider further, in the *Faits divers,* an extract dated
1927 from a Moscow newspaper and published by Gide
under the title "A Superman at the Bar of Justice." This
is the story of a perfectly normal young man, we are
told, who during the course of a conversation in which
Nietzsche and Dostoevsky are frequently quoted, declares himself capable of anything and, when chal-
lenged, coldly assassinates a young girl (who lends herself, quite as extraordinarily, to the experiment) to
"prove his will" and without any motives of jealousy,
cupidity, or vengeance . . . A character who reminds
us of Raskolnikov's theories, in whom Gide sees a pre-
cursor of the doctrine of Nietzsche's superman by his
distinction between ordinary and extraordinary men, the
latter being entitled "to authorize their consciences to
surmount certain obstacles . . ." I scarcely need remind
the reader that in analogous cases Dostoevsky sees a
real spiritual bankruptcy, due to impiety, for "if God
doesn't exist, everything is permitted." —But here too, in
the actual murderer of the girl, in Raskolnikov, or in
any of Dostoevsky's other characters, the action's motivation, if exceptional, is no less clear; the character

wants to prove the infinitude of his will, even at the risk of his life, and without concern for the moral obstacles that would stop a theoretician less intense and less influenced by his reading (although he might have arrived at conceptions just as dangerous on his own—the case is not impossible); the girl lets herself be killed in order not to seem to lack courage; Raskolnikov kills in order to take his place in the category of extraordinary beings . . .

In his Lafcadio, Gide has subtilized, refined, quintessentialized gratuitousness; he has aspired to a crime that is committed absolutely without reason. He is alone in thinking so. Julius has never been convinced of the gratuitousness of actions; as soon as he learns that Fleurissoire has been murdered, he decides that the motive is theft; influenced by a conversation with Lafcadio, he thinks he has arrived at the notion of inconsistent characters on his own, but when he is told that theft was not the motive of the crime, he exclaims: "There is no crime without a motive," as any judge would, as Gide himself does later, and he supposes Amédée has been murdered by the gang that has kidnaped the pope and wanted to get rid of a witness who knew too much. Of course Gide ridicules Julius by making him fundamentally incapable, despite his—quite temporary—pretensions to create an inconsistent character, of understanding an action without a motive. But Gide's quarrel with Julius, as with the judges who believe only in the interestedness of an action, is not very fair, for he himself admits that there are always secret motivations. All he can reproach them for is their lack of a sense of complexity, their insufficient concern with rare or obscure motives . . . Even so, we should no longer doubt these insufficiencies so much, for after all, many of these gentlemen have read Gide.

By an aesthetic attitude—a gratuitous one, we might say—Gide has dug an artificial moat between two kinds of actions, some familiar and classified, others exceptional and obscure; all relate to one and the same psychology, without which, moreover, any attempt at explanation would have to be abandoned. There is no gratuitous act, no free act, no inconsistent act, no detachable act—this is the very postulate of science. And Gide knows this is true, despite his reserve about a basic and inexpressible residue, the metaphysical extension of problems of action and personality which, on the psychological level, cannot be posited or even conceived, save according to a determinism of principle and of method.

In positing the gratuitous act as a distinct entity, Gide has thereby based his work on a paradox. It remains for us to see if Gide has managed to give it the appearance of truth, or, if one prefers, to confer upon it that artistic truth which satisfies the reader and which is the emotional equivalent of truth; for in the domain of the imagination, the power of illusion precedes authenticity. Has Gide at least given us the *aesthetic illusion of the gratuitous act*, or has he merely implanted a disappointing hypothesis in a skillful fable?

It will be recalled that Lafcadio's crime is inserted in a huge comic apparatus intended to lead the victim into the adventurer's hand. This encounter is a pure effect of chance, like that of the Miglionnaire and of Coclès. Amédée Fleurissoire, salesman of religious objects in a provincial town, has joined a crusade to liberate the pope, whom he believes to have been kidnaped by Freemasons and taken to the Castel Sant'Angelo by an underground tunnel from the Vatican (whence the work's title); this sequestration is intended to permit the secret substitution of a false pope, acting in conformity with the association's objectives. As a matter of fact, Fleurissoire is the victim of an enormous confidence trick played on a group of naïve and wealthy Catholics by the Mille-Pattes gang; he unwittingly becomes part of a plot he is in a position to expose, following the indiscretion of one of the unconscious dupes of this machination, headed by a monster impostor known as Protos, who happens to be a former schoolmate of young Lafcadio. I am omitting the savory imbroglio of characters and events which makes this book such an amusing parody of the picaresque novel, and to which the shade of Eugène Sue and the genius of Fantomas would subscribe. Lafcadio is still quite unaware of this matter when he takes the train from Rome to Brindisi; this illegitimate youth, as seductive as he is disturbing, has just discovered his father, on the eve of the latter's death, in the person of a rich ambassador, Count Agénor de Baraglioul, who had fathered him on a beautiful *demi-mondaine* in Bucharest, where he occupied a diplomatic position; without letting him enter the great, closed world of "family," Lafcadio's father has nonetheless provided him with a comfortable inheritance which permits him to travel. Fleurissoire takes the same train; following his misadventures in Italy, he has fallen into the hands of Protos' gang, which passes itself off as an organization of priests disguised for the deliverance of the Holy Father, and which has entrusted Amédée with the mission of cashing in Rome a check for six thousand francs, which sum he will then bring to Naples. He enters the compartment where Lafcadio is musing over various recent and remote memories:

"Oh! ! What kind of ark can that strange old man have come out of?"

The sliding door into the corridor had just let in Amédée Fleurissoire. Fleurissoire had traveled in an empty compartment as far as Frosinone. At that station a middle-aged Italian had got into his carriage and had begun to stare at him with such glowering

eyes that Fleurissoire had made haste to take himself
off.

In the next compartment, Lafcadio's youthful
grace, on the contrary, attracted him.

"Dear me! What a charming boy!" thought he;
"hardly more than a child! On his holidays, no doubt.
How beautifully dressed he is! His eyes look so can-
did! Oh, what a relief it will be to be quit of my suspicions for once! If only he knew French, I should
like to talk to him."

He sat down opposite to him in the corner next the
door. Lafcadio turned up the brim of his hat and
began to consider him with a lifeless and apparently
indifferent eye.

"What is there in common between me and that
squalid little rat?" reflected he. "He seems to fancy
himself too. What is he smiling at me like that for?
Does he imagine I'm going to embrace him? Is it
possible that there exist women who fondle old men?
No doubt he'd be exceedingly astonished to know
that I can read writing or print with perfect fluency,
upside down, or in transparency, or in a looking glass,
or on blotting paper—a matter of three months' train-
ing and two years' practice—all for the love of art.
Cadio, my dear boy, the problem is this: to impinge
on that fellow's fate . . . but how? . . . Oh! I'll offer
him a cachou. Whether he accepts or not, I shall at
any rate hear in what language."

"*Grazio! Grazio!*" said Fleurissoire as he refused.

"Nothing doing with the old dromedary. Let's go
to sleep," went on Lafcadio to himself, and pulling
the brim of his hat down over his eyes, he tried to
spin a dream out of one of his youthful memories.

. . . .

Lafcadio, though his eyes were shut, was not
asleep; he could not sleep.

"The old boy over there believes I am asleep," thought he; "if I were to take a peep at him through my eyelids, I should see him looking at me. Protos used to make out that it was particularly difficult to pretend to be asleep while one was really watching; he claimed that he could always spot pretended sleep by just that slight quiver of the eyelids . . . I'm repressing now. Protos himself would be taken in. . . ."

The sun meanwhile had set, and Fleurissoire, in sentimental mood, was gazing at the last gleams of its splendor as they gradually faded from the sky. Suddenly the electric light that was set in the rounded ceiling of the railway carriage, blazed out with a vividness that contrasted brutally with the twilight's gentle melancholy. Fleurissoire was afraid, too, that it might disturb his neighbor's slumbers, and turned the switch; the result was not total darkness but merely a shifting of the current from the center lamp to a dark blue night-light. To Fleurissoire's thinking, this was still too bright; he turned the switch again; the night-light went out, but two side brackets were immediately turned on, whose glare was even more disagreeable than the center light's; another turn, and the night-light came on again; at this he gave up.

"Will he never have done fiddling with the light?" thought Lafcadio impatiently. "What's he up to now? (No! I'll *not* raise my eyelids.) He is standing up. Can he have taken a fancy to my portmanteau? Bravo! He has noticed that it isn't locked. It was a bright idea of mine to have a complicated lock fitted to it at Milan and then lose the key, so that I had to have it picked at Bologna! A padlock, at any rate, is easy to replace. . . . God damn it! Is he taking off his coat? Oh! all the same, let's have a look!"

Fleurissoire, with no eyes for Lafcadio's portmanteau, was struggling with his new collar and had taken his coat off, so as to be able to put the stud in more easily; but the starched linen was as hard as cardboard and he struggled in vain.

"He doesn't look happy," went on Lafcadio to himself. "He must be suffering from a fistula or some unpleasant complaint of that kind. Shall I go to his help? He'll never manage it by himself. . . ."

Yes, though! At last the collar yielded to the stud. Fleurissoire then took up his tie, which he had placed on the seat beside his hat, his coat, and his cuffs, and going up to the door of the carriage, looked at himself in the windowpane, endeavoring, like Narcissus in the water, to distinguish his reflection from the surrounding landscape.

"He can't see."

Lafcadio turned on the light. The train at that moment was running alongside a bank, which could be seen through the window, illuminated by the light cast upon it from one after another of the compartments of the train; a procession of brilliant squares was thus formed which danced along beside the railroad and suffered, each one in its turn, the same distortions, according to the irregularities of the ground. In the middle of one of these squares danced Fleurissoire's grotesque shadow; the others were empty.

"Who would see?" thought Lafcadio. "There—just to my hand—under my hand, this double fastening, which I can easily undo; the door would suddenly give way and he would topple out; the slightest push would do it; he would fall into the darkness like a stone; one wouldn't even hear a scream. . . . And off tomorrow to the East! . . . Who would know?"

The tie—a little ready-made sailor knot—was put on by now and Fleurissoire had taken up one of the cuffs and was arranging it upon his right wrist, examining, as he did so, the photograph above his seat, which represented some palace by the sea, and was one of four that adorned the compartment.

"A crime without a motive," went on Lafcadio, "what a puzzle for the police! As to that, however, going along beside this blessed bank, anybody in the next-door compartment might notice the door open and the old blighter's shadow pitch out. The corridor curtains, at any rate, are drawn. . . . It's not so much about events that I'm curious, as about myself. There's many a man thinks he's capable of anything, who draws back when it comes to the point. . . . What a gulf between the imagination and the deed! . . . And no more right to take back one's move than at chess. Pooh! If one could foresee all the risks, there'd be no interest in the game! . . . Between the imagination of a deed and . . . Hullo! the bank's come to an end. Here we are on a bridge, I think; a river . . ."

The windowpane had now turned black and the reflections in it became more distinct. Fleurissoire leaned forward to straighten his tie.

"Here, just under my hand the double fastening—now that he's looking away and not paying attention—upon my soul, it's easier to undo than I thought. If I can count up to twelve, without hurrying, before I see a light in the countryside, the dromedary is saved. Here goes! One, two, three, four (slowly! slowly!), five, six, seven, eight, nine . . . a light . . ." Fleurissoire did not utter a single cry. When he felt Lafcadio's push and found himself facing the gulf which suddenly opened in front of him, he made a great sweep with his arm to save himself; his left hand clutched at the smooth framework of the door, while, as he half turned round, he flung his right well behind him and over Lafcadio's head, sending his second cuff, which he had been in the act of putting on, spinning to the other end of the carriage, where it rolled underneath the seat.

Lafcadio felt a horrible claw descend upon the

back of his neck, lowered his head and gave another push, more impatient than the first; this was followed by the sensation of nails scraping through his flesh; and after that, nothing was left for Fleurissoire to catch hold of but the beaver hat, which he snatched at despairingly and carried away with him in his fall.

"Now then, let's keep cool," said Lafcadio to himself. "I mustn't slam the door to; they might hear it in the next carriage."

He drew the door towards him, in the teeth of the wind, and then shut it quietly.*

If we study the succession of Lafcadio's thoughts closely, we discern:

—His astonishment at Fleurissoire's entrance.

—His disgust upon examining him, his sense of a lack of any community of species.

—His notion of the surprise the smiling Fleurissoire would feel if he were to become aware of Lafcadio's special talents.

—His desire to intervene in Fleurissoire's destiny, manifested by the offer of the cashew.

(All this is a mere priming, tinged with antipathy.) Then Lafcadio withdraws his interest from Fleurissoire; subsequently he returns to him:

—Idea of his pretended sleep, accompanied by attention.

—Impatience with the changing light provoked by the manipulation of the switch.

—Curiosity as to Fleurissoire's actions, which makes him open his eyes.

—Remark concerning Fleurissoire's unhappy expression.

—Impulse to help him put on his collar.

* *Lafcadio's Adventures.* Copyright 1925 by Alfred A. Knopf, Inc. Translated by Dorothy Bussy. Reprinted by permission.

—Real help given by turning on the light.

(All this suggests a kind of pity.)

—Sight of the bright squares of the windows silhouetted against the slope, and of Fleurissoire's shadow in one of them, the others being empty.

—Idea that no one would see if Fleurissoire were pushed out.

—Notion of the ease with which the door could be opened, and imagination of the crime and of the impunity with which it could be accomplished.

—Remarks concerning the possibility of being seen, and reflections gravitating around the idea of the crime.

(All this wakens the suggestion of the possible crime.)

—Lafcadio's curiosity relating to himself rather than to events. Would he be capable of anything, without drawing back when confronted by action? Distance between imagination and action. Impossibility of revoking an action once it is performed.

—Mental progression: If the risks were foreseen, the game would lose all its interest. Implication that the risks must be left in the game. Elimination of prudence.

(All this, which seems to digress from the notion of the crime itself, creates a state of challenge. There remains only to link this *virtuality* with the suggestion.)

—The observed crossing of a river does not alter the train of thought.

—The increased ease of the lock's functioning, accompanied by Fleurissoire's looking away, immediately determines a kind of wager. Fleurissoire's life is to be gambled with as in a game of chance: saved if while counting slowly to twelve no light is seen in the countryside. Beginning of the game, the countdown. And here Lafcadio passes from imagination to action by the intermediary of *the game,* an unreal action through which one enters reality almost unwittingly. He slows down the count—no doubt in order not to cheat, to abide by the convention—which augments Fleurissoire's chances, so to speak, of being executed: he sees the light only at ten; if he had not slowed down after four, he would have reached twelve before the light, and Fleurissoire would have been saved.

—At ten, a light. Instantaneous push from Lafcadio. No reflection. He is caught in the game. He plays it to the end, without stopping himself.

—Probably, sudden perception of Fleurissoire's attempts to hold himself back with his left hand on the smooth door jamb, his right on Lafcadio's collar.

—Disgust at feeling a hideous paw fall on the back of his neck; Lafcadio lowers his head and gives a second push, more impatient than the first. It is difficult to interpret this second push; Lafcadio could think twice about his action; he completes it. Why? Not because he is afraid it has been understood by Fleurissoire; is it out of disgust at being clawed by "the animal," as he says later? Or is it rather out of a hatred of retouching? To go all the way? Or because it is very difficult to inhibit a rapid action as it is being performed, even if one wants to? Such a thing does not even seem to have occurred to him. Moreover it matters little; the gratuitous act would have been the same had it been prevented at the last moment, once it had been initiated. But Lafcadio is not a man to look for attenuating circumstances.

From the analysis of the crime, we must conclude that Lafcadio did not know Fleurissoire and had no reason to kill him. This is what makes the act gratuitous. But by *demotivating the crime*, Gide has *made it incredible*. It is only by the artifice of the narrative that he establishes its genesis. Consider all the details of the analysis we have just listed, and set aside those which concern the action itself; place in another list those which concern Lafcadio's nature, and you will discover that the former are inadequate to explain the act (which is no doubt what Gide wishes); they are sentiments of the moment, the circumstance, and without bearing; neither disgust, impatience, nor curiosity as to Fleurissoire's trifling actions impels him to the murder; the kind of pity he inspires is ineffectual, even in restraining Lafcadio. On the other hand, everything which concerns Lafcadio's profoundest self is here expressed in order to bring the gratuitousness of the act into play. *By motivating the character, Gide thereby impels the reader to fill the gap between the act and its author.* If the act is disinterested, it seems no less interesting for Lafcadio. Fleurissoire's personality is relegated to the background; it plays no role; anyone else might have suffered the same fate—with this reservation, that he be as anonymous, in order not to have awakened any powerful effect in Lafcadio's mind which might have deprived him of the freedom to make the individual into a mere pretext. It was essential that sooner or later Lafcadio take this step, and it is in doing so that this so-called free man is a slave. The key lies in that passage where he discovers the distance between imagination and the act, and where he is tempted to prove to himself that nothing is stopping him. All the rest is accessory, the velleities of prudence; perhaps they merely augment, in fact, the *temptation* (it is surprising that Gide doesn't use this word) by the notion of risk they inspire in our gambler.

But why, we may ask, does he commit this crime precisely at this moment, upon this victim? *By chance,* or, more precisely, because circumstances lend themselves to it; further: they suggest the notion of the crime, doubtless not for the first time (although Gide has not informed us on this point). Lafcadio has nevertheless experienced the instability in the equilibrium of two contrary actions when, having taken on his shoulders an old woman's bag, he felt in kissing her that he might just as well have strangled her. In any case the circumstances are presented with enough consistency so that the act can be introduced here with the *maximum* of facility. This is the meaning, in my opinion, of such details as the shadow projected on the slope and the play with the lock on the door—added, of course, to the wretched Fleurissoire's *optimum* position in front of the glass. Analogous circumstances would inevitably have presented themselves one day or another; one may suppose that Lafcadio would not have yielded—and then one diminishes his profound motivation—or think that he might have behaved in the same way, in which case one reinforces his tendency to commit the gratuitous act. In either case it is a second reason for regarding this free man as a slave: here a slave of circumstantial determinism, as before of the fatality of his nature.

The pretext of Fleurissoire and suggestive circumstances—such are the modes of an act whose essential and permanent element is Lafcadio's personality, or, if one prefers, the system of ideas which proliferates in his thought like a cancer and which lives there in an independent manner, without criticism whatever he may think of it, without links to the rest of his being, and which must conclude so dangerously in what Renouvier would have called "a mental vertigo." He himself will say later that he "did it very quickly" while he had a desire to do it; "I was living unconsciously, I killed as in a dream." He yields to the hypnotic fascination of an idea. Certainly he is not mad; on the contrary he is quite lucid, but only exceptional, abnormal, monstrous —which would not keep him from seeming true if Gide had convinced us.

One may cite analogous cases, but the problem is to know, in these cases, whether one does not always find a motivation, not only in the character (as Gide has done so superbly), but also in the *action* which he commits (which Gide has refused on principle to do), and particularly a motivation for the latter in the former. Now if Gide has admirably succeeded in the character (consider the full-length portrait of Lafcadio to be found in the book, which is sufficiently lifelike to have escaped its author and perilously influenced an entire generation of writers after World War I), he has not won our adherence to the action, and he has not really succeeded in relating them to one another. This is the weakness of *les Caves*. Lafcadio exists; his gratuitous crime seems unreal to us, and we have particular difficulty in believing that he committed it.

I think that Gide might have come to realize the contradiction in which he was to imprison his hero if, instead of starting from the critique of ideas of psychology and justice, he had started from the critique of a logical idea such as causality. It is in fact astonishing that Gide never uses the word *cause* apropos of Lafcadio's actions. Criticism of the notion of cause has led certain philosophers to denounce its imprecision and to substitute for it the notion of *function* and of variable factors (in the mathematical sense of the phrase). Thenceforth the psychological progression is no longer the simple succession of motive and act; the act is the product of a great quantity of factors, almost impossible to measure, but whose existence prevails at any moment of our lives and whose complexity leaves no flaw through which a truly undetermined action might slip.

If Lafcadio's gratuitous crime distresses us, in short, as a logical scandal, it also shocks us as a moral scandal. Though we may tolerate the event with a maximum of complacency, may rival the author in broad-mindedness, Fleurissoire's murder is hard to swallow. In the first place Gide has made Amédée absurd, but he has not made him odious; and by accumulating his misadventures, in which his good faith is constantly ridiculed, he has finally made him touching; this effect is reinforced by the sympathy he wins from Carola, the good-hearted whore who can recognize a saint in this ninny; by launching Amédée on his nonsensical crusade, Gide has made him into a kind of burlesque hero who approaches Quixote in disinterestedness (here is the true gratuitous act) and Parsifal in chastity. —Next, Lafcadio, by an inverse error, has been burdened with too many attractions. The reader is suspicious of his good deeds, and it must be admitted that the scene of the rescue of the two children from the fire is terribly contrived. As for the petty dishonesties committed out of bravura, they are amusing from only one point of view, and disagreeable from all others. The sympathy we are supposed to accord them is not steadfast, nor can it be; it is only a quite temporary complicity. —Lastly, Gide proposes an untenable bargain. He was no doubt artistically justified in taking his adventurer to the extreme limit of his tendency, but the act itself changes everything. One is no longer the same before and after a crime. Lafcadio's crime may be gratuitous, but to us it appears unjustifiable. Apropos of Merimée's *Partie de tric-trac*, Gide writes in his *Journal*: "There is no *essential* difference between the honest man and the scoundrel. That the honest man may *become* a scoundrel is what is terrible and true. In the paths of 'sin' it is only the first step that counts. As someone has already remarked, it is easier for a woman to have no lover than to have only one. That is the story of Lafcadio." But progression into evil cannot pass for an excuse. Moreover it is not between the honest man and the scoundrel that there is no difference, it is between the honest man and the *criminal*, for we can all commit a crime—by a sudden lapse of conscience, by a mental deficiency, by a lack of resistance to circumstances—but we will become scoundrels only by maintaining a profound solidarity with the crime. Now Lafcadio, if he is more or less sickened by his crime, if he has difficulty explaining it to himself, and if he is thereby shocked to hear himself called a *criminal*, feels absolutely no remorse for it and, faithful to his nature, regrets only that the contest should be simplified by the arrest of Protos in his place, which diminishes his risks and the pleasures of the game. If he were a Russian, he would confess publicly or turn himself in. If he momentarily thinks of doing so, it is only to show himself worthy of the respect which, in spite of everything, Julius' daughter Geneviève shows him; but once she has given herself to him out of love, he thinks only of freeing himself from this new connection, for "he esteems her a little less now that she loves him a little more," which is not only disagreeable but actually impious, although still within the logic of the character, for there is a terrible and inescapable logic of inconsistency which condemns Lafcadio to perpetual evasion; and at the end there is no longer any question for him of sacrificing his freedom and the promises of life by giving himself up to the police for the meager pleasure of deserving his mistress' approval.

Gide's indulgence for his hero must not make us forget that he condemns him, however modestly. Such indulgence derives from the notion of *the virtue of evil*, which Gide has acknowledged elsewhere and in which he sees a resource that may serve the good, on condition that its energy be directed toward it, thereby becoming more capable of serving its cause than the lukewarm conformity of an untested honesty. This is the first lesson that can be learned from *les Caves du Vatican*. It is indeed about Lafcadio that one can say, with Gide, that "collaboration with the demon is necessary in the work of art," and that "it is with good intentions that one makes bad literature." But Lafcadio, by his very inconsistency, is essentially a *virtual* being. To Julius, who sees him as ready for anything, he answers, "Ready for nothing." It is not impossible that

Lafcadio may be saved. His crime has suddenly limited him, reduced him to the unilaterality of the determining action and separated him from the love of men, whom he despises but whom he needs. It is not impossible that he should one day put the virtue of evil to the service of good, if he consents to forget himself a little. In any case Gide does not mean to identify himself with his young hero, and it is altogether an error, as Gide has remarked, to regard *les Caves* as "an affirmation of nihilism." Despite appearances, Gide does not intend to destroy; he aims at constructing; above all he aims at moral progress.

Ultimately, in this critical work, Gide has not shown enough irony with regard to Lafcadio—there are only traces of it—and this is what risks blurring the book's meaning. It is curious to see that almost the same thing happened to him apropos of the only important character in *les Nourritures terrestres*, Ménalque, whose morality he has elsewhere explicitly reproved, in fact regretting, despite one or two touches of an almost ineffable irony, not having been able to accentuate or emphasize the latter.

He could perhaps have spared himself the trouble with regard to a scoundrel as obvious as Protos, one of Lafcadio's masters, who has completed the strange education Lafcadio had received from the collection of uncles his mother had provided him with. Protos, moreover, is a conformist in his own way; he knows that one leaves one society only to enter another, which has its own laws, and he consequently attempts to subjugate Lafcadio to it. But Lafcadio is a free man who has no taste for "circles."

Gide has spread his irony thickly over the characters living in bourgeois conformism, the Catholic Julius, the Freemason Anthime. He has made it more stinging by satirizing their futile attempts to escape from it—Anthime's conversion and Julius' new artistic conceptions. But these are only dodges, and both men return to their ruts as soon as interest demands it.

Alongside this satire on impotent or insincere attempts at nonconformity, Amédée's crusade is the caricature of sincere action and fervor. Gide has belabored this character as though he wanted to stamp out the remains of his former mysticism by ridiculing it outrageously. Of all the characters in *les Caves*, Amédée is the only one who has "an eagle."

The conclusions of *les Caves* are therefore rather disappointing, and somewhat negative. Gide's ulterior motive must no doubt be sought outside the book. If one notices that none of the characters, neither Protos nor Lafcadio, nor Julius nor Anthime nor Fleurissoire, manages to perform a satisfactory act, a "correct" act, and if one observes further that they represent virtually every level of intelligence, one concludes that what they all lack is a sound notion of the relations that obtain between intelligence and action. Yet we know Gide's position on this problem. He has expressed it in various places, notably in his *Conférences sur Dostoevsky* and in his *Conversation avec un Allemand quelques années avant la guerre*. In general he is convinced that the mind may not act, but causes action. In action, man compromises and limits his thought. "Thinking that because I have done this, I could no longer do that—that is what becomes intolerable." Here again is the horror of choice which produces impotence in action but plenitude in thought. That there is an antagonism between life and art Flaubert had already noted, and Gide's first interest is to reach a practical conclusion for the benefit of the artist. But since Gide is also, in the second place, a moralist and even a pedagogue, he cannot be indifferent to action; he has had to discover a way of acting indirectly, without entering into action himself, by means of interposed characters, by means of the effect which his thought, served by his *insinuating* art, exerts on their consciousness: Gide has always dreamed of being the writer of his time who would have most *influence* in fifty years. By the diversity of his works, complementary but divergent, he has assured this influence possibilities of spreading in every direction; he has thereby promoted, in the best manner, the freedom of his person, by expressing it completely in all its complexity.

5. Récits

That Gide is a novelist is contestable. We shall have to decide the question apropos of *les Faux Monnayeurs*. Yet he is universally recognized as a master of the *récit*. *L'Immoraliste, la Porte étroite, Isabelle, la Symphonie pastorale* are four authentic masterpieces which enrich that magnificent tradition of French literature which includes *la Princesse de Clèves, Manon Lescaut, René, Adolphe, Carmen, Dominique* . . .

These *récits* have often been misunderstood, primarily because they have been taken for more or less fictionalized confessions, secondly because they have been read without being "placed" in the ensemble of Gide's works, and finally bcause their hidden irony has not been discerned. Gide explicitly states in one of his *Feuillets:* "With the single exception of my *Nourritures*, all my books are *ironic* works; *they are books of criticism. La Porte étroite* is the criticism of a certain form of romantic imagination; *la Symphonie pastorale*, of a form of lying to oneself; *l'Immoraliste*, of a form of individualism."

The *récits* therefore constitute a part of the same series of tendentious works to which the *soties* be-

longed. They too are satires, although Gide has hedged
a bit here ("'Criticism' doesn't mean the same thing as
'satire'"), but of a special nature: they are serious and
indirect satires. We all know that a portrait painted
with great fidelity and complete submission to the
model can be infinitely more cruel than caricature, especially since, being truthful, it leaves no margin for .
the illusion of a systematic distortion against which the
model could protest. Gide's *récits* are like those im-
placable portraits in which the painter's very love for
his subject serves only to reinforce—emotionally—the
severity of his vision by a deliberate accuracy.

What further differentiates the *récits* from the *soties*
is the role of irony. Whereas *Paludes* and the *Prométhée*
are steeped in it, and though it circulates freely in *les
Caves du Vatican*, aiming even at Lafcadio in places
(though rarely; this character, merely grazed by it, is
in fact treated in the manner of the heroes of the
récits, whom irony illuminates but does not overpower),
there is no direct attack in the *récits*. The characters
the narrator encounters may well be ridiculed by him,
but only from his own point of view, not that of the
author, who stubbornly remains in the wings. It is in
order to attain a higher degree of objectivity that Gide
has handed his pen to the four characters who tell these
stories, and whose nature must indeed be ignored in
order to mistake them for him; any comparison elo-
quently testifies to this separateness: a fierce individual-
ist (the hero of *l'Immoraliste*); a fervent Protestant,
amorous and yet apathetic (Jérôme in *la Porte étroite*);
a sentimental university student who dreams of being a
novelist (Gérard Lacase in *Isabelle*); a Swiss pastor
who confuses the voice of conscience and the voice of
instinct (the minister in *la Symphonie pastorale*). One
certainly divines, or is expressly told in the *Journal* and
in *Si le Grain ne meurt . . .* , what Gide's personal
experience may have contributed to the life of these

beings, and with what supple skill he has wisely made them speak in the first person; we see how well he could mimic himself, but each time by exploring only a part of himself, driving himself to absurd extremes— Gide, who always wanted to be at the *extrême milieu,* who always dreamed of equilibrium and proportion, whom Claudel defined as "a mind without propensity." Still we must make this reservation, that Gide's sympathy, his interest in others, permits him an objective mimetism that produces the pastor who tells *la Symphonie pastorale* and whom he nonetheless opposed from the bottom of his heart. Gide's mastery seems to me to consist precisely in utilizing all his powers of sympathy and antipathy; by sympathy, he makes these *first persons singular* speak with an accent of truth unequaled in French fiction, and the author's *I* realizes possibilities far beyond the *I* of Gide the man; by antipathy, he maintains all his reserve, marks the distances which separate him from his creatures, and keeps a margin of irony between the frame and the drawing of these figures, executed with a mixture of attachment and detachment that is classical in its sureness.

The surface interest of these *récits* has obscured their critical aspect; readers let themselves be carried away, and react naïvely to the story they are being told, and this is indeed part of Gide's intentions; but he also intends the reader to withdraw his identification, either by the story's end or, perhaps still more, as it is being told.

The extension of the adventures of these singular spirits in the reader's mind, and the accompaniment to them, is a critical reflection which detaches him from them and keeps him from granting a predominant, excessive importance to the total emotion he may be tempted to derive from them. If the immoralist Michel horrifies him, if Alissa pierces his heart with pity, if Isabelle disillusions him, if the pastor irritates him, he must not allow his feelings for the fate of these heroes to turn against their author; instead he will praise Gide for having been able to provoke with such intensity a response that attests to the artist's sureness of touch and powers of evocation. He will avoid the naïveté of asserting his own feelings as a reproach to Gide's. For Gide is horrified by his "superman"; he admires Alissa and is distressed by her demanding virtue; Jérôme's apathy seems ruinous to him; he despises the seductive Isabelle and ridicules Gérard's over-obliging imagination; he is irritated by the pastor's unconscious hypocrisy. In fact the irony begins only after a perfect comprehension of these beings, and for Gide, no doubt, of himself. The irony consists in not accepting them, however human or superhuman they may be, and however touched we are by their motives or their condition, by value or virtue, by sanctity itself. We must, however much it goes against the grain, reject them. They are dangerous examples. The Gidean irony lies in this transcendence, which always costs us something, for there is a kind of horrible courage in Michel, an exalting appeal in Alissa's renunciations, a pietistic respect in Jérôme's inaction, a charm in Gérard's romanticism, an intoxicating seductiveness in the portrait of the unreal Isabelle, an evangelistic fervor and kindness in the pastor. It is a heroic irony. Hence the deep resonance of these unforgettable works, even after we have plumbed their secret. Rereading them, we always fall under their spell again.

And yet Gide has seemingly wished to keep us at a distance. His advice is always not to follow whatever path he has shown us: "Nathanaël, throw away my book." The irony of these works is curiously placed. In l'Immoraliste it is in the conclusion that the reader will draw from it, the relentless story not having left him time to collect himself before Marceline's dreadful death march and the exhaustion of the hero's inhuman tendency. In *la Porte étroite*, Jérôme's respectful inaction wakens a muted irony at each of his self-effacements, but the last lines of the *Journal d'Alissa* burn with a despairing irony at the notion of her anguish when she divines the total futility of her ascent toward virtue and her solitude achieved without God. More muted, the irony of *Isabelle* is in the movement that erodes our mysterious enchantment; it accompanies the decrescendo of the fictional illusion, the wretched collapse of an imaginary charm. In *la Symphonie pastorale*, as in a comedy, the irony lies in the gap between the pastor's naïve words and the unacknowledged feelings they conceal, between his conscience and his unconscious; it makes him the reader's pathetic plaything.

If this irony, sometimes muted, sometimes lightly etched upon the story's transparency, sometimes concealed in an intention that exceeds it, yields the secret of each of these *récits*, none gives us Gide's whole thought. To arrive at this, we must complete them by each other; and it is obvious, for example, that the excesses of egoism in *l'Immoraliste* and of sacrifice in *la Porte étroite* counterbalance one another; but for a total view, we must actually take all of Gide's work into account, oppose the impotent exasperation of *Paludes* to the harsh energy of *l'Immoraliste*, the parody of sanctity in the *Prométhée* to the sublimity of *la Porte étroite*, the destructiveness of *Saül* to the enrichment of *les Nourritures*, the altruism of *le Roi Candaule* to the egoism of *l'Immoraliste*, etc. . . . The most cursory indication of these necessary comparisons suggests that Gide's entire work is a kind of symphony whose significance is not in this or that part, but in their harmony, their unison, and by this I mean their contrast as much as their concert. There are only two books in which Gide has tried to put all of himself—prematurely, in *André Walter*; at the peak of his maturity, in *les Faux Monnayeurs*. We understand why Gide has reserved for this last book alone the designation *novel:* a novel worthy of the name must, in effect, communicate a whole world, represent an author's entire vision, orchestrate all the parts of his imagination. In a sense, the total of Gide's *récits* and *soties* would be the substance of a vast novel integrating them in a varied unity. *Les Caves du Vatican* might be said to afford something like a rough draft of this polyphony, with the contrasts of its double plot, the variety of its characters, their varied situations in society, but in tone and intention it is not so much a novel as a parody of a novel, the comedy of the novel—moreover, one admirably executed. And here again Gide has contrived a relation with another of his works: *les Faux Monnayeurs* corresponds, on the serious level, to this farcical work. Moreover we know that in an initial plan, Lafcadio was to be the narrator of *les Faux Monnayeurs* and enter into relations with the novelist Edouard; Gide was certainly right to cut the links that united the two conceptions and to set apart, at the summit of his work, this great attempt to objectify his entire inner world. I shall study this work later, and if I refer to it here, it is because it allows us to see more clearly the nature of these *récits* without which Gide could doubtless not later have conceived and mastered such a network of intersecting intentions. Each of the *récits* is in fact remarkable for the purity of its line, the elegant singleness of its contour, the sobriety of its development and, for once to use this word in praise, its *unilaterality.*

I think that what distinguishes the tale from the novel is its minimum of intricacy, its continuous *melody.* Without proliferating incident or episode, Gide has admirably understood the technical purity this genre requires, as opposed to the novel, where only proliferation and interconnection can give the impression of total life. In the tale, one takes a sounding which of course respects divagations but must especially preserve, in its elegant abstraction, the separateness of its singular object. At the core of *l'Immoraliste,* of *la Porte étroite,* of *Isabelle,* of *la Symphonie pastorale,* we find a simple *donnée,* a single germ; and Gide's art has been precisely to bring this seed into flower, not forcing it, but encouraging its bloom with the patience and the love of a good gardener. One human being who prefers himself to everything and sacrifices everything to himself, another who prefers everything to herself and sacrifices herself totally; the disillusionment of an overweening imagination, the blinding of desire by the lies of conscience—such subjects sufficed to give these tales the *élan* of classical perfection.

The art of the novel tends to create in the reader emotional states which approach those of poetry. In French this tendency is called, in fact, *le romanesque.* It would not be difficult to show that Gide's *récits* achieve powerful effects and that, on this point, he is a match for the most spellbinding storytellers. We need merely to recall our horrified admiration for the immoralist's criminal madness, the hideous impression of Marceline's death, the anguished and despairing sublimity to which we are swept by the ascetic renunciation of Alissa's mysticism, the contemptuous melancholy on which *romanesque* illusion is wrecked in *Isabelle,* the outraged pity the blind girl's suicide wakens in us, the culmination of the self-duped pastor's folly. The whole range of feelings, from the most powerful to the most subtly tinted, is explored by Gide. It is difficult to surpass the pathos of Alissa's growing solitude.

We realize how readily the novel may contain all genres: tragedy, comedy, poetry. And the tale can, precisely, isolate—whereas the novel must mingle—any one of these great fundamental emotions which are at the core of the ensemble effects by which the genres may be distinguished. From this point of view, then, these

four *récits* of Gide's are tragedies: they are all determined by deaths, save one, *Isabelle* (not counting the
deaths of the minor characters), which ends in a collapse of the heroine that is worse than death. As a
bloodless tragedy, all things considered, it is Gide's
Bérénice. And apparent in all of them, more than the
romanesque, is a profound poetry consisting of our distressed sympathy for all these splendid themes of true
suffering, for all these excesses of unchecked vitality, of
elevation to the absolute, of the romanticizing of reality,
of mortal hypocrisy. It is against this poetry—abjured
yet so deeply felt—that resolute irony gains a footing,
not without regrets, not without bitterness.

But if the novel borders on poetry by these affective
fulfillments even as it approaches the drama by the
creation of characters and the imposition of their destiny, it seems to me that the true pleasure proper to the
novel is to achieve an original vision of the world by
the invention of a fictional universe which does not
duplicate the one we live in but takes its inspiration
from it in order to recreate it, or rather to reinterpret it
and thereby give us a new explanation of it, astonishing,
if not shocking. I therefore propose to define the novel
as a metaphysic of the intelligence, regarding that
pleasure proper to it as an intellectual pleasure. We
shall return more forcefully to this conception apropos
of *les Faux Monnayeurs*, but it is necessary to suggest
it here with regard to Gide's tales. For even an author
of tales who never writes a true novel, one rivaling life
itself in complexity, has his metaphysic nonetheless: he
merely disperses it in fragmentary aspects (like Mérimée, like Maupassant) instead of centering and organiz-
ing it in huge ensembles (like Balzac, like Dostoevsky).
To grasp this metaphysic in the author of tales, we
must gather up and compare in an ideal gallery these
separate portraits of a world even more his own than
that of reality. And though Gide has given us his total

vision in *les Faux Monnayeurs*, the four *récits* we are considering here do not fail to present certain common characteristics. All are narratives of *disappointment*. All touch us, distress and irritate us; but intellectually they show us characters imprisoned in a formula, captives of a rule, a law, a convention or a habit, and victims of themselves. They have all *chosen* and have found themselves prisoners of a choice—of a choice whose distinguishing mode is, respectively, harshness, narrowness, facility, or deception. The reader will recognize once again the horror of choice, a sign in Gide of rigidity and ossification in an attitude, a sign of thralldom, of impoverishment, and no doubt of imbecility, of weakness, of deficiency, whether its source is the absolutism of desire, the exaltation of virtue, the seduction of the imagination, or the complacencies of conscience. The fraudulence of his goal imprisons man in a fatality. If these tragic works are cruelly crowned by irony, it is because for Gide intelligence is an essential value; it is because the critical spirit is at the basis of all true progress and, no doubt, of all true love as well. That even the critical spirit is liable to distortions, Lafcadio has shown us. One might follow it at work in everything Gide writes, notably in his plays and above all in *les Faux Monnayeurs*, where I am tempted to see it, more than the devil in whom Gide has not succeeded in making us believe, as the true protagonist.

The work of a novelist or a storyteller might theoretically be regarded as the result of an impulse to analyze and an impulse to synthesize. Out of reality, which he starts from and which comprehends his inner life as well as the spectacle of the outer world, his imagination abstracts elements which interest it and to which it accords a new place, role and value in an original recomposition, guided by his intellectual metaphysic.

The error of certain novelists is to confine themselves to analysis. Every work of art is synthetic and organic. Consequently each novelist, each storyteller has his own way of resolving the problem of the relations of reality and imagination. Gide's method may be expressed in two words: *development* of possibilities, and *transposition.*

In the web of events and characters which forms the basis of the *récit,* Gide does not start with actions or circumstances, he starts with the actors; more precisely, he starts with a complex of feelings which has moved him, and whose communicative warmth he wishes to restore. He has explained himself on this matter in *Un esprit non prévenu.* There are, he says, two ways of depicting life. "The one, external and commonly called 'objective,' first sees the gestures of other men, the event, and then explains and interprets them.

"The other, which is primarily attached to the emotions, to thoughts, invents incidents and characters most suitable to express these emotions—and risks remaining incapable of painting anything which has not first been experienced by the author. The latter's resources, his complexities, the antagonism of his too-diverse possibilities, will permit the greatest diversity among his creations. But it is from him that everything emanates. He is the sole guarantee of the truth he reveals, and the sole judge. The heaven and hell of his characters are in him. It is not himself that he paints; but what he paints he might have become had he not become everything himself . . ."

It is, then, a personal method, one which claims to draw everything from the self. But it does not proceed by a naïve expression of the novelist's dreams; it proceeds by abstraction, isolating a tendency and causing it to fructify by yielding to its impulse. "How many buds we bear within us . . . which never flower in our books! They are 'sleeping eyes,' as the botanists call them. But if, out of determination, we get rid of them all, save one, how it grows then, how it swells! how quickly it monopolizes the sap! To create a hero, my recipe is a simple one: Take one of these buds, put it in a pot—all alone—and an admirable specimen soon results. A word of advice: preferably select (if it is true that you have a choice) the bud that bothers you most. You get rid of it at the same time. This may be what Aristotle called the purgation of the passions . . ."

In this way Michel, Alissa, and the pastor represent not Gide, but possibilities of his soul, and are authentically his creatures. The mistake begins when one claims to limit Gide to them. In their author's real life, these characters have never been tolerated; they have been opposed to each other and balanced: "That there is a bud of Michel in me goes without saying; but this is a case of those opposing passions Pascal describes so cleverly, which maintain themselves in equilibrium because we cannot yield to one save to the other's detriment." To reduce Gide to one of his characters is to diminish him wrongly. "If I were only the hero (I don't say: the author) of *l'Immoraliste* . . . I should feel myself diminished."

As a matter of fact, Gide possesses a second method, for he has not modeled quite all his characters on himself. There are doubtless some whose germ was not within him. Nothing could be further from his nature than Jérôme's apathy or Marceline's weakness. But this second method, a complement of the first, eventually unites with it, in an odd way. For to abandon yourself in imagination to one of your tendencies, submitting to its demands, is not far, in practice, from the converse operation, which consists in borrowing from the external world a disposition which is alien to you and lending yourself to it with such force of sympathy that little by little it seems to become natural to you, and personal. In the first case Gide encourages the budding;

in the second, he performs a graft, and perhaps I admire the artist in the second instance even more. In both, submissive attention replaces an active *parti pris*. The flowering is observed with the same patience. But if Gide has perhaps not clearly distinguished these two operations on account of the equivalent sympathy they require (whether for a part of oneself or for another person's tendency), nothing better suggests how greatly they are opposed in origin than this curious passage where the mimetism of the external world is resolved in the disappearance of the self: "Nothing is accomplished if I have not been truly able to become this character I am creating, and to depersonalize myself in him until I put my readers on the wrong scent and risk incurring the reproach of never being able to paint any portrait but my own, however different Saül, Candaule, Alissa, Lafcadio, the pastor of my *Symphonie*, La Pérouse, or Armand may be among themselves. It is returning to myself that embarrasses me; for to tell the truth, I no longer know who I am; or, if you prefer: I never am, I become."

No doubt there are also cases—this would be a third kind—where the invasion of the self by a borrowed nature is based on a scission of the personality, in one part of which it finds an echo: this, I presume, would be the typical case of Alissa, whose heroic nature has found an analogy in Gide's early mysticism. But Gide has not taken all of Alissa from himself. He has received a suggestion from the real world and reinforced it by his personal fervor (or the memory of that fervor).

It would be an oversimplification not to take into account the fact that Gide must also have struggled against too complete an abnegation of himself. The latter, in certain cases, would have resulted in a stalemate. Becoming once again as mystical as his pastor, he would have failed to make us aware of the deceptions of his conscience; he would have adhered to his duplicity instead of showing it to us. It is not surprising that this subtle stratagem awakened his impatience during the writing of *la Symphonie pastorale:* "Suddenly I want to regain a state of fervor, and I am reluctant to let myself be caught in it: I pull on the reins and use the whip at the same time . . ."

How different Gide can be, actually, from what he has most tried to resemble is shown best in his skill at detaching himself from all his heroes and judging them at a great distance from himself:

". . . No, I don't think Michel will ever write. His warmth, as you can tell, is only ardor; it burns without giving heat; the words would disintegrate under his pen. Believe me . . . it is only because I am not Michel that I could tell his story 'so remarkably well,' as you say."

And it is here, as the end of this passage proves, that the development of possibilities, of virtuality, is linked in Gide to *transposition.* Actually his art lies in that miracle which reconciles attachment and detachment. These are actually a painter's properties. Love and criticism are here marvelously united to produce that combination of warmth and impartiality which gives Gide's *récits* that extraordinary power of personal life and of serene objectivity. We can walk around these characters, as around real persons. The sense of life is not communicated, as in other great creators, by a kind of blood transfusion brutally forced upon us, or by the warmth of an insolent or embarrassing contact, but by the animation of independent creatures whose umbilical cord has been carefully cut.

"Only what has ceased to serve is suited to become the substance of art." Gide here reveals one of his secrets. By memory, he recovers the warmth necessary to the life of his heroes. By the detachment of the past, he achieves the *sang-froid* which assures his technique and keeps his hand from trembling. The more ardent the original experience has been, and the more complete his liberation from it, the better the work unites the domination of a faultless art with the palpitation of recovered life. There is in Gide an incomparable clarity in this separation of sentiment and intelligence, of the romanticism of passion and the classicism of expression. It is Gide who defines true classicism as *romanticism mastered*. This desire to purify substance is already quite apparent in the earliest and most intransigent of his *récits, l'Immoraliste:* "I spent four years not writing but living it; and I wrote it to transcend it; I have had this book the way you have a sickness . . . I no longer admire any books save those the author has only barely managed to survive." It is the work in which he has succeeded least, moreover, in achieving that sovereign domination of the object and which, from this point of view, contains a certain technical impurity. There linger in it too many "tatters of himself." Later, he will "absent himself" from his *récits*. The temptation had been too strong, the fever too violent (this cure is indeed the crucial phase of Gide's life); but if we sense a certain effort in the admirable *domestication* of the powers of anarchy from which the book is born, we must not presume that elsewhere Gide has required any such strife. He knows that flexibility, even cunning, is often the condition of an artistic success which severity or harshness would destroy. It is with the greatest ease that the *Journal d'Alissa* and her letters were composed: "how easy it is for me," he says, "how voluptuous to yield to a being less complicated than myself and who, by that very fact, expresses herself with less difficulty."

We need only compare Gide's confidences as to the circumstances which inspired these *récits* with the use he has made of them to see how far he is from naturalistic methods, from the documentary techniques of the slice-of-life school. Nor is there anything in him of the visionary, of Balzac's overblown amplification or

Zola's epic overexcitement. He enlarges no more than
he reproduces. One scarcely dares say that he transforms. He *transposes*. He brings to another plane certain selected elements, following their secret or significant directions, and not their picturesque or exotic
details. This is as true of his landscapes as of his characters. We know from *Si le Grain ne meurt . . .* that
Anna Shackelton's death had first suggested a *récit*
which was to be called *Essai de bien mourir*. But he
effected another transposition:

"I was extremely affected by the thought that neither
my mother nor myself had been able to be with her at
her last hour, that she had not said goodbye to us and
that her last glances had met only strangers' eyes. For
weeks and months I was filled with the anguish of her
solitude. I imagined, I even heard the desperate call
and then the collapse of this loving soul deserted by
everything save God; and it is the echo of this call that
reverberates in the last pages of my *Porte étroite*."

Alissa's Journal, October 15.

Joy, joy, tears of joy . . .

Exceeding human joy and beyond all pain, yes, I
foresee this radiant joy. This rock I cannot surmount,
I know it has a name: happiness . . . I understand
that all my life is in vain if I do not attain happiness
. . . Ah! yet, you promise it, Lord, to the soul that
renounces and is pure. "Blessed now," says your holy
word, "blessed henceforth are those who die in the
Lord." Must I wait until death? It is here that my
faith stumbles, Lord! I cry out to you with all my
strength. I am in darkness; I wait for the dawn. I cry
out to you until I die. Come and slake my heart. I
thirst for that happiness . . . Or must I persuade
myself I have it now? And like the impatient cock
that crows before the dawn, summoning not an-
nouncing the day, must I not wait for the night to
pale before I sing?

October 16.

Jérôme, I would teach you perfect joy.

This morning, a fit of vomiting weakened me terribly. Once it was over, I felt so weak that for an instant I almost hoped for death. But no; first a great calm came over my whole being; then an anguish seized me, a shudder of the flesh and the spirit; it was like the sudden, disenchanted illumination of my life. It seemed to me that for the first time I saw the hideously bare walls of my room. I grew afraid. Even now I am writing to reassure myself, to calm myself. O Lord! If only I could have gone to the end without blasphemy.

I could still get up. I fell on my knees like a child . . .

I would like to die now, quickly, before having understood again that I am alone.

In the second part of *l'Immoraliste*, the Caux landscape has not tempted Gide to a description *à la* Flaubert; his interpretation transforms its role from that of décor to a more affective existence: "It is this valley which I have painted, and it is our house, in *l'Immoraliste*. The countryside has not only lent me its setting; throughout the book, I have sought its likeness."

Just as he abstracts in order to encourage the flowering of a particularity of his nature, or as he grafts an alien sensibility onto himself in order to develop it, with the same freedom Gide detaches from the chaos of experience some combination of circumstances, some anecdote even, some natural setting or episodic figure, provided he finds significance and promise in it, and he preserves their profound meaning by contriving a liberation which renders them more faithful to themselves, so to speak, than they were in the confusion and compromise from which he drew them. This double sense of what must be necessarily arbitrary in art and of its inner deepening has entirely freed Gide's *récits* from the vulgarity of the naturalistic tradition and from the banality of facile psychologizing.

Sympathy and transposition were, moreover, obvious resources for a storyteller like Gide who has not a great deal of imagination and who refuses to transcribe nature literally. We have seen how his subjects grew from the germination of an inner tendency. Nonetheless the subject of *Isabelle* is borrowed from reality, as well as the setting, which is furnished by the estate of Formentin, near La Roque, Gide's property; most of the characters actually existed. The other *récits*, moreover, are laid in countries with which Gide was familiar: North Africa, Italy, Normandy (La Roque-Baignard in *l'Immoraliste*, and Cuverville-en-Caux in *la Porte étroite*), and last of all the Swiss Jura: it is at La Brévine that the action of *la Symphonie pastorale* is situated; *Paludes* had been written there, and Gide retained an unpleasant memory of a hostile population. When the social milieu is significant, Gide paints it with the same concern for likeness as his heroes, the same sobriety of means, the same power of hidden suggestion. Landscapes or interiors are inseparable from the beings who inhabit them. We can no longer think of Jérôme and Alissa without seeing the garden of their childhood and the little kitchen-garden gate; of Michel without imagining the apartment surrounded by terraces in the Biskra hotel.

In *Isabelle* the atmosphere plays the leading role. It is created not only by the old estate, its huge grounds, its old house and the summer-house where Gérard finds the telltale letter, but just as much by the faded *bizarrerie* of the beings who inhabit La Quartfourche. Here the characters create the décor, so strange do they seem. Recall the Floche household, and above all the Saint-Auréol couple, who in a museum "would immediately be classified among the extinct species," and whom Gide has described with a brief and picturesque humor that recalls the Chateaubriand of the *Mémoires d'Outretombe*. *Isabelle* is distinguished by this *sotie* aspect.

Emotion in it is less serious than in the other *récits*, because the supposed narrator is not deeply committed. *The Pathetic Illusion* (this was Gide's first title) is not deadly, like Alissa's utterly futile heroism; the dissolution of the *romanesque* is endurable and could not lead to suicide, like the despair of the blind girl who recovers her sight in *la Symphonie pastorale*. It is an ambiguous charm that imbues this "half-playful interlude between two over-serious works." The erotic reverie which nourishes the *romanesque* interest and the narrator's passionate curiosity is plunged into a milieu of a burlesque unreality where everything seems to grimace.

Isabelle has come by night, in secret, as is her custom, to seek help from her aunt:

Madame Floche, poor old thing, was still holding her bunch of keys in one hand and in the other the meagre little bundle of notes she had taken out of the drawer; she was just going to seat herself again in her arm-chair, when the door opposite that at which I was posted was suddenly flung open—and I could hardly restrain a cry of stupefaction. The Baronne was standing stiffly in the doorway, décolleté, rouged, in full ceremonial attire and her head surmounted by what looked like a gigantic feather brush of marabout. She was staggering under the weight of a great six-branched candelabra in which all the candles were burning, flooding her with their flickering light and shedding tears of wax all over the floor. She had come, no doubt, to the end of her strength, for she began by hastily making for the table and setting down the candelabra in front of the looking-glass; then, taking four skips back to her position in the doorway, she once more advanced, solemnly and with measured steps, stretching out at full length in front of her a hand loaded with enormous rings. In the middle of the room, she stood still, turned stiffly towards her daughter and, with hand still outstretched, shrieked in ear-splitting accents:

"Get thee behind me, ungrateful daughter! Your tears can no longer move me and your protestations have for ever lost the way to my heart."

The whole speech was delivered with no variation of tone at the topmost pitch of her voice. In the mean time, Isabelle had thrown herself at her mother's feet and taken hold of her dress; as she pulled it to one side, revealing two absurd little white satin slippers, she herself continued to strike her forehead on the floor, where a rug was spread over the boards. Madame de Saint-Auréol did not lower her eyes for an instant; still looking straight before her, with glances as piercing and icy as her voice, she continued:

"Is it not enough for you to have brought poverty into the dwelling of your parents? Are you contemplating a further . . ."

Here her voice suddenly failed her and she turned towards Madame Floche who, making herself as small as she could, sat trembling in her arm-chair:

"And as for you, Sister, if you are still so weak . . ." (she took herself up) "if you are still so unpardonably weak as to yield to her entreaties, even for one kiss—even for one groat—so true as I am your elder sister, I leave you—I recommend my household gods to Heaven, and I leave you, never to set eyes on you again."

I seemed to be looking on at a play. But since they were unconscious of being watched, for whose benefit was it these two marionettes were acting this tragedy? The attitudes and gestures of the daughter seemed to me as exaggerated and as artificial as those of the mother. . . . The latter was facing me, so that I saw Isabelle from behind, still prostrate in the posture of a suppliant Esther; all at once I caught sight of her feet; the boots she wore, as far as I could see through the coating of mud that covered them, seemed to have tops of puce coloured poult-de-soie; above them showed her white stockings, across which the dripping, muddy flounce of her lifted skirt had left a smear of dirt. . . . And instantly the long story of adventure and wretchedness told by these poor witnesses spoke more loudly to my heart than all the old woman's declamatory tirades. A sob rose in my throat; I made up my mind to follow Isa through the garden when she left the house.

In the mean time Madame de Saint-Auréol had taken three steps towards Madame Floche's chair:

"Come, give me up those notes. Do you imagine I do not see the paper you are crumpling in your hand? Do you think me blind or mad? Give me the money, I tell you!" And seizing the notes, she held them melodramatically to the flame of one of the candles in the candelabra: "I would rather burn them all" (needless to say, she did nothing of the sort) "than let her have a groat."

She slipped the notes into her pocket and resumed her theatrical attitude:

"Ungrateful daughter! Un-natural daughter! My bracelets and my necklaces, you know what road they took! Let my rings go the same way!"

So saying, with a dexterous movement of her outstretched hand, she let two or three drop on to the floor. Like a famished dog after a bone, Isabelle flung herself upon them.

"Now go! We have nothing more to say to each other; I no longer acknowledge you."

Then, having fetched an extinguisher from the bed-table, she extinguished one after the other all the candles in the candelabra and departed.*

* "Isabelle" from *Two Symphonies*. Copyright 1931 by Alfred A. Knopf, Inc. Translated by Dorothy Bussy. Reprinted by permission.

The composition of these *récits* shows great narrative mastery in the chronological organization of events, in the rhythm of the scenes, in the progression of effects. In *l'Immoraliste*, Michel's cure is a wild *allegro* balanced by Marceline's death march, her persistent agony; between these two sections, rising and falling, occurs something of a plateau, formed by Michel's experiments in normal life; but this central portion is itself composed like the whole; Michel's attempts at being a landowner and his dawning disgust with the property frame the exalting conversations with Ménalque which determine the hero's orientation. In *la Porte étroite* it is enough to mention in passing the double illumination of facts by Jérôme's narrative and by Alissa's journal or her letters, with the deepening the latter produce in the former's pathos. Jérôme's narrative of the ruined walk is followed by the letter from Alissa it inspired. Similarly Jérôme's unhoped-for return during the night is presented from two complementary perspectives. And the asceticism by whose light Alissa believes she must send Jérôme away can be understood entirely only if we compare it with the young man's terror at the heroic dissimulation confessed in the young mystic's journal. Neither of the two knows everything about the other; it is only at the book's end that Jérôme will have, too late, a complete comprehension of a situation whose interest Gide has doubled by giving us Alissa's heart-rending journal.

The organization of *Isabelle* is even more skillful; it presents the facts not according to their genesis, but according to the order of their discovery, and this permits the narrator to maintain his illusions while disturbing him by unexplained details, and finally deflates them by the revelation of the banal reality. The composition of *la Symphonie pastorale* is more on one level, advancing steadily, although we can observe a series of parallels between events and their moral effects in Gertrude's transition from blindness to sight at the same time as from happiness to despair, and in the pastor, from blind exaltation to the bitter consciousness whose expression gives a contrasting tone to his two notebooks. —Notebooks kept by the pastor during the wintertime and spring in La Brévine; —Gérard's tale told to his friends Jammes and Gide after their conversation and visit to La Quartfourche; —recollections written by Jérôme, frequently alternating with fragments of Alissa's letters and, before the appendix of the journey to Nîmes, concluded by the pages of Alissa's journal; —Michel's narrative to his friends at night on the terrace of his house at Sidi B. M.—these are the means of presentation Gide uses with an equal ease. Despite the ingenuity of the breaks, the interruptions that he contrives in the notebooks and diaries to indicate a sudden change, a development, or the effect of time on the feelings, some readers may prefer to this mosaic the continuity of an ampler narrative. Nothing equals the splendid drive of *l'Immoraliste*. If the subtlety is greater in *la Porte étroite*, Gide himself, who was unable to return to it "without an unspeakable emotion," complains, with splendid frankness, that "the transitions" are not "exempt from preciosity." To make us discern the pastor's pious comedy on himself by giving us only his journal is a virtuoso performance; we may prefer that the progressive disclosure of the truth be effected with less cleverness, by the very progress of the narrative, as in *Isabelle*. Gide's art is eminently concerted, and it is of course when this organization is invisible that it functions most effectively.

Economy of means is another quality of this art of the *récit*. In Gide, every line counts. None is without its edge. From this point of view, *l'Immoraliste* is of a magnificent hardness and speed, whereas in *la Porte étroite* there are certain rare places that seem somewhat overworked, a little too satisfied with their own effects.

But where Gide excels is in the reverberation, the *reprise* of a detail; the reader will recall the scissors stolen by Moktir which are later found and returned to Michel by Ménalque. How one and the same sentence can affect the development of a soul according to the different values attributed to its meaning is shown in *l'Immoraliste* by a remark made by Marceline to Michel, and which he later addresses to Ménalque. The art of preparations, whose power is particularly prized in the theater, is no less necessary to the novel, but gains in discretion without losing any of its suggestiveness. Consider, for instance, how the second of these two passages is cruelly sensitized by the recollection of the first:

Antoine, Etienne and Godefroi were discussing the last vote in the Chamber, as they lolled on my wife's elegant armchairs. Hubert and Louis were carelessly turning over some fine etchings from my father's collection, entirely regardless of how they were creasing them. In the smoking-room, Mathias, the better to listen to Leonard, had put his red-hot cigar down on a rosewood table. A glass of curaçoa had been spilt on the carpet. Albert was sprawling impudently on a sofa, with his muddy boots dirtying the cover. And the very dust of the air one breathed came from the horrible wear and tear of material objects. . . . A frantic desire seized me to send all my guests packing. Furniture, stuffs, prints, lost all their value for me at the first stain; things stained were things touched by disease, with the mark of death on them.*

Here is the second passage:

Meanwhile the horrible clot had brought on serious trouble; after her heart had escaped, it attacked her

---

* *The Immoralist.* Copyright 1930 by Alfred A. Knopf, Inc. Translated by Dorothy Bussy. Reprinted by permission.

lungs, brought on congestion, impeded her breathing, made it short and laborious. I thought she would never get well. Disease had taken hold of Marceline, never again to leave her; it had marked her, stained her. Henceforth she was a thing that had been spoiled.*

By making his main characters speak or write, Gide has obliged them to paint their own portraits. A method which admirably suits the tale and perfectly justifies (etymologically) the title *récit* that Gide affects. It was essential to lend each of these narrators a tone of his own. Here Gide's sympathy has served him further. His method seems indeed to have consisted of *listening* in himself to the voice of his characters. Hence that timbre, those particular inflections which make us recognize them so certainly, without Gide's having to bother with all those clumsy "he saids" which encumber the prose of novelists incapable of giving their protagonists a characteristic tone. Michel's harsh, unconceding tone, Gérard's *interested* tone, Jérôme's fervent and rather suave tone, Alissa's ardent, secret, strained and yet bare tone, the pastor's pious and somehow complacent tone—all are of an admirable rightness we must particularly admire in the nuances and tacks of emotion.

The characters described by the narrators also have their own tone, dissonances that are to be integrated into the basic tone. They make it more apparent, as Abel's expansiveness contrasts with Jérôme's reserve; or they complement it, as the characters' outbursts in *Isabelle* set off Gérard's polished and amused moderation. Consider if, in Michel's tone, we succeed better than the man who tells his story in distinguishing "pride's share from that of strength, of coldness, or of modesty?":

* *The Immoralist.* Copyright 1930 by Alfred A. Knopf, Inc. Translated by Dorothy Bussy. Reprinted by permission.

It had been very cold that morning. Toward evening a burning simoon sprang up. Marceline, exhausted by the journey, went to bed as soon as we arrived. I had hoped to find a rather more comfortable hotel, but our room is hideous; the sand, the sun, the flies have tarnished, dirtied, discolored everything. As we have eaten scarcely anything since daybreak, I order a meal to be served at once; but Marceline finds everything uneatable and I cannot persuade her to touch a morsel. We have with us paraphernalia for making our own tea. I attend to this trifling business, and for dinner we content ourselves with a few biscuits and the tea, made with the brackish water of the country and tasting horrible in consequence.

By a last semblance of virtue, I stay with her till evening. And all of a sudden I feel that I myself have come to the end of my strength. O taste of ashes! O deadly lassitude! O the sadness of superhuman effort! I hardly dare look at her; I am too certain that my eyes, instead of seeking hers, will fasten horribly on the black holes of her nostrils; the suffering expression of her face is agonizing. Nor does she look at me either. I feel her anguish as if I could touch it. She coughs a great deal and then falls asleep. From time to time, she is shaken by a sudden shudder.

Perhaps the night will be bad, and before it is too late I must find out where I can get help. I go out.

Outside the hotel, the Touggourt square, the streets, the very atmosphere, are so strange that I can hardly believe it is I who see them. After a little I go in again. Marceline is sleeping quietly. I need not have been so frightened; in this peculiar country, one suspects peril everywhere. Absurd! And more or less reassured, I again go out.

There is a strange nocturnal animation in the square—a silent flitting to and fro—a stealthy gliding of white burnouses. The wind at times tears off a shred of strange music and brings it from I know not

where. Someone comes up to me. . . . Moktir! He
was waiting for me, he says—expected me to come
out again. He laughs. He knows Touggourt, comes
here often, knows where to take me. I let myself be
guided by him.

We walk along in the dark and go into a Moorish
café; this is where the music came from. Some Arab
women are dancing—if such a monotonous glide can
be called dancing. One of them takes me by the
hand; I follow her; she is Moktir's mistress; he comes
too. . . . We all three go into the deep, narrow room
where the only piece of furniture is a bed. . . . A
very low bed on which we sit down. A white rabbit
which has been shut up in the room is scared at first
but afterwards grows tamer and comes to feed out of
Moktir's hand. Coffee is brought. Then, while Moktir
is playing with the rabbit, the woman draws me toward her, and I let myself go to her as one lets oneself sink into sleep. . . .

Oh, here I might deceive you or be silent—but
what use can this story be to me, if it ceases to be
truthful?

I go back alone to the hotel, for Moktir remains
behind in the café. It is late. A parching sirocco is
blowing; the wind is laden with sand, and, in spite
of the night, torrid. After three or four steps, I am
bathed in sweat; but I suddenly feel I must hurry
and I reach the hotel almost at a run. She is awake
perhaps. . . . Perhaps she wants me? . . . No; the
window of her room is dark. I wait for a short lull in
the wind before opening the door; I go into the room
very softly in the dark. What is that noise? . . . I do
not recognize her cough. . . . Is it really Marceline?
. . . I light the light.

She is half sitting on the bed, one of her thin arms
clutching the bars and supporting her in an upright
position; her sheets, her hands, her nightdress are
flooded with a stream of blood; her face is soiled

with it; her eyes have grown hideously big; and no cry of agony could be more appalling than her silence.*

In *la Symphonie pastorale* we can admire how the pastor's tone, when he admonishes his elder son, can dissimulate his unconscious jealousy under the virtuous indignation he believes he is suffering. Finally I would point out as especially interesting the effects of tone *against* tone. The sublime fervor of Alissa surpasses, but often accompanies, Jérôme's more tepid but nonetheless sincere fervor. Ménalque's conversation with Michel marks, in the two characters, two degrees of a related but still unequal tension.

We need not insist on the point. Gide's style here retains all the qualities we have discerned in his poetic prose. But since it is the expression of characters who say "I" but are not Gide, the language is barer, soberer, more direct, and carefully avoids those *recherché* turns of speech and those violations of syntax by which Gide inflects his own sentences. These are not artists talking; these are human beings. But here too Gide never forgets that art is transposition; and the perfect stylization of his characters' dialogue shows that while respecting the particularity of their personal idiom, the author purifies it in order to render it still more faithful to his meaning, and raises it, by the finish he imparts to it, to the level of art, whose truth is less that of reproduction than that of representation.

Passionate yet measured; their composition so clear and sober, their passion so contained, their *attention* so loving, their diligence so skillful; stripped of all superfluity (one only appreciates to what degree Gide's tales are without digression when one reads other storytellers), these *récits* irresistibly remind us of the great portrait painters of the French school, especially, perhaps, in their exclusion of pomp and prettiness and sentimentality, of the perfect honesty of a Clouet.

If the little series comprising *l'École des Femmes,* *Robert,* and *Geneviève* does not keep to this level, it is because Gide has taught us to be demanding; it would make the reputation of anyone else. But if the old ease of his manner is still here, the originality is less urgent, the *romanesque* is increasingly sacrificed to the desire to *convince.* Under skillfully concealed pretexts we arrive at theses which Gide would once have been careful not to formulate, for art has nothing to do with proving. We may still admire, in *l'École des Femmes,* the delicate painting of the "decrystallization" of the love of a generous woman unhappily married to a virtuous braggart; or in *Robert,* its skillful counterpart, an indirect satire on the sincerely deceptive justification, which recalls the subtlety of *la Symphonie pastorale.* But the satire on conformism, so suggestive in *Paludes,* so funny in *les Caves,* yields to direct exposure and to polemics, to out-and-out discussion. In *Geneviève,* a series of amusing dialogues between young girls, the *thesis* assumes an increasingly large place. It is no longer a satire on marriage which we can disengage from the *récit;* it is a declaration of the *jeune fille's* rights to maternity. One does not question the audacity of the thought. But Gide seems to have abandoned all his art, and the lack of taste for literature which he attributes to Geneviève is only a pretext authorizing him to express his ideas, scarcely transposed into another key. There remains only the patina of his talent as a storyteller. The irony is dead, and the poet no longer supports and sustains the moralist.

Gide has gradually, imperceptibly shifted from indirect satire to precise demands, from criticism to polemic, from irony to apology. Without breaking a single string, he has untuned an instrument whose perfect pitch once won all our admiration.

6. Plays

The plays of André Gide occupy a place apart in his work. They might be removed without seriously disfiguring it, for he has expressed elsewhere most of the ideas that animate these dramas; yet who would consent to lose three plays as representative of their author as *Saül, le Roi Candaule,* and *Oedipe?* All three have been performed, without gaining the success they deserve; *Saül,* in fact, had to wait twenty-five years for a public, the same public, in fact, that after World War I belatedly perceived Gide's importance in contemporary literature. As for *le Roi Candaule,* it failed in the heyday of Edmond Rostand's triumphs. *Oedipe,* a late work, is distinguished from the others in that it was apparently not intended for the stage; it emphasizes the ideological character and the schematic viewpoint toward which this attempted purification of the theater had already tended.

It is regrettable that his efforts were not better rewarded, for Gide evidently had the makings of a dramatist if not powerful, at least original and ingenious. His entire work bears witness to his sense of pathos and his sure hand in writing dialogue. *Le Retour de l'enfant prodigue* was found to be stageworthy. Gide has often been tempted by the dramatic form (we have remarked elsewhere that he cast his *Philoctète* and his *Bethsabé* as plays), but without submitting it to stage requirements. He drafted a kind of mythological opera, *Proserpine* (which he later made into the dramatic symphony *Perséphone* for Ida Rubinstein), where we hear the echo of the spring songs used too in the *Nouvelles Nourritures*. He had abandoned an *Ajax*, unable to resolve its contradiction. His *Journal* contains plans for plays which we can only regret were not executed, for the subjects seem most suitably Gidean. "Strange how much Humanity's stock has risen since the Greeks, or even since Shakespeare. Nothing does more harm to the drama than this excessive valuation." We have already encountered an analogous notion apropos of the *Prométhée mal enchaîné*. Gide wanted to make it the subject of a drama to be called *Sylla*. On another occasion he planned to write a play with the title *l'Échanson* (The Cupbearer). "I don't know why procurers have always been made into monsters and vile creatures. I have been thinking of an admirable drama about Joseph; and in particular the prison scene: Joseph between the steward and the cupbearer." Compare this note with a passage from Gide's Weimar lecture *"On the Importance of the Public,"* where he divides writers into true and false providers (citing the authors of thesis plays as an example of the latter), illuminating his distinction by an interpretation of the character of the cupbearer, who slakes men's thirst (Ganymede, for instance), and the steward, who stays men's hunger (Prometheus, for instance). Gide makes the curious observation that only the true providers deserve the hatred of men and gods alike; they must know how to do without the public, or at least how to wait for it. As for the rest: "O false providers of today, you may rest easy! If no one thinks of hanging you, it is because you bring nothing to eat. But you do not make us drunk either, and that is why you are detestable!" It is doubtless a drama of complex interest we have lost here. Gide also gave thought to the character of the illegitimate son; some of his reflections doubtless turn up in the role of *Oedipe;* and the reader will recall that this is Lafcadio's condition. Gide also wanted to write a comedy, and the domestic scenes of *Saül* and *le Roi Candaule,* the irony of the dialogue in *Oedipe,* and all we know of his satirical gifts in other works make us regret the abandonment of this intention. The playlet entitled *le Treizième Arbre* (written in 1935, first staged in 1939), which Gide modestly baptized "a joke in one act," is little more than a lively sketch; with a deliberately conventional setting and *dramatis personae* (a château with its countess, its vicomte, its curé, its old gardener, and stereotyped guests), Gide has amused himself by cunningly weaving around a scabrous incident (an obscene figure has been drawn on the bark of a tree) the threads of his diverse antipathies to conformism, the clergy, and psychoanalysis; the witty misunderstandings brought to light by the curé's disgraceful police interrogation of the two men of learning, a philologist and a doctor, to which the countess lends a complacent ear, are enough if not to animate, at least to color his puppets with an irony that occasionally reminds us of *les Caves du Vatican;* without turning to caricature, Gide's playful realism, which suggests a social register Henri Monnier, insinuates into the mechanical action of a proverb a kind of discreet horseplay which analysis would soon show to be far from anodyne. One wonders if Gide would today be as hard on Jules Renard's acid little masterpiece *la Bigote,* which in 1909 made him want to throw himself into holy water. Let us mention, for the record, that a play based on *les Caves* was performed at their annual festival by the Belletriens de Lausanne, that Gide's later version was performed at the Comédie Française, and that he kept among his papers the scenario for *le Curieux mal avisé*, referred to in the *Journal des Faux Monnayeurs*, and published, in *Littérature Engagée*, *Robert ou l'Intérêt général*, a work concerning which Gide regretted "an effort to return to realism."

It will be noticed that among these subjects, many are inspired by mythology or history, with a predilection for Greek and biblical antiquity. This is entirely the perspective of classical tragedy. And indeed *Saül, le Roi Candaule,* and *Oedipe* are tragic subjects which have inspired many authors of the past. One finds them treated, even in our day, in diligent Alexandrines by one or another of the countless neo-classic or pseudo-classic imitators which the posterity of Corneille and Racine, and of Voltaire too, nourished quite lately, though meagerly. The remarkable thing about Gide's tragedies is that they are treated in a modern spirit. Nothing betrays the pastiche. Indeed public taste would have to have been long and diabolically perverted by pre-World War I theater, whose collapse is almost complete today, to overlook how contemporary Gide's plays are, in the best sense of that word. In recent years we have seen a superb revival of the great subjects of the classic theater. It is only fair, in hailing the miracle wrought by Giraudoux, and not forgetting the less pure, but still provocative magic of Jean Cocteau in *la Machine infernale*, to recall that Gide, whose entire *oeuvre* is imbued with Greco-Latin mythology and biblical subjects, was the first to revive them on our stage in a spirit of youth.

We also find in these three plays certain Gidean preoccupations quite alien from those that might have concerned the heroes he borrowed from the Bible, from Herodotus, and from Sophocles. It would therefore be pointless to study the discrepancies these plays afford when compared with the texts they have taken for their points of departure. These fine subjects cannot be improved; they can only be enriched. They are like those poetic images whose symbolic value can constantly change and always reflect new preoccupations. Implicitly Gide's tragedies, which were already the condemnation of a literature of pastiche, are also a condemnation of the historical theater, whose attempts to reconstruct (we shall not say resurrect) the past are doomed to failure. This is because historical drama is still a form of realism; it is a realism of the past. And Gide has perfectly understood realism's error. "Dramatic art" he says in his *Journal*, "must no more attempt to give the illusion of reality than painting; it must make something out of its particular means and seek effects which derive only from itself."

This is because there is a specific aesthetic of the drama. Gide has given us his conception of this aesthetic in his lecture *"On the Evolution of the Theater,"* in which he contended with not only the realist tendency, but also what he called "episodism" (whose chief representative was Rostand). He aligns himself with the classic authors in their attempt to make the dramatic work "a work deliberately and manifestly artistic" instead of "pursuing an illusion of reality, which even when realized would serve only to produce a pleonasm with reality itself." This is why he praises the classic drama's alienation from familiarity and its respect for the unities, and considers the advice to return to nature a misunderstanding. In his *Journal*, he declares that "insubordination to the rules results from an unintelligent subordination to realism."

The unities are basically of little importance to Gide. With the exception of unity of action, by which he abides almost to excess, as in his *récits*, he does not observe them. In *Saül* there are eleven changes of scene; in *Candaule*, three; the duration of *Saül* is of a Shakespearian indeterminacy; *Candaule* takes place in three days, or rather in three nights. What counts for Gide, and not only in the art of the theater, are the salutary constraints, the rules; and here this admirer of the strict form of the sonnet, which, by the way, he has never employed, approaches Valéry. He prizes the obstacle, which "serves as a springboard" to the great artist. Gide has even invented a new dramatic unity which he calls "the unity of the spectator"; he wants the "poetic re-creation to be addressed, for its entire duration, to the same reader or auditor"; yet is this not the kind of dramatic requirement a novelist would conceive?

On the other hand Gide saw clearly that our tragedy was dying "of a dearth of characters." The theater, he explains, has moved closer to life; hypocrisy and coercion, the effects of social and Christian morality, by "imposing a common ideal on each man" have etiolated individuality. The tragic conception of *characters* has been replaced by that of *situations*. The theater must turn away from life and propose to humanity "new forms of heroism, new figures of heroes." Gide was no doubt thinking of his Candaule at the time, for the character of Saül can scarcely be proposed as exemplary. But later on, the virile Oedipe will indeed fall into this category. Moreover Gide has a peculiar manner of considering his heroes. Recalling Racine's remark that "our respect for heroes increases the farther from us they are," Gide adds: "this respect for the characters put on the stage is perhaps not indispensable." Here Gide reveals one of his ulterior motives. Indeed, he will treat neither Saül nor Candaule nor Oedipe "respectfully." In a sense his dramas are still *soties*, works of criticism. Intelligence always keeps watch on the roof-tree of his creations.

Aside from this spirit of investigation that so curiously illuminates Gide's theater, intelligence plays a more fundamental role: it is at the very origin of his plays. *Saül* results from a need to counterbalance the *Nourritures terrestres*. It constitutes its antidote, opposing the eulogy of perpetual escape, the acceptance of all desires and the rejection of choice, by the tragedy of a man enslaved by his temptations, annihilated by his surrender to all that seduces him, and whose will has entirely dissolved in the rejection of action. In the preface to *le Roi Candaule*, Gide insists on "putting in the foreground the intellectual structure" which formed "the skeleton of his drama." It derives both from his reading of Herodotus and "in part from an article where an author of talent, 'pleading for moral freedom' proceeded to reproach the possessors of art, of beauty, of wealth, in short the 'ruling classes,' for not attempting to educate the people by instituting exhibitions in their behalf. The author did not say—was careful not to say—whether the people would be allowed to touch. I suspect that, being too intelligent to be unaware that the question's interest began only at this point, he preferred to evade it, regarding the consequences as too serious and fearing his incapacity to describe them." As for *Oedipe*, it is obviously intended to promote a certain conception of man. If Gide's theater is careful not to fall into the trap of the thesis play, it is nonetheless secretly fed by a certain ideology.

This is probably the only point, though it is a crucial one, where one might attack Gide's theater. Elsewhere, it seems to me, none of the qualities necessary to the dramatist are deficient in André Gide: elegance of architecture, sacrifice of the superfluous or the secondary, individuality of character, sureness of the dialogue (and monologue), appropriateness of tone, clarity of style, continuous, if subdued, poetry (with the exception of *Oedipe*, which represents Gide's last, driest manner). These dramas lack neither action nor movement: their development is perfectly controlled; they fail in not being raised to a higher degree of energy. It could not be otherwise with so conscious, so intellectual a point of departure. True drama is not content with representing an action; it is itself an action. It is not, like the novel, the product of intelligence, or like poetry, the fruit of sensibility; it is a gesture of the will. What constitutes the dramatic work is an energy affirmed by the invention of a universe peopled with beings who are not, like those of the novelist, opinions of their observer, but creatures of a power that engenders them. The drama is a metaphysic of the will. It is the diversification of this energy, the detail of its employment, its distribution, that one must constantly encounter in the analysis of a truly dramatic work, even when it presents us with the will's failures, whether a consequence of fate, in tragedy, or of human weakness, in comedy. For the dramatist's creative energy dispenses his gifts unequally to his children.

Intelligence, moreover, is as necessary to the dramatist as sensibility, but it cannot by itself furnish him with those germinative cells from which the whole drama takes its source. Where the intelligence assumes its function is in the disposition of the action, in the elimination of parasitical inventions, in the modifications of detail. Intelligence distributes and purifies; it does not create.

Gide has perfectly understood the importance of technique in the theater, and he has wrought his own to a high degree of ease and purity. He is particularly aware of the framework in which the drama functions: "As a painting is a space to be actuated, a play is a duration to be animated."

If Gide's dramas result from intellectual preoccupations rather than from an irresistible impulse to create complexes of characters and events, it would nonetheless be unfair to argue that he failed to see the necessity of strongly animating the drama. The remark just quoted proves this, as well as the importance which we find him according to characters. If he has not the dramatist's will, he has at least the intelligence of that will;

he has it to the point of being able to simulate it out of sympathy, and this is what gives his plays a certain life; they are flooded with light, if they are a little lacking in warmth. Precisely the opposite is true of Claudel's dramaturgy, where sheer vitality dispenses with the refinements of the critical spirit.

Actually Gide attempted to make himself into a playwright combining moralist with aesthetician, both excellent, who might furnish each other a maximum of co-operation. This is suggested in the comparison of two notes from his *Journal*. Here, first, is the remark of the moralist: "It is worth considering that of the two most solemn dramas antiquity has bequeathed us, *Oedipus* and *Prometheus*, one discusses the notion of good and evil, or better, of permitted and forbidden, in its most arbitrary aspect, the other the notion of punishment, etc." And here is the aesthetician's doctrine: "It is not only a question of inventing the event most likely to reveal character; it is character itself that must necessitate the event. (See *Coriolanus, Hamlet*.) The series of events is the development of character (Macbeth—who cannot escape his own fulfillment). Or else, quite the contrary, let the revealing event come first (Sophocles, Ibsen) and the drama be its gradual enlightenment; the typical example of this: Oedipus, who passes from happiness in ignorance to knowledge in misery." Saül, precisely, is a character "who cannot escape his own fulfillment", with this refinement, that fulfillment, for him, is defeat or destruction.

Saül's subject is the dissolution of an individual who surrenders to all his desires. The play's movement consists in the slow disaggregation of a soul, but King Saül has no conflict with external characters, at least evades any such conflict that might engage him; he must struggle only against himself, against his disposition to indulge. He is a man in isolation, who avoids or abandons the responsibilities of power and obeys only his impulses. He is therefore a character whose dramatic aspect is entirely interior, and who might have constituted the hero of a *récit* parallel to *l'Immoraliste*. He is an excellent subject for interior monologue, and Saül's monologues and his asides, put end to end, would sum up the entire play superbly. To adjust it to the stage, Gide has had the ingenious idea of doubling his character by exteriorizing Saül's temptations in the form of demons. These demons, to whom the play's exposition is entrusted, will subsequently intervene in it every time Saül is alone, and will ultimately not leave him alone even in the presence of other characters. It must be admitted that Gide has successfully resolved all the problems of credibility which the stage raises in Saül's relations with his symbolized desires. Without turning them into allegories, he has wisely preserved their metaphysical status which, while still necessitating their picturesque presence, makes them less a reality than a projection into the concrete world. Their degree of existence is about that of the devil. Do we believe in the devil?

The other characters, though incisively drawn, are only silhouettes. They gravitate around Saül without managing to influence his destiny. It is the development of Saül's character that leads him by degrees to the complete dissolution of his being, of which madness will be only the sign, and death the final seal. He *passes through* events, and the other characters are only the pretexts of the tragic fatality he bears within himself.

Not that this play lacks a sufficiently complex action, one freely drawn from the Book of Samuel; however discreetly he has treated it, this action gives Gide's play a heightened vitality. But by nature, Saül fluctuates in this frame. His will, before dissolving completely, intervenes only in spasmodic and unsuitable actions, fits of madness which make him the victim of a God who has withdrawn from him. It is Saül's disorientation

157

which makes him both a pathetic and a ridiculous figure. Out of this profoundly isolated character, whose
impulses continually yield to temptations until he foun-
ders in a kind of madness conscious of its own impotence, out of this character by nature suited to the
récit or to the confessional tone of the intimate journal,
Gide has nonetheless extracted the maximum of dramatic potential.

In the first act the demons invade the king's palace
at dawn and humorously assign each other their roles.
A monologue reveals Saül's uncertainties. Since God no
longer answers him, he has interrogated the stars and
discovered that his son Jonathan will not succeed him
on the throne. In order to keep this secret from being
learned, and to be alone in knowing the future and hoping thereby to be able to change it, Saül orders all the
wizards and astrologers of Israel to be killed. Conversations among the servants, and between the high priest
and the queen, reveal that for the last month Saül has
escaped the influence of these last two characters. Saki,
the king's cupbearer, is too young, too naïve, and too
loyal to help them spy on Saül. They hope, with the
help of the royal barber, whom the king often heeds,
to place a new spy at his side; but Saül, his suspicions
aroused, refuses the harpist David who is offered to
him. Meanwhile he has killed the messengers who have
come to announce the death of the wizards. But young
David, introduced into the palace, asks the queen for
authorization to combat the giant Goliath, who has
hurled a challenge to the bravest soldiers of Saül's army.
The Philistines are in fact encamped about the city (all
this information is given by rapid allusions, with a remarkable lightness of touch). The queen is won over
by David's beauty, youth, and courage; she presents him
to her son Jonathan, a weakling who is attracted to his
new comrade at first sight; and David, having refused
the king's helmet and armor, prepares himself for battle.

In the second act we learn from the crowd's excited comments about David that Samuel has anointed this young shepherd, as once he had anointed Saül, the chosen of God. A few words from Jonathan tell us that David has conquered Goliath. Upon Saül's entrance, the stage empties: "Solitude is mine—but it is because they flee from me." Infuriated by David's popularity and jealous of the boy, he calls him in and is immediately seduced by his youth, his beauty, and his devotion to the throne (his loyalty, one might say, which is the leading feature of this character). He attaches David to himself as harpist, even when he learns that he is the very person the queen had intended for the office. The queen attempts to induce David to become a useful spy who will report Saül's words to her, and against his respectful resistance uses every means within her power; enchanted moreover by his person, she attempts to seduce him . . . But Saül, who has been watching, kills the queen with his javelin, and we realize that he is far more jealous of David than of the queen. —Saül, who believes himself alone in his room, meditates on his situation, but the demons are there and increasingly intervene in the development of his thoughts. "They would know my secret, but do I know it myself? I have many secrets." The queen's murder inspires no remorse: "I understand now why I loved the queen so little. In my youth I practiced chastity too easily. I have practiced many virtues . . ."; he decides to rid himself of the high priest as well. Then he becomes familiar with the demons, whom he gradually perceives around him; he drinks with them, they press close to him, and their insinuating temptations reveal that Saül is obsessed by the image of David. The end of this act, in an atmosphere of externalized nightmare, possesses an incomparable demoniac poetry.

The queen's murder has terrorized the palace. In Act Three everyone flees upon Saül's approach, as he stalks through the halls, spies on the court, hides behind curtains, attempts to surprise conspiracies. With insinuating proposals the barber offers David his faction against the exhausted Saül and the weakling Jonathan; David, devoted to God, to the king, and to his son, rejects him. Then Saül re-enacts with David and Jonathan the scene which had led to the queen's murder; after having dressed Jonathan in the royal robes to rouse him to an awareness of his powers, he leaves him alone with David, but hides behind a drapery; Jonathan, exhausted by the weight of the crown and of the purple, strips them off and puts them on David, who wears them without difficulty; the scene's dialogue is more amorous than amical, and gradually excites Saül's jealousy. He intervenes; David flees, though without haste, casting off the robes; Jonathan faints, to Saül's disgust. The king has an interview with the terrified and obedient high priest, who is stupefied with fear and whose stumbling replies provoke Saül's impatience and his boredom when the priest recites the list of God's commandments. —An interview between the king and the barber shows how alien affairs of state have become to Saül: "There are affairs more important than those of the realm—and they concern myself alone." He scarcely realizes that the Philistines are returning and thinks only of David, whom he cannot bring himself to detest, and yet he is anxious: "I would give much to know," he tells himself, "that it is not David I must fear." To please the youth, he has his own beard cut off. "It hid me." (We recognize this symbolic motif of shaving the beard, which we meet again in *l'Immoraliste* and in Gide's own biography.) The barber suggests to the king a means of protecting himself against his obvious fears: he must consult a witch who has escaped his ban, the witch of Endor, whom Saül knows, for when he was a young shepherd she had predicted his kingship to him. Saül tries in vain to pray, and exits.

The central scene of the play occurs here. Gide has succeeded in creating a witch quite different from those ordinarily met with in the theater. He has made her affecting, pathetic. Near death, she recognizes Saül (who is annoyed by this) and conjures up the shade of Samuel, who reveals Saül's nature and destiny to him in striking phrases:

> Saül! Saül! There are other enemies than the Philistines to conquer; but the one who oppresses you is one you have welcomed unto yourself . . .
>
> Think you that God, in punishing you, has not already known, and long since, the latest waverings of your soul?—He has set the enemy before your door; your chastisement is in their hands. Behind your door that is even yet ajar, they are waiting; but they have long since been met. You, too, feel in your heart the impatience of this waiting: what you call fear, you know that it is desire.

Saül faints and fails to hear Samuel's last prophecies; coming to his senses, he cruelly tries to tear them from the witch, who takes pity on him, and whom he kills. In her agony, she gives him her last advice: "O King deplorably ready for surrender—close your door . . . close your eyes! Cover your ears—and may the perfume of love . . . no longer find access to your heart.—All that delights you is your enemy . . . Free yourself! Saül . . . Saül! . . ." Saül realizes that henceforth he will "struggle alone in the darkness."

Saül has not understood, as Gide has said elsewhere, that it is "by climbing up that one must follow one's inclination." The virtue of effort is indissolubly linked to the search for originality; otherwise, there is only cowardice and dissolution, anarchy of being.

The futility of this tragic lesson is immediately shown in the following scene, at the same time as the old king's incurable frivolity. David attempts to awaken Saül's courage by martial songs; he succeeds only in making him yawn: "Don't you know something more entertaining?" During their conversation, Saül's futile, furious, and bitter coquetry conflicts with David's dignity; Saül's agitation turns to senile madness; tempted by all that is contrary to him, he even invites David to unite with him against God and offers him the crown; he loses control of himself, and even as he struggles to keep his lips from releasing his secret, he indirectly avows his passion to David. The latter flings away his harp, which breaks, and leaves, crying to an awakened Saül: "Henceforth your secret is no longer intolerable to you alone." Old Saül's madness deserves more space than I can allow, for in it Gide has expressed, with consummate control of the motifs which provoke it and of the accidents which punctuate it, the wild complication of a soul which is no longer its own master, its order routed.

The fourth act consists of a series of scenes in different settings. The composition is somewhat less firm. In a *garden*, we observe the touching farewells of David and Jonathan. David will put himself at the head of the Philistines in order to assure Jonathan the crown Saül cannot defend. He arranges to meet him in a cave. —In the *desert*, under the burning sun that "evaporates the wisdom of kings," Saül, with neither crown nor royal mantle, wanders in search of she-asses (as in the time of his youth, when he was happy . . .). A demon in a brown cloak mocks him, strips him of all his dignity, and sends him on the path to his perdition. —In the *palace courtyard* the crowd reports Saül's degradation: the old king has been brought back to the palace singing and dancing. He enters, the crowd manifests its scorn and abandons Saül when he mounts his throne and clumsily attempts to make a speech amid mocking laughter; they leave the king for a more interesting spectacle: David's army has arrived. Only little Saki, his cupbearer, remains; the child touches the senile old king by his despair and his loyalty. In order to stay and talk with him, Saül refuses to heed the high priest. Playfully he asks Saki to try on the crown (this is a symptomatic and symbolic obsession with him) and in a scene where he tries to elicit tales of David and Jonathan's intimacy from the innocent child, Saül grows angry and cruelly thrusts the crown upon Saki's head. It is impossible to convey here the volatility of the contradictory sentiments to which Saül is prey and by which Gide, with clinical certainty, paints the incurable collapse of a soul in agony.

Then comes the caricature of escape; Saül asks Saki to run away with him and search for she-asses. —We next find Saül in a *cave*, accompanied by a demon whom he takes for Saki and who shows him David and Jonathan at their appointed meeting place. David advises Jonathan to make Saül take refuge with him in this cave. But Saül, whom the demon advises to feign sleep, suspects treason. Jonathan, catching sight of his father, warns David, who is praying and refuses to interrupt his prayers. Finally David approaches the trembling Saül, places his crown beside his head, and so that Jonathan may persuade him of his loyalty, cuts a piece from his purple; Saül will understand that he could "take his life." Once the two young men have left, Saül laughs derisively at seeing himself inadequately covered by the cloak: "How kind they are to me!" His destiny is to be deaf to all that might save him and, like Gide's other heroes, he drains his personality to the dregs.

In the last act, in a mountainous place where Saül has pitched his tent, we learn that all the Hebrews have become David's partisans. As for Saül, "defeat is already consummated in his heart." Jonathan, who desires to act, finds himself in conflict with his father's sluggishness, all of Saül's resources are drained, but his intelligence formulates his collapse as a theory: "When I took action I did not understand that there is a time for action—and a time to repent for having taken action. My son, understand that there are things more important for the soul than the victories of an army . . ." Jonathan asks him: "When have you taken such great action, my father?" And Saül replies: "I know; I know; above all I have desired. But for that, too, my child, the time comes when I would repent." He can only talk now, and complains when his son leaves him briefly; Jonathan has not even been able to make Saül promise to follow him when he returns.

—Saül remains alone, with Saki unnoticed at first. The demon calls Saül plaintively from the wings, while the latter attempts once again to pray, but after a few words, distraction prevails upon him and gives way to his obsessive love for David. "My God, what am I before you that you should overwhelm me with desires? When I seek a place to support myself, it yields. I have nothing solid within me. (Absently) What I love most in him is his strength. Splendid is the suppleness of his loins! . . . Enough, my lips!" The demon still calls to Saül. Saki tries to keep him from opening the door (we recognize the symbol and the advice of the witch of Endor), but Saül: "O, closed little heart! Do you not hear that someone calls me?" He walks out of the door, finds a tiny, trembling demon, carries him in and warms him . . . Saki leaves. Jonathan discovers the "little child" which Saül has taken in. "Oh! my father, do you not love me any more than this little thing?" Saül, almost sobbing: "You do not know how difficult it is!" But his absurd pride does not abandon him: "My worth is in my complication." Moreover he is still convinced that David and Jonathan have organized his defeat, and when Jonathan tries to lead his father away, Saül dismisses him, first reciting his new proverb: "With what will a man console himself for a defeat, if not with what has defeated him?" Momentarily forgetting the demon, he has a last impulse: "Ah! Why is it that I hesitate to rise up and act? My will! my will! I call to it now as a shipwrecked sailor hails a bark he sees riding in the distance—disappearing! . . . disappearing . . . I encourage all things against myself. The demon tells Saül that he will never rest again, and answers his complaints with a cruel truth: "Pity! Come, Saül! You cannot tell me that if you called me here, it did not give you pleasure . . .", and knowing his victim, he incites him to new temptations: "Yet if you wanted to have pity . . . I am not alone; there are many others out there," and Saül, incorrigible, already enticed despite himself: "Where are they . . ." and lets them all in. "I would be afraid [we recognize the counterpart of an idea expressed in *les Nourritures*] that if I refused even one, it might be the one that is most charming— or perhaps most wretched." He forbids Jonathan to enter, darkens the stage with his cloak. Riot of the demons; Saül's vain attempt at prayer; the demons press Saül further and further: "I am done away with." Indeed, Saül no longer exists: he is no more than the chaos of his vices and his desires; his own personality has been completely effaced, has melted under the assaults of external temptations which nothing in himself has opposed. The play is virtually over, but it could not be ended by a scene so purely symbolic. The day dawns, a trumpet call rings out, the demons vanish. Saül snatches his cloak from the doorway and says: "It is too late!" He kneels in the cool grass, a prey to one last temptation: "Now is the hour when the goatherds bring the herds from the stables. —There are grasses bathed in dew . . . I am tempted." He does not see one of his former servants, who creeps up behind him, his sword raised, but murmurs mysteriously: "Oh! Oh! Oh! This one is a cowardly temptation; it assails me from behind." The sword falls and kills Saül. The crown is taken to David, who orders the murderer to be put to death: "He has let this crown fall with all its weight upon my head";

he learns of Jonathan's death: "I have done what I could do, Jonathan, my brother"; and he orders a solemn funeral rite. The cortege forms to the sounds of a dead march.

I scarcely need indicate how superbly this play is contrived for the stage. Not only is the inner drama proper to Saül skillfully objectified, but it is framed in a kind of discreet ceremoniousness, animated by an economical but nonetheless telling use of extras. The action's complexity, as we have just seen, is so ingeniously devised that it suggests, even at a first reading, no sense of complication. On the contrary, the impression the play leaves is one of elegant architecture, without parasitical ornaments. The wealth of implications is counterbalanced by the sobriety of the developments; above all, an impeccable placing of details gives this hierarchy of combined elements a perfect ease. The style's rightness of touch, its precision and restraint complete the sense of admirable order which makes Saül a skillful composition; its ease is that of a consummate artist mastering all he undertakes.

This magnificent drama, of such mature thought and expression, was the work of a writer twenty-eight years old. The actor de Max was to play the role of Saül; the play had been accepted by Antoine, on condition that the success of a work by Brieux permitted him to risk the production; yet Saül was not performed at the time of its completion, in 1896; it was only published seven years later, and had to wait until 1922 for the Vieux-Colombier to produce it, with only moderate success. One understands Gide's complaint in his Journal at this period, and shares his feeling: "Why . . . should I be surprised that Saül should be received so coolly by the critics? They saw only declamation in it, as they saw nothing but phrases in my Nourritures. Can't you recognize a sob, then, unless it sounds the same as your own?" For my part, what strikes me most on rereading this forty-two-year-old work sixteen years after that performance is that it hasn't a single wrinkle. The critics will one day be astonished, when they turn to the history of our theater, to realize that the great works of the early twentieth century are far from being those which made the most noise. They will notice that the author of *Knock* was above all the author of *Crome-deyre-le-Vieil*, and, in this revision of values, we can be sure that *Saül* will hold a high place in twentieth-century true drama, which will ultimately have been, without our having even realized it, a poetic drama.

Le Roi Candaule, a play in three acts, was performed (in 1901) under the direction of Lugné-Poe, who played the role of Candaule; de Max played Gygès. The major newspapers didn't make much out of it. The play was performed in various European cities. In Berlin, in 1908, its failure was complete, and the author was covered with insults (*"eine solche Schweinerei"*) and crushed by the comparison with Hebbel's play *Gyges und sein Ring*, held to be as superior to Gide's as Kleist's *Amphitryon* was to Molière's.

There was much in *Candaule* to feed the critics' fires —first of all, a new character who was no less natural for being exceptional, as Gide pointed out in his *Préface:* "As if the common was more natural than the rare! Lead more natural than gold!" He reminds us of Nietzsche's phrase about Candaule: "Generous to the point of vice" and his remark: "It is curious to see that excessive generosity is always accompanied by a loss of shame." "Shame is a reservation," Gide puts it. The play, moreover, has further implications: "Perhaps . . . it is not impossible to see in it the defeat, the suicide almost, of an aristocracy which is disarmed by its excessively noble qualities until it can no longer defend itself . . ." and the entire ideology this generalization provoked in the person of Candaule: "If Candaule, too great, too gener-

ous and driving himself to extremes, permits the ignorant Gygès first to see, then to touch and share what he
learns slowly and yet too fast to love—to what, to whom
could this communism not extend?" At the time only
Charles Maurras discovered in "this subtle and powerful
little book . . . profound political allusions" whose "discretion" did not seem to him "to exclude precision."

The ideological background thus seems more evident
here than in *Saül,* but we must remember the extraordinary delicacy of touch with which it is inserted into
this play, made out of such slight substance. The intellectual suggestions are indicated with so light a hand
that they have readily passed unnoticed. It is perhaps
the least "stressed" of all Gide's works. He has chosen to
draw with probity "at a time when everyone paints,
when no one or almost no one draws any more," and
to avoid "lyric excess" and "bombast."

Indeed, *Candaule* is a purified tragedy, imbued with
a transparent light, and gives off a crystalline ring. It is
not written in the plain prose of *Saül* nor in regular
verse, but in what appears to be *vers libre* (less precious
than the latter would have been in the attempt to
achieve a musical effect); actually the form is a kind of
"accented prose" whose moderation does not exclude
vigor, but envelops it in a constant nobility.

Gide has greatly altered Herodotus' narrative. He has
made Gygès a fisherman instead of a shepherd, and
the role of the magical ring has been entirely transformed.

After a *Prologue* consisting of a proud soliloquy by
the fisherman Gygès—who, in order not to miss the next
day's tide, leaves Candaule's palace, where a great banquet is being prepared—the first scene presents the conversations of the idle or flattering lords whom Candaule
keeps at his court by "a kind of wavering generosity"
and not out of policy or foolishness. Candaule insists
that Queen Nyssia honor the banquet with her presence,

and repeats as much to his guests. The banquet begins, although the queen in her modesty is reluctant to yield to Candaule's pleas to unveil her face. Interrupting the guests' compliments, Candaule attempts to explain his state of mind (Gide here establishes the basis of a character which will be completely developed in the second act.):

> No, my lords do not thank me
> For offering this banquet the queen's beauty;
> In truth, I suffered too much, knowing it alone.
> The greater my admiration for her,
> The more I felt I was depriving you.
> To myself I seemed a greedy monopolist
> Unjustly withholding the light.

Carried away by his thoughts (and this, I submit, is the essential feature of his character), Candaule declares:

> . . . I fear lest I steal from all
> The wealth I alone enjoy

Without realizing that it is Nyssia he is speaking of, who then reproaches him:

> Fie, my lord! You seem to forget
> The riches you speak of are myself.

As for the queen, she replies to a question about sharing:

> That there are certain kinds of happiness
> One kills in trying to share . . .

Yet Candaule is not convinced, only irritated:

> Yet that too depends with whom . . .

Soon afterward one of the guests breaks two teeth on a ring concealed in a fish. Since it bears a mysterious inscription, "I hide happiness," the fisherman is sent for, and meanwhile there is a debate on happiness, as in a

Platonic dialogue, furnishing the occasion for the impulsive Candaule to explain his own doctrine:

> My happiness seems to gain
> Its force and violence in others.
> Sometimes it seems to me to exist
> Only in what knowledge of it others have,
> And that I possess nothing
> Save when I am known to possess.
> I vow, my lords, it would matter little
> Were I to possess all the earth
> If in doing so I lived there alone,
> Or if no one were to know it.
> My lords, believe me, it is most of all
> When you profit by my wealth
> That it is mine.

And, addressing himself to Phaedrus, the most intelligent of his guests:

> After all—for myself—what does happiness
> Matter to me? Truly, is it not worthy
> Only of the poor to care about being happy? . . .
> Each thing one possesses
> Carries its new desire to test it—
> And to possess, for me, is to experiment . . .
> To risk! That is the other kind of happiness:
> The rich man's kind . . . It is my own.

Gygès arrives, dignified, reticent. His wife, returning drunk from the palace kitchens, has accidentally set fire to his hut and his nets. Candaule, affected by such a misfortune, sends for Gygès' wife. But one of the courtiers lets it be known that she has granted him her favors. Candaule grows indignant. Gygès, in grim resolution, seizes a knife on the table and kills his wife. Candaule decides to make Gygès not his servant but his friend. The final portion of this act is executed with an affecting warmth.

In the second act, the following day, Gygès has been installed in the palace as a lord, but he has lost nothing of his *sang-froid*. Candaule's attitude is incomprehensible to him. He believes in his pity, not his friendship. His conversation with the king shows the latter's new concern to vanquish the misery he is ignorant of. It is by trying to make Gygès share in all his goods, attempting to make him taste happiness that Candaule, saddened by his protégé's regret for his wife, by his belief in her love, arrives at a "disturbing thought" he scarcely dares admit to himself:

> Louder, speak louder, my newest thought?
> Where would you take me?

He asks Gygès if it greatly embarrassed him to know that his wife did not belong to him alone, and he finally offers to let him see the queen. Gygès does not understand and asks the king if he does not love her. —The rest of the scene is devoted to providing a means of realization to the strange motive that drives Candaule on: the ring, which Candaule has discovered renders its wearer invisible. Candaule disappears and reappears "like a god" before Gygès' eyes. The queen approaches. Candaule puts the ring on Gygès' finger, and he becomes invisible. The royal couple prepares for bed, and Candaule, struggling against himself and against the effect of Nyssia's words, which implicitly condemn his secret plan, drinking to keep up his courage, admonishes himself:

> Candaule, you weaken!
> Who then would ever do this thing,
> If it be not you?

With renewed enthusiasm he takes advantage of the darkness (Gygès has thrown to the floor the torch that illuminates the bedroom at the very moment Nyssia is

about to drop her last veil) to exit, ordering Gygès to
remain.

The third act develops the consequences of this folly.
Gygès, after the night, is filled with remorse, shame,
terror, and love for the queen. As for Candaule, he
cruelly expiates his generosity: Nyssia declares herself
intoxicated with bliss, and Candaule falls prey to a
jealousy which nonetheless astounds him and which he
scorns:

> You, Candaule, jealous! For shame then!
> Wicked passion, you shall be still.

Gygès, who has heard their conversation, tears off the
ring and, in a soberly measured confession, gradually
reveals the whole truth to Nyssia, who is conscience-
stricken as he proceeds; with a remark that reveals all,
he hands her a dagger to kill him with. Seized with a
profound horror, Nyssia presses Gygès instead to kill
Candaule:

NYSSIA: Go, stab him with it.

GYGÈS: (*letting the dagger fall to the ground*) I
cannot. My friend! . . .

NYSSIA: He was my husband too! Kill him.

GYGÈS: I cannot . . . It is he who gave me . . .

NYSSIA: It is he who betrayed me. (*She rends her
veil.*) He is coming back— One of you must die. Be
quick . . . Put on the ring again. Stab him! Stab
him!

GYGÈS: How then? Without being seen?

NYSSIA: You were hidden from me, were you not!

GYGÈS: He gave me the ring.

NYSSIA: (*exasperated by this resistance*) Oh! Yet one
of you must be jealous! (*She seizes Gygès and
kisses him wildly on the lips.*) Oh! You will stab
him, Gygès. . . . Oh, you will stab him!—

The ring! Put on the ring, now. (*She slips it on his finger.*) Vanish then! He is here.

Candaule, however, confides to Phaedrus his desire to abandon his luxurious life:

This palace, these feasts must now
Belong to myself alone. And Nyssia . . .
And Nyssia, you know, I shut her away now . . .

He has followed his notion to its extreme conclusion, like all Gide's heroes, but can no longer endure its burden. Urged on by Nyssia, the invisible Gygès strikes Candaule, who suffers only a painful surprise:

I felt within me nothing but kindness,
Nyssia . . .

He asks to see Gygès again, who, horror-stricken and desolate, kneels beside his friend. Nyssia forces him to his feet, declares him her husband, puts the crown on his head, and invites the lords to the banquet that is about to begin. Gygès' attitude shows him to be a ruler who will not fall victim to Candaule's weaknesses:

GYGÈS: (*who has gradually recovered*) Sit down, my lords. (*hostilely, in Nyssia's direction*): That lovely face, Madame, I thought it was to remain veiled.

NYSSIA: (*scornfully*) Veiled for you, Gygès. Candaule has torn my veil.

GYGÈS: (*brutally pulls a piece of her garment over her face*) Well then, sew it together.

SYPHAX: (*amid the murmur this action provokes*) Come, gentlemen, let us drink to Gygès' happiness.

The character of Candaule could not fail to provoke astonishment. Gide, in a projected *Nouvelle Préface pour Candaule*, writes: "Difficulty of getting an idea admitted as a motive." We recall an earlier, analogous difficulty in Lafcadio's gratuitous act. But in his *Journal*, Gide has illuminated another point in *Candaule*, seeking corroborators in Rousseau and Dostoevsky. In his *Confessions*, Rousseau declares, speaking of Madame d'Houdetot and of Saint Lambert: "I have never for a moment considered her lover as my rival, but always as my friend. It will be said that this was not love: that may be, but in that case it was more." And Gide also recalls Rousseau's position between Madame de Warens and Claude Anet, as well as that of Prince Mishkin between Rogozhin and Nastasia Philipovna. "The expression of this feeling (which is also that of my Candaule)—which I have found only here—is of the greatest importance." Candaule was a hero—not false, but one too rare for the theater: his purpose and his lack of jealousy met with little sympathy. It is likely that here, too, a *récit* would have been more appropriate to the development of his feelings. However skillful Gide has been in suggesting them, there is a certain awkwardness in Candaule's asides when he gradually becomes aware of the idea that intoxicates him as it floods his mind.

On the other hand, the character of Gygès is the most vigorous of any Gide has put on the stage. His pride in his poverty, his energy in action, his vigorous adaptation to circumstances make him a strikingly virile and rugged figure. The harsh simplicity of his words completes a physiognomy which proves, like his Michel in *l'Immoraliste*, that Gide is not incapable of a savage tone.

I shall not analyze the structure of Gide's *Oedipe* in detail. A drama in three acts, each preceded by an epigraph, it is intended to be read, not performed. Yet it has been staged a number of times, first by Pitoeff in 1932. Gide has stripped this play of all glamour. The extremely simple, natural style, verging on the commonplace without succumbing to it, rather Voltairian in its acuity, of a certain dry charm, suits this kind of blueprint, which is less psychological than social. At the "pathetic" moments it is so intellectual that it leaves us quite without emotion. On the other hand more than one of Oedipe's declarations touches us by its grandeur. The action, rapid but without any attempt at dramatic interest, borrows only a few points of reference from tradition and serves exclusively to advance a series of interpretations which Gide has made of the classical characters for his own use. It belongs with his treatise on the Dioscuri—less poetic, more social. Without expressly seeking anachronistic effects, Gide has deliberately furnished all his characters with modern, even contemporary states of mind, and the play shamelessly alludes to current ideas and events. Etéocle has written reflections on *"Le Mal du Siècle"* subtitled "Our Anxiety." With his brother, Polynice, he shares a doctrine of the repression of desires and of their realization in dreams which counters Freud's. It is easy to assign Tirésias the name of a Catholic critic hostile to Gide. But it is the entire web of ideas which is of our time. Consequently there is no poetic distance, as in the classics, or as in *Saül* and *Candaule*. This is Greece in the twentieth century, this is Paris, and with nuances that vary according to the characters, the language is that of our own bourgeoisie. The work is less interesting for its dramaturgy than for the study of Gidean ideology. A critical work, again, but bearing the same relation to the dramatic series as the trilogy of *l'École des Femmes* to the series of *récits*. The drama is only a pretext, however skillful, for new views concerning various problems which Oedipe's case suggests by the various links it offers with a number of powerful situations. Gide has therefore, like Freud, created his own Oedipus complex—in an altogether different sense, of course, and humorously speaking. Yet the significance of this ideological tragedy is not diminished because he has treated it throughout in that familiar, bantering tone which appeared only occasionally in *Saül* and which —remotely—suggests the philosophical tragedy *à la* Voltaire. Here ideas, always a danger in the theater, have invaded the characters until they become merely mouthpieces. It is the extreme but natural consequence, and this time without aesthetic counterweight, of Gide's tendency to start his plays from an idea.

The chorus, which represents the people, is less religious than clerical: "It is good to put the gods on one's side. But the surest way is to put oneself on the side of the priest." Its prudence is mitigated by a latent skepticism: "And if we have fasted this year it was no doubt in penance . . . but also because we had nothing left to eat."

Tirésias is the priest who increases his power by teaching the fear of God and always acting in His name. His policy is a cunning one. He convinces Créon "to crack open . . . Oedipe's impious happiness. Through this unhealed crack, God will penetrate into his heart." Intrigue and unction are his natural attitudes. He always has the last word.

Jocaste is the bigot in the priest's faction, and the prudent wife who urges her husband to persevere in the ignorance which protects their happiness, instead of calling his attention to certain points which no historian has yet remarked on.

Créon, who prefers to enjoy the advantages of power without assuming its responsibilities but is always ready to fill the interim gap between two reigns, is the prudent conservative who considers religion good for the people and useful to those who govern, and is pleased to inherit the virtues and the wealth attached to a high birth: he leans on them.

Créon regards Oedipe's sons as tormented spirits.

Etéocle and Polynice are postwar intellectuals who
seek from their reading authorization to do evil, "the
approbation of indecency," but despite or because of
their common tastes, they are destined to destroy each
other, if only in their incestuous lust for their sister
Ismène, a frivolous society girl. Antigone, on the other
hand, has that demanding purity of spirit which impels
her to become a nun and reconvert her father, but she
ultimately discovers that her true duty is to accompany
him. She says to Tirésias: "I listened to you when you
taught me God until this day; but now, even more
piously, I shall listen only to the teachings of my reason
and my heart."

Oedipe is a man who believes himself happy because
he owes his happiness entirely to himself. He has vanquished it, being better suited to action than to reflection, "inconsistent like all impulsive men," as Créon says.
Hostile to Tirésias as a freethinker to a curé, he fears he
will become infatuated in his happiness, which he
wants to deserve. He is a man who tries to win everything from himself. "It does not even displease me to
learn I was a bastard. In the days when I believed I
was Polybius' son, I applied myself to imitating his
virtues. What did I have, I asked myself, that was not
first given by my fathers? Heeding the lessons of the
past, I expected that yesterday alone would dictate my
so-be-it. Then suddenly, the thread broke. A child of
the unknown, with no more past, no more models, nothing to lean on, everything to create: fatherland, an-
cestors . . . to invent, to discover. No one to take after,
save myself. What does it matter to me now whether
I am Greek or Lorrainese? O Créon! So submissive, so
dutiful, how could you understand the beauty of this
demand? Not to know who one's parents are is a call to
valor!"

This modern Oedipus believes in progress, in democ-
racy, in human value. In a tone which mingles an au-

thentic grandeur with familiar simplicity, he sets forth his faith in his advice to Polynice and Etéocle, whose disappointing conversation he has listened to; but he has praised Polynice for believing "less willingly in the gods than in the heroes." "Rest assured that humanity is no doubt much farther from its goal which we cannot yet imagine, than from its point of departure, which we already no longer make out." "Tirésias bores us with his mysticism and his morality. I had been taught all that under Polybius' roof . . . Tirésias has never invented anything and cannot approve of those who seek and those who invent. However inspired by God he may claim to be, with his revelations and his birds, he could not answer the riddle. I understood, I alone understood that the only password to keep from being devoured by the sphinx is 'Man.' No doubt it required a little courage to say it, that word. But I had it ready long before I heard the riddle; and my strength is that I admitted no other answer, whatever the question might have been.

"For you see, my children, each of us, as a youth, meets early in his course a monster who raises some riddle before him which might keep us from advancing. And though this particular sphinx asks each of us a different question, my children, rest assured that for each of her questions the answer remains the same: yes, there is only one and the same answer to all these various questions: and that one answer is: Man; and that one man for each of us is: Self." After Tirésias urges him to explore his past, Oedipe, who does not wish undeserved happiness, "as if happiness were what he had ever looked for," reproaches himself for having grown "numb with recompense." He rouses himself from this lethargy and proceeds, in his manner, to the famous interrogation. "I have no desire for happiness that consists of ignorance and error." He understands that by marrying Jocaste, the courageous bastard had once again become the prey of heredity. "In vain the future called me, Jocaste drew me back." But he reproaches God for his "cowardly betrayal." The crime has been imposed upon him by God, who "ambushed him on his road," even before his birth. Either the oracle was lying, or Oedipe couldn't escape. He was hunted down. He realizes he was the victim of a destiny quite different from the one he admitted when he supposed himself guided by a god toward glory, not toward a crime whose horror has been concealed from him. All this is a criticism of the ancient conception of taboo and of divine sanction. After having put out his eyes in order to punish them for not having been able to warn him, he sarcastically asks Tirésias if this offering, too, was foreseen. But, like Gide's other heroes, he drives himself to the logical extreme, explaining his immolation in terms of a sublime clarity: "I had reached a point I could not get past save by turning against myself." He will bear happiness to the men of the land where he is to die, since "a great benediction is promised to the land where his bones find their resting place." Tirésias corrects him: "It is not their happiness you must seek, but their salvation." This modern Oedipus replies: "I leave it to you to explain that to the people."

7. *Les Faux Monnayeurs*
and the Art of the Novel (i)

Les Faux Monnayeurs is André Gide's most complex
work, and undoubtedly one of the most complex in all
literature. The wealth of interconnected intentions, the
subtlety of its composition, whose firmness results from
counterpoint and whose freedom is contrived by a
syncopated progress, the abandonment of developments
almost before they have begun, the reliance on the
reader's imagination, intelligence, and capacity for attention, the rapidity of the suggestions and the ease of
the style all make this bulky book not only impossible
to summarize but, what is more serious, impossible to
summarize without betraying it. One always has this
impression, of course, in attempting to account for a
work of great authority, but here we are confronted
with a difficulty more peculiar still: the substance to be
studied appears to evaporate upon analysis, so volatile
is its essence by nature. This also accounts, I think, for
the irritating quality of *les Faux Monnayeurs* so often
described by readers, even those most familiar with
Gide's work, and which we must also take into account,
it seems to me, for it too must have entered into the
author's intentions. One must already be a perverted

reader, in other words a critic, to be convinced that the
nuance of annoyance a book provokes can be, in certain privileged cases, an additional charm.

But on this occasion I hope the critic is entitled to
speak of a book while supposing it to be entirely present
in the mind of his public; this is a little too much to
ask in the case of a work so luxuriant, but that is precisely why one must ask it. Too many practical reasons
make this hope quite futile, particularly since it is not
enough to have read *les Faux Monnayeurs* (I have
made the experiment) to remember it in detail; the
book only begins to live in the privileged domain of our
imagination, to take shape there, after it has been reread. The advantage of a community of recollection
between public and critic, of the sort we count on in
dealing with a universally appreciated masterpiece,
would be to skip this breathless attempt at a theoretical
reconstruction, so bloodless and absurd in the case of a
major work where nothing can replace direct vision, and
which suggests the pallid description of paintings for
the use of those who have not seen them, or those
verbal accounts of inaudible symphonies which give
the impression of translations for the deaf.

At the same time one would obtain a second advantage: to replace quotations by allusions. Allusion
has this advantage over quotation, that it creates a
complicity between critic and public; it has another,
too, for the critic: that of not humiliating his prose.
Audiences enjoy quotations, and with reason, for it is
generally the finest passages of a great writer that are
quoted, and often the great writer gives them a rest
from the bad lecturer. It is no less true that allusion,
presuming it is understood, flatters a certain snobbery,
and adds connivance to rapidity. It is above all this
last feature that the critic would retain, for it leaves
space for aesthetic analysis, instead of monopolizing it
for a fragmentary reproduction which pulverizes the

masterpiece into crumbs, even if they are the best crumbs. In *les Faux Monnayeurs,* quotations are extremely difficult to extract from the body of the text, and this, I think, is the first quality one may discern in the book: a novel must, by nature, resist dissection; you will find abrupt halts in *les Faux Monnayeurs,* a certain coquetry of restraint; you will not find—as in *les Nourritures,* for example, where it was quite suitable—a marquetry of aesthetic effects. No isolated phrases for effect, no maxims to be detached, no anthology pages carefully contrived for press reviews or future high school textbooks. Such discretion has its own savor.

Faithful to my method, I shall continue, on the one hand, to illuminate the text under consideration by statements borrowed from the author's *Journal* which expressly refer to it, or by passages from his critical writings which permit us to grasp his intention better (thus we may gain a view of a work consonant with its spirit); and on the other, to apply to it some principles of an aesthetic I am attempting to use as my touchstone, even as I invent it upon contact with its objects and rectify it when necessary, for even though aesthetics dominates criticism, it has value only if it sanctions the latter, and there must be a constant exchange between them which assures and articulates both (this is what permits us, once we have attempted to attune ourselves with a maximum of sympathy to the original vibration, to detach ourselves for a moment in order to judge it). With *les Faux Monnayeurs,* this double procedure has its work cut out for it. It is not easy to participate in an attempt so complex, divergent, disconcerting, and sometimes deceptive. It is not easy, either, to apply to the book criteria which prove quite fruitful in the case of less artful works.

But to reconcile our sympathies with *les Faux Monnayeurs,* Gide has given us a document of great importance—*le Journal des Faux Monnayeurs,* in which, during the years this enormous work was elaborated, he kept a kind of logbook recording the events and the notable mishaps of this strange navigation of a writer toward his masterpiece. The technical and human interest of this document are such that the *Journal* has become inseparable from the novel and no doubt exceeds the intrinsic interest of such an undertaking (consider, for example; Flaubert's letters to Louise Colet, which permit us to follow the progress of *Madame Bovary*), because, from a certain viewpoint, *le Journal des Faux Monnayeurs,* although located outside the novel which bears this title, constitutes virtually its chief subject. At one point, Gide was tempted to turn this whole *Journal* into his novel, since indeed the latter's hero, the novelist Edouard, is also writing *les Faux Monnayeurs,* since the effort to disengage a novel from reality is his constant preoccupation, and since he too plans to make his chief character a novelist. If Gide rightly abandoned putting this *Journal* into his book, it is no doubt because Gide is not Edouard, although he has given him a good deal of himself, but it is also because the chaos of his *Journal* could not be inserted *as it was* into a transposed and harmonized creation: the same is true of the *Journal* as of reality: to appear in the novel, it would have had to undergo a particular treatment—and we have only a few extracts from Edouard's *Journal* particularly devoted to his literary projects, to his intentions as a novelist. Gide's *Journal des Faux Monnayeurs* is content to gravitate around his book, and it is not easy to distinguish which of the two, the star or its satellite, sheds light on the other. In any case, the *Journal des Faux Monnayeurs,* adding to it the *appendix* in which Gide has grouped a number of important documents and drafts of a first version, and not omitting certain indications from Gide's personal *Journal,* affords an inestimable contribution to the understanding of his only novel.

I think that in order to analyze a work of this nature somewhat closely, it would be wise to consider it as the product of a double architecture. One, which would be its profound or internal architecture, concerns not so much the appearance of the work as the mental or ideological structure that controls it. It would be, so to speak, the psychical system which we feel to be operative in the novel. I shall postpone consideration of this system for the second chapter on *les Faux Monnayeurs*, which will be devoted to applying the aesthetic of the novel to *les Faux Monnayeurs* as we might apply it to a novel by Balzac. But *les Faux Monnayeurs* is an extraordinary, exceptional, unprecedented novel, a unique case that is not only inimitable, but should not be imitated. It requires a supplement in critical method —I dare not say a refinement. I therefore propose to examine first the surface architecture Gide has chosen to give his novel, this composition rich in superstructures that oblige us, in order to attempt to account for them, to resort to a rather barbarous terminology, but which we cannot neglect without depriving the work of one of its most striking characteristics. There is, one might say, a novel in *les Faux Monnayeurs* which might be told—all differences of temperament apart—by Balzac or by Dostoevsky, with certain narrative techniques which are quite special but with which, after all, we have grown familiar. And then there is this same novelistic substance manipulated, elaborated, spun out, cut up, crisscrossed, superimposed, echoing itself, as Gide has worked it into this light, elegant, and perforated monument which suggests a tower in which two spiral staircases are intertwined around a same axis, so that certain parts communicate, though two people on landings at the same level can no longer see each other—or else a high order of labyrinth where traffic would be facilitated by a series of signposts and arrows: it is im-

possible to get lost here, on condition one has good
eyes and a good memory.

I shall therefore not ask my reader to reread *les Faux
Monnayeurs* with me (this would be pleasant for me,
but a little long for him) but to survey it from above,
noting its salient features, the accidents of the terrain.
I hope that in this way its prospect will seem less confused.

But so that this summary view may assume its full
meaning, fall into some kind of order, I must urge the
reader to keep ever present in his mind a double distinction which I believe will illuminate this first super-
ficial analysis.

Like every novel, *les Faux Monnayeurs* tells us an
invented story, and like every novel, it attempts to
present this story as a true one. Let us, therefore, place
ourselves within this story, and, forgetting that we are
its readers, forgetting that we have read *le Journal des
Faux Monnayeurs*, which explained its genesis to us,
let us quite conventionally regard the events, and characters that will pass before us as facts, as reality. Alongside this reality (which is fictive, ideal, even artistic),
we find in *les Faux Monnayeurs* an effort to make a
novel out of them; this is the preoccupation of the character of the novelist, named Edouard; this Edouard,
invented by Gide and whom we provisionally regard
as authentic, decides he will create a fiction out of
reality. Since *his* reality is the events invented by Gide,
the novel Edouard will produce from them will therefore be fictive to the second degree. So long as all we
need to know is that what Gide has invented is Edouard's reality, and that what Edouard has invented is
fictive to the second degree, there is no difficulty; the
distinction is a simple one. It would continue to be so
if the *Journal* kept by Edouard were content to note
his reflections as provoked by reality, his hesitations as
a writer and a moralist (all of which are still imaginary,

fictive things), and especially his sketches for his novel, *les Faux Monnayeurs;* Edouard's *Journal,* confronting events, would correspond both to Gide's *Journal* in relation to his personal life and to the *Journal des Faux Monnayeurs* in relation to the novel Gide was elaborating. But—and here everything becomes complicated—Edouard's *Journal* is not content to note his reactions; it has become one of the instruments of narration Gide has used to tell the story of *les Faux Monnayeurs.*

One must therefore introduce a second point of view and distinguish the objective presentation from the indirect presentation of events whose narrative forms the plot of *les Faux Monnayeurs.* The story of *les Faux Monnayeurs* is told to us not in one manner alone, as in many novels, but in two: sometimes by the author, sometimes by his hero Edouard. And we see at once that this distinction between the *objective narrative,* as we find it in the body of the novel, and the *indirect narrative,* as we find it in most of Edouard's *Journal,* does not symmetrically coincide with the first distinction between the fictive to the first degree (which is *les Faux Monnayeurs* by Gide) and the fictive to the second degree (which is *les Faux Monnayeurs* by Edouard).

By making Edouard participate in the narrative of the supposedly real events out of which he claims to create *afterward* a novel which transforms them, Gide has no doubt skillfully interwoven the two threads of his plot, but we also have the impression that he has thrown matters into confusion. We are invited to become acquainted with a certain part of reality through Edouard, and his "idiosyncrasy," we must admit, also impels him, like his creator, to a spirit of broad-minded impartiality. Edouard's narrative succeeds, on the whole, in being objective. Then—aside from a concern for variety—why not have narrated directly those scenes where he intervenes (though rarely as a novelist), with the same independence as the rest? I see a reason to entrust them to Edouard's *Journal* in only two cases: 1) if the fact that they are in his *Journal* can advance the plot—and this occurs at the beginning of the novel, when young Bernard, having stolen Edouard's suitcase, reads certain pages of Edouard's *Journal* which inform him of the events in which he will eagerly participate; 2) if these scenes are noted by Edouard for use in his novel: the pretext is too broad and not in proportion to the cause, for in this case Edouard could have told the entire story if necessary (it had occurred to Gide, moreover, to have the story told by another character altogether whom he eliminated from his plan, and that character was none other than our old acquaintance from *les Caves*, Lafcadio). I concede the scene (Georges Molinier's attempted theft from the bookstall) which Edouard will later transcribe as he projects it for his future novel. But this case is unique in the entire book. Edouard who, like Gide, has meanwhile written at one sitting the first thirty pages of *les Faux Monnayeurs*, has not given them to us. We regret the fact. This is what we were hoping to find in Edouard's *Journal*, and not the account of events in which he has taken part and which Gide might have narrated as well as he.

It is understandable that Gide reluctantly abandoned having a number of scenes in his novel narrated by one of its principal characters. Perhaps to some extent because the entire book was originally to be written in the first person, which, as we have noted apropos of his *récits*, he regarded as a factor of superior objectivity; more probably because he enjoyed making Edouard's "I" speak—narrate—for him. This indirect presentation of events, which Gide, according to his own *Journal*, discussed at great length with Roger Martin du Gard, is indeed a method dear to Gide's heart and which he controls with a master hand. It must have cost him considerable effort to abandon it in *les Caves* and in *les Faux*

Monnayeurs, and occasionally we sense that he is a little less at ease in objective narrative. At least he has introduced, even into the latter, certain elements of indirect presentation; in *les Faux Monnayeurs* we find *letters* (from Laura, from Olivier, from Bernard) and above all a number of events reported to us in the course of *conversations* by one of the characters by means of whom Gide discharges himself, as often as he can, of the responsibility of *telling:* he does so, moreover, with that consummate art of dialogue and personal narrative which we have admired in the *récits,* in the *soties* and in the plays. The description of events then depends on the psychology of the individual character. And when the event is familiar to us from several aspects, the slight distortion it suffers or the interpretation it suggests gives the novelist resources of subtle penetration. But it is not only into the objective narration that Gide has introduced something of this indirect method; he has frequently managed to intervene as narrator, to *comment,* somewhat in the manner of Stendhal but more critically, and one of the curiosities of *les Faux Monnayeurs* is the last chapter of the second part, which is entirely devoted to the author's review of his creatures' destiny: alongside Edouard's chapters, it is Gide's chapter which dominates the second slope of the work.

Les Faux Monnayeurs is divided into three parts, the first and the last of equal length (eighteen chapters), the central part conspicuously shorter (seven chapters): it does not constitute the heart of the action at all; it is a kind of plateau between two slopes. Whereas the two outer parts take place in Paris and are animated by violent events, the central part takes place in Switzerland, in secluded Saas Fée, during vacation, and the characters' principal activity is conversation.

In the first part everything seems to project into the

future; there is a general movement forward, a somewhat acid but youthful *allegro*. In the third part, after the rest period of the vacation, the destinies that have been dealt coast toward their conclusions; it is a *presto agitato;* things disintegrate or get lost in the confused continuity of life, which absorbs and reabsorbs everything and, above all, continues.

Let us consider only the asperities, the peaks of these great movements, the exterior schema of events, drained of the complex sentiments that color them, merely taking into account the perspectives from which they are presented to us.

The novel begins with seven chapters of *direct narration*. Young Bernard, a candidate for the *baccalauréat,* has discovered a correspondence proving that he is not the legitimate son of Judge Profitandieu; he decides to abandon his family and, having joined his comrades in the Luxembourg, persuades his best friend, Olivier Molinier, to let him sleep at his house for the night. —A *conversation* between the two judges, Profitandieu and Molinier, informs us that the courts are racked by a scandalous case: young people, minors for the most part, are conducting orgies in a Paris apartment. Returning home, Profitandieu finds the dreadful *letter* in which Bernard announces his departure. Profitandieu announces the fact to his wife, to his elder son Charles, who is a lawyer, to his daughter Cécile, and to Bernard's younger brother Caloub. —*Conversation* between Bernard and Olivier in the latter's bedroom, which Olivier's younger brother Georges overhears while pretending to be asleep. Olivier describes to Bernard how his older brother Vincent has abandoned his mistress, who came to plead with him at night, and also tells Bernard what he knows about his Uncle Edouard, the writer, whom he greatly admires. We make the acquaintance of the young doctor Vincent Molinier at the house of Count Robert de Passavant, whose father was in Vincent's care and who has just died. Vincent, the author tells us in a résumé, encouraged by Robert de Passavant, has gambled away the five thousand francs which his mother had put aside to facilitate the start of his career and with which he had intended to help his mistress. Passavant offers him five thousand more francs to gamble with. He will meet him later at Lady Griffith's. We divine that Passavant has his own reasons to be interested in Vincent: he has designs on his young brother Olivier. Meanwhile the body of Passavant's father is watched over by his youngest son Gontran and by an old servant. —Cynical *conversation* between Lady Griffith and Passavant: we discover that she is in love with Vincent and has managed to separate him from his mistress, and that Vincent has confided his whole story to her: at Pau, where they were both being treated for a more or less imaginary tuberculosis, Vincent and Laura, believing they were soon to die, had given themselves to each other. Vincent arrives, having won fifty thousand francs; Lady Griffith says good-by to her guests, but secretly gives Vincent a key which will permit him to return shortly. Passavant is not deceived. —Bernard noiselessly leaves Olivier's bedroom; facing the future, he delivers himself of a *monologue* and falls asleep on a bench. —*Conversation* between Vincent and Lady Griffith, with whom he wakens; she lectures him and confides strange recollections (the shipwreck of the *Bourgogne,* hands chopped off with axes to keep swimmers from climbing into the overcrowded lifeboats: she makes a symbol out of this for her own purposes).

It is in the eighth chapter that we make the acquaintance of Edouard and of his *Journal.* On the Paris express he is annoyed with the success of Passavant's book, *The Horizontal Bar,* which has just come out. He rereads a *letter* in which Laura Douviers asks him for help; she dares not tell her husband or her parents the truth: she is pregnant and, abandoned by her lover, does not know where to turn. He rereads the pages of his *Journal* devoted to Laura. Edouard's *Journal* thus serves, first of all, to motivate present events by the narration of previous events. This is a retrospective device. Among diverse reflections on sincerity, psychological analysis, and "decrystallization," we learn that Laura formerly exercised a great influence over Edouard and that he once loved her; nonetheless he did not consider himself a suitable husband and therefore advised Laura to marry an honest professor, Félix Douviers, who teaches at Cambridge. Edouard jots down a few reflections on the "pure novel" and on Passavant, and arrives in Paris.

Two short chapters of *direct narration* present the meeting of Edouard and Olivier. They like each other enormously, but mutual embarrassment keeps them from understanding each other. However, Bernard, who has decided to go to the Gare Saint-Lazare to meet Olivier, feels a strange emotion—of jealousy and exclusion—upon seeing him on Edouard's arm. He picks up the cloakroom ticket Edouard has absent-mindedly dropped and succeeds in obtaining his suitcase, which thereby affords him the resources he needed.

The following three chapters are exclusively devoted to Edouard's *Journal*, aside from a few lines recording the passionate interest Bernard takes in reading it, particularly since it is about his friend Olivier and people about whom the latter has told him very little. Bernard thus learns quite a few *underlying facts*, and above all to appreciate Edouard. Edouard writes how he had surprised a young *lycéen* trying to steal a secondhand book from a bookstall. It is none other than his nephew Georges Molinier. He plans to use the episode in his *Faux Monnayeurs*. Georges, meeting Edouard at his house later, is not at all abashed. Edouard notes his relations with his half-sister, Pauline, and her family,

all of whose members he still knows only slightly.
—Edouard's half-sympathetic, half-annoyed reflections
concerning Douviers, with whom Laura has discussed
him. Long account of Laura's wedding. Discussion of
Laura's family, the Vedel-Azaïs, who run a boarding
school. Detailed portrait of a Protestant *milieu*. The
grandfather Azaïs, who is the principal of the boarding
school, is a former pastor whose honesty is equaled only
by his gullibility, and who imposes hypocrisy on all
around him. We learn that his students have founded a
kind of secret association which the poor old man takes
for a league of virtuous emulation. Pastor Vedel is entirely taken up by his functions. His wife is a sentimental
imbecile. Their children appear to be turning out badly
in this atmosphere: Sarah flirts outrageously with Olivier and shows Edouard a series of strange veiled avow-
als in her father's diary; Armand masks his sensitivity
by a merciless cynicism which respects almost nothing
around him. Edouard, who once lived in this boarding
school himself and describes his memories of it to Laura,
decides to give a chapter of his *Faux Monnayeurs*
with an epigraph from Bourget, "the family: that social
cell," this title: "Solitary Confinement." Reflections on
errors in education. Praise of illegitimate children, who
alone are entitled to be natural. We have glimpsed,
meanwhile, the noble figure of La Pérouse, Edouard's
old piano teacher, and been given a recollection of a
disturbing inmate of the Vedels' establishment, the
swindler Strouvilhou. —Edouard describes his visit to
La Pérouse. The old La Pérouse couple is profoundly
disunited, and both suffer odiously from their life in
common. La Pérouse confides to Edouard that his only
link to the world is a thirteen-year-old grandson whom
he has never seen, little Boris; his son, who is dead,
fathered the child on one of his pupils, a young Russian girl, a splendid musician now living in Poland.
Edouard's reflections on the tragedy of morality. The in-

frequent encounters between Edouard and Olivier continue to be evasive. All too *eager* to remain, Edouard, depressed, decides to leave for London.

Four more chapters of *direct narration:* Bernard, reading the letter from Laura to Edouard, realizes that she is the "abandoned mistress" Olivier was telling him about. He bravely decides to save Laura. He finds her at her hotel, astonished at this visit from a stranger. During their conversation, Edouard arrives, wryly amused to meet his thief again. Laura tearfully asks him to take her away, and Bernard ardently urges him to make him his secretary. —Robert de Passavant, to whom Vincent has sent Olivier on his request, suggests that Olivier become editor in chief of a new literary review he is starting, and that he spend his vacation with him; he gives Olivier a copy of his new book with an ambiguous inscription. —Analysis by the author of the stages of Vincent's development by which the devil has gained the upper hand. His conversation with Lady Griffith shows that his conscience has not yet completely foundered. She gives him useful advice, for she is ambitious in his behalf. —Lady Griffith, Passavant, and Vincent dine together. Vincent interests Lady Griffith deeply by his remarks on submarine fauna. After dinner Passavant urges Vincent to obtain his parents' permission for Olivier to spend the summer vacation with him as his secretary. Vincent is not deceived.

The first part concludes with another fragment of Edouard's *Journal.* Having lost his suitcase, he had bought a notebook, and in it we read *notes contemporary with events.* The *Journal,* which has hitherto served as a *retrospective explanation* of events, now becomes a mirror parallel to reality. What is essential in this passage is the account of a second visit to La Pérouse. Received by the old couple, Edouard records their dissension, each of them calling him to witness. Alone with Edouard, La Pérouse announces that it can go on no longer and that he has resolved to commit suicide at the end of three months' time (Edouard does not seem to attach any special significance to this declaration). He asks Edouard to give his grandson, after his death, an annuity which Madame La Pérouse knows nothing about. Edouard offers to visit this grandson, who is at Saas Fée in Switzerland, and to do everything possible to bring him to see his grandfather. La Pérouse distracts Edouard's attention by lively remarks when the latter asks him to stop thinking of dying.

The second part consists of six chapters of the novel and a special chapter in which Gide speaks as novelist. The novel portion is framed by two *letters,* the first from Bernard to Olivier, the second from Olivier to Bernard. Bernard tells Olivier what he does not know about his brother Vincent's adventure with Laura, and describes the life he himself is leading at Saas Fée with Edouard and Laura, with whom he confesses he has fallen in love. But Olivier sees in Bernard's letter only the fact that he himself has been supplanted both in Bernard's heart and in Edouard's. Out of spite, he hurries off to Count de Passavant.

Edouard's *Journal* tells us about the idyll of little Boris and Bronja, the angelic daughter of the lady doctor who is trying to restore this neurotic boy to health; his mother has confided Boris to her care for the vacation. Madame Sophroniska has undertaken a cure which Edouard describes by a *conversation* with the lady doctor, and which obviously derives, without our being told so much, from the psychoanalytic method. In the succeeding chapter a long analysis first explains Laura's distress at being forced by circumstances to assume a role contrary to her nature, which requires observance of the proprieties. On the other hand it is Edouard whom she loves, whom she would have liked to marry, whom she sought even in Vincent's arms. She finds no comfort save in Bernard's virtual cult for the

author, and with Bernard she plays a role of godmother
or elder sister. As for Bernard, he is annoyed that Edouard does not make use of his talents. A certain awkwardness begins to develop between Laura and Bernard. This analysis leads to a curious *conversation* in
which Edouard, Madame Sophroniska, Laura, and Bernard take part. Edouard impulsively and clumsily attempts to explain to his listeners—reticent, ironic, and
unconvinced as they are—what his book *les Faux Monnayeurs* will be like, and he is led to explain his ideas on
the novel. I regard this dialogue on aesthetics as a key
passage in the entire book, and I cannot avoid returning to it when we study that *novel of the novel* which is
Gide's chief concern in this complex work. In the brief
fragment of his *Journal* that closes the chapter, Edouard regrets having permitted himself to speak so freely.
Fortunately he was interrupted by the two children,
Boris and Bronja, coming back from a walk. He opposes
the mysticism praised by Madame Sophroniska. He
notes Victor Strouvilhou's name preceding his own in
the Saas Fée guest book (this detail must be remem-
bered with regard to future information concerning
the activity of this character, already mentioned in
Edouard's *Journal* as his schoolmate at the Vedels' establishment). I nearly forgot to mention that during the
course of the conversation about the novel, Bernard took
out of his pocket a counterfeit coin given him by the
grocer of Saas Fée, to whom it had been passed.

The succeeding chapter consists of a *dialogue* between Laura and Bernard, who clumsily and yet skillfully declares his love, or rather his veneration. She
rejects him kindly. She is not free. She has decided to
confess everything to her husband, and Douviers, in reply, implores her to come back, swearing to love the
child that is about to be born as if it were his own.
Laura and Bernard continue their frank conversation
about their feelings for the characters involved in this

drama: Douviers, Vincent, Edouard . . . and Bernard's future.

Edouard's *Journal*. He glimpses the subject of his book. He is opposed to the realists, including Bernard, with whom he fears he will be unable to reach an understanding. He now agrees with Sophroniska's opinion as to the value of mysticism. Account of Boris' cure, at least according to Sophroniska, who has at last discovered the hidden origin of Boris' problems. She had given a certain Strouvilhou the parchment which little Boris wore in a pouch around his neck and which contained five words by which he and his little schoolmates of the *lycée* in Warsaw, under the leadership of an older schoolmate who initiated them into clandestine practices, believed they were performing magic (the talisman reappears in part three). Edouard is not convinced of the cure's success (we are given a transposed critique of Freudianism), but he decidedly does not consider himself as a mystic (these oscillations in Edouard's mind reproduce the familiar Gidean rhythm). Edouard has suggested that little Boris be sent to the Azaïs school; he imagines old La Pérouse's pleasure on seeing his grandson.

A bragging *letter* from Olivier to Bernard describes his life with Count de Passavant, who is keeping him in luxury and idleness. Bernard is upset by the changes he discerns in his friend, and he detests Passavant. A conversation between Bernard and Edouard proves that they realize that they were both mistaken in joining forces; Bernard decides he will take a temporary job as an under-master at the Vedel-Azaïs school, where he will watch over little Boris and remain at Edouard's disposal if the latter needs him.

The second part ends with a curious chapter which might easily be removed from the novel, but which is extremely instructive because it enlightens us as to Gide's attitude toward his characters. In rereading it, we see how his sympathy is constantly held in check by his judgment.

The third part begins with three chapters of Edouard's *Journal*, each devoted to one of the characters of the novel. —Edouard has taken Boris to his grandfather (Madame de La Pérouse has gone to a "home"), but the child and the old man were not able to get along. Judge Molinier, during a conversation which Edouard scrupulously reproduces, confides his problems to Edouard; a docile, because guilty, husband, he has just discovered that his correspondence with his mistress has vanished from his desk; he fears Pauline has found it, and he is in terror of her jealousy. We learn incidentally that Vincent has left on a cruise (Lady Griffith had promised to recommend him to the Prince of Monaco and to facilitate his new career as a biologist). Molinier congratulates himself upon the excellent company his children are keeping, Vincent with the Prince, Olivier with Passavant, and Georges (who is about to return to the Azaïs school for the new term) with the son of a senator (named Adamanti: we shall come across this name again). He tries to console his colleague Profitandieu, who has not been so fortunate, and whom young Bernard has abandoned . . . Edouard assures Molinier of Bernard's probity, without, it is true, mentioning the stolen suitcase. Molinier then confides that Profitandieu is hearing the very case which a conversation between the two judges had referred to at the beginning of the novel, and that he risks finding his own son implicated (we note here that Molinier is misinformed; it is not Bernard, but his younger brother who is mixed up in this scandal . . . but Gide wants the reader to make his own corrections). —Then Edouard is asked to call by Rachel, one of the Vedel girls, the sister of Laura and Sarah; she is devotion itself, and the burden of the entire establishment rests on her shoulders. She asks Edouard for a temporary loan. Armand explains to

Edouard that Rachel, who has already given up half
her dowry to increase Laura's, is also paying off the
debts of her older brother Alexandre, who has left for
the colonies. Aside from Armand, who venerates his sister Rachel as much as he despises the other members
of his family including himself, no one, neither old
Azaïs, nor Vedel, nor the pastor's wife, is aware of
Rachel's perpetual sacrifice, though its manifestations
are before their eyes every day. —A visit to La Pérouse
shows the wretched old man's increasing degradation.
He gives himself up for dead, and expects to be treated
as though he had ceased to live at a specific date, the
one when he lacked the courage to pull the trigger of a
pistol pressed to his forehead. In his despair he constructs an anti-Christian theory in which God figures
as a devil who amuses himself by letting men believe
in their freedom. He agrees to come to the Azaïs boarding school instead of living alone.

Two chapters of *direct narrative* describe the students
returning to the Azaïs school and the disturbing remarks
of some of them who are involved in the orgy scandal;
the gang is headed by a certain Ghéridanisol, who describes the activities of his cousin . . . Strouvilhou.
Bernard passes his *baccalauréat* and argues aggressively
concerning the subject of the French composition with
Olivier, who is crushed . . . Meanwhile the gang that
includes Ghéridanisol, Georges Molinier, and Adamanti
. . . begins to put into circulation counterfeit coins
whose origin is known only to Strouvilhou, who has
persuaded his little cousin to assure the complicity of
the *"kids of good family,"* because in case of danger
the parents will be sure to hush up the affair, and to
compromise these parents in advance by making the
children hand over documents damaging to the honor of
their ancestry.

Olivier and Bernard have an affectionate *conversation*
in which they discuss their literary aspirations. Bernard

promises to take Edouard to a meeting where the editors of *Argonautes* are having a banquet with those of *Avant-Garde*, the review financed by Passavant and of which Olivier is to be editor in chief. During the course of this conversation, several phrases of Bernard's concerning suicide committed out of enthusiasm, excess of vitality, lead Olivier to murmur that he conceives of suicide as following a joy so great that afterward all life would seem pale . . .

Edouard's *Journal* relates his conversation with Pauline Molinier; she is a very intelligent woman, not at all deceived by her husband's infidelities, resigned to endure what she cannot prevent, but anxious about the future of her children, Olivier and, particularly, Georges: she suspects that Georges has stolen a hundred-franc note from her, and when Edouard tells her of the missing correspondence, she immediately realizes, without saying so, who is responsible for the theft.

Four chapters resume the *objective narrative*. One of them is devoted to Armand, whose psychology—consciously impotent, cynical, and secretly despairing—is illuminated by a magnificent dialogue with Olivier; another, to the wild *avant-garde* literary banquet, where Edouard's irony and Passavant's insolence cross swords. A real person appears in this brilliant scene—Alfred Jarry, whom Gide easily and without exaggeration makes into a caricatural figure of great verve. We find Passavant, eager to distract public attention from his private life, ostentatiously flirting with Sarah Vedel, who on her side makes unequivocal advances to Bernard; he finally takes her to her room and spends the night with her, with Armand's bizarre complicity. During a dispute instigated by Jarry, Olivier has provoked someone to a duel; disgusted by this milieu for which Edouard and Bernard have nothing but contempt, he begs Edouard to take him away. Bernard has spent the night with Sarah, and in the morning Armand arranges to waken him in time to escape without his presence being known. Meanwhile Edouard finds Olivier missing when he gets up; he discovers him in the bathroom, half dead: the boy has tried to commit suicide by turning on the gas heater . . . The arrival of Bernard and one of his friends permits Edouard to discover the motives of this suicide; Bernard reports to him the conversation he had had with Olivier on this subject, when Olivier declared he could understand committing suicide after supreme joy. Nothing of what the reader is intended to guess for himself is expressed, but only suggested.

A *letter* from Laura informs Edouard of the imminent arrival of Douviers, who intends to provoke Laura's lover to a duel and demands to know his name. *Dialogue* between Edouard and Bernard about Laura and Douviers. Pauline comes to see her son, and it is Edouard's *Journal* which tells us about this visit and the extremely odd conversation Pauline has with Edouard: she is not scandalized by so peculiar a situation, but cannot help feeling a certain jealousy. On the other hand, Edouard's happiness, particularly when Olivier regains consciousness, is unalloyed.

Before returning to Edouard's *Journal*, we learn how Edouard visits Passavant to pick up the things Olivier left in his house; incidentally, a fragment of a *letter* from Lady Griffith informs Edouard that the vamp and her victim, Vincent, have begun to hate each other; they are now in Africa. Passavant offers Strouvilhou the job as editor in chief of his review in the course of a lively dialogue in which the insolence of the two interlocutors is well matched, yet in which Strouvilhou distinctly triumphs.

Edouard's *Journal.* Edouard, filled with joy, has written thirty pages of *les Faux Monnayeurs* without faltering. He has seen Douviers, whose jealousy seems to have diminished. Reflections on the inconsistency of characters in the novel. Olivier's influence on his work.

Unexpected visit from Profitandieu who comes to inform Edouard of a new situation, a more critical one, in which his nephew Georges is implicated: the affair of the counterfeit coins. He urges Edouard to warn Georges, before it is too late, to end his precocious life of crime. And suddenly the old judge, filled with anguish, confides to Edouard his grief at Bernard's departure, for he has always preferred Bernard to his own children, precisely because he felt something unconquerable and rebellious in him. Profitandieu would like Edouard to ask Bernard to come back, and also tells him that Bernard's mother has just left him for good. Edouard is moved. But no sooner does Edouard mention the counterfeit coin Bernard found in Saas Fée than the father is completely transformed into the examining magistrate.

Two more chapters of *narration*. The first, quite strange: Bernard meets an angel in the Jardin du Luxembourg who takes him to various places—the chapel of the Sorbonne, a political meeting, a poor neighborhood—and at night Bernard wrestles in bed with the angel until morning, though neither antagonist gains the upper hand. At dawn Rachel asks to speak with him. Her voice is so sad that Bernard begins to hate Sarah. We next see him returning to Edouard's, after he has left the boarding school. They discuss Bernard's future and the best employment of his talents. Until Bernard solves the problem, Edouard will try to find him a job on the *Grand Journal*. —Meanwhile, Rachel cannot bring herself to let Sarah "go to perdition," but the latter, unwilling to be saved, decides to join a friend in England.

Edouard visits La Pérouse at the boarding school, where he has become the proctor and the butt of all the boys' teasing. It is Edouard's *Journal* which relates this conversation, in which the old man's degradation is tragically evident. Then Edouard tells how he has decided to warn Georges against the dangers of his behavior: he makes him read several lines of his novel, in which Audibert and Hildebrand are worried about young Eudolfe, and in order to warn him agree that Audibert will take down what they say and give it to Eudolfe to read. Georges conceals his true reaction—he finds the name Eudolfe ridiculous; actually he is flattered to have attracted Edouard's attention. But the judge's threat, communicated by his uncle, makes him grow pale, then blush. —Edouard notes that these pages of *les Faux Monnayeurs* are bad. Georges warns his schoolmates. Ghéridanisol gets rid of the counterfeit coins. That same evening Strouvilhou takes steps.

From this point on events move at a rapid pace. It is Armand who finally assumes the editorship of Passavant's review; he tells this to Olivier, who does not conceal how much he pities Armand. During the conversation Armand shows Olivier a *letter* from his brother Alexandre relating the arrival of a madman who believes himself to be the devil. We gather that Lady Griffith has been drowned by this unknown person . . . it does not occur to Olivier that the murderer is his brother Vincent, whom he supposes to be in America and from whom he has had no further word.

The following chapter describes the pathetic situation of little Boris, in despair over Bronja's death, isolated in the boarding school, where he is cruelly disregarded, or rather, despised, by his schoolmates. Ghéridanisol's wickedness inspires him to let Boris see the talisman his cousin Strouvilhou has given him, and the poor child falls back into his bad habits. But this is not enough for Ghéridanisol, who out of hatred for Boris creates the "League of Strong Men" to which the wretched child, surrounded by hostility, greedy for a little sympathy, is to be admitted; he will be the victim, not just the dupe, of a dreadful machination. Under the pretext of a test of courage, and by means of a rigged drawing of straws, Boris agrees to shoot himself in the temple during the study hour under old La Pérouse's monitorship; the poor old man falls to the floor, paralyzed by a stroke; Ghéridanisol was the only one to know that there was no need for the pistol to be loaded; it is the one with which La Pérouse had decided to commit suicide long since and which had remained loaded in its case. The police do not recover the pistol, which Georges has got rid of. The child's corruption finally gives way to horror, and he flings himself into the arms of his mother. —The book ends with a brief extract from Edouard's *Journal*. He will not use little Boris' suicide in his *Faux Monnayeurs*. After the scandal, Azaïs has had to disband the school. Old La Pérouse has fallen into a mystical despair: he regards cruelty as the first attribute of God, who "sacrificed his own son to save us." Bernard has returned to his father's house; Edouard begins to be interested in Bernard's young brother Caloub, whom he is very curious to meet . . .

The reader will have been struck, I imagine, by two characteristics of this composition: 1) the equilibrium which keeps these divergent plots going; 2) the occasionally wearisome discontinuity of the development. One gets tired of a diversity which constantly interrupts the progress of the narrative.

We can therefore understand why Gide should complain, in the *Journal des Faux Monnayeurs*, about "the extreme difficulty" he "suffers in making [his] book advance." Aside from the subject's complexity, he has imposed exceptional constraints upon himself: "With each chapter, I have to start over from scratch. Never take advantage of momentum—that is the rule of my game," and "the difficulty is not to construct the rest of my novel as an extension of the lines already drawn . . . a perpetual welling-forth; each new chapter must pose a new problem, be an overture, a new direction, an impulsion, a forward plunge of the reader's mind. But the latter must leave me, as the stone leaves the sling. I am even willing for it to return and strike me, like a boomerang."

Let us note, further, how Gide planned to end his novel: his book "will be concluded suddenly, not by the exhaustion of the subject, which must give the impression of being inexhaustible, but on the contrary by its enlargement and by a kind of evasion of its outline. It must not be stoppered, but squander itself, overflow . . ." He wanted somehow to cause it to re-enter the continuity of life itself.

The composition of *les Faux Monnayeurs* was laborious, but it was natural; it consisted of a spontaneous movement, a slow but sure growth, directed but not forced. In certain parts, at least, it seems to have taken a curious turn, to have gone in a regressive and justificatory direction, as the following notes from the *Journal des Faux Monnayeurs* bear witness: "A need to go farther and farther back in order to explain any given event. The slightest act requires an infinite motivation."

"My novel is developing in reverse, strangely enough. That is to say, I am constantly discovering that this or that, which has happened before, ought to be told. Consequently the chapters do not accumulate one after the other, but continually push further back the one I originally conceived as the first." One is reminded of a vegetal movement, taking root ever more deeply; add to this the observation that most of the chapters are, on the contrary, like bounds forward which suggest the drive of the sap that extends divergent branches, and one has a sufficiently distinct image of the organization —never abstract, pulsing with life—which under the appearance of intellect prevails over the flowering of the Gidean fiction. Intellect controls, but from without, in order to judge, or to suggest judgments; it is careful not to intervene. Hence there is nothing forced or artificial in this development. Gide may not be a novelist, but he is certainly a born storyteller. His plots are not manufactured. They animate themselves. And now we may examine the profound architecture of this strange novel.

8. Les Faux Monnayeurs
and the Art of the Novel (ii)

Any theory of the novel must contend with *les Faux Monnayeurs*, and this already suggests the importance of this work. Personally I am inclined to regard the novel as a product of the faculty of thought, not so much as it is directly exercised in science or philosophy, but become artistic. Intellect, acting aesthetically, effects this production of mental universes which are the worlds of Stendhal, Balzac, Flaubert, Zola; of Fielding, Defoe, Dickens, Thackeray; of Tolstoy and Dostoevsky; and which use the real universe only as raw material, a starting point. The original interpretation they give us is, ultimately, both very close to and very remote from it. Creation or re-creation—in any case an imaginary vision where the subjective manipulates the objective in its own way—the novel is indeed a metaphysic of the intellect.

That a work like *les Faux Monnayeurs* is charged with intellect is only too obvious. That it is altogether a novel is not so easy to decide. It seems rather a work in progress toward the novel, a creation which has stopped a little before the last stage of the novelistic progression. And there is in the subject itself a kind of reinforcement of this suspension. After all, Gide wanted to give us not so much *les Faux Monnayeurs* as the attempt of a novelist to extract it from the chaos of the real. In this sense, if we were to admit that Gide has entirely succeeded in treating this subtle subject, we might absolve ourselves critically by repeating that *les Faux Monnayeurs* is the novel of the novel. But we shall contest this claim a little later on.

If one considers *les Faux Monnayeurs* as an abstraction consisting of this self-reflection, one will find in it, I think, instead of a novel, the fragments of a novel curiously connected. Gide of course was not wrong to see in *les Faux Monnayeurs* the substance of half a dozen novels. Their integration has been carried quite far, and it is indisputable that he has established extremely close links between these several possible novels—which I prefer to denominate *récits*, quite similar by their purity of line to those we have already admired, but whose very clarity of development differentiates them from the complexity and even the diffusion proper to the true novel. One may wonder whether the interlinking of a dozen *récits* really constitutes a novel. It seems to me that a novel's architecture is of another order, although it is not easy to distinguish. But what is certain is that the spirit which presides over the conception of the whole is quite different. Which, perhaps, accounts for the somewhat sporadic, diffuse, flickering impression *les Faux Monnayeurs* makes as a whole.

But this brings me to a more direct contestation of the book. The metaphysic which dominates and controls the fictonal creation, (that may, as we recall, be distributed in a series of tales), and which in Gide's *récits*, as we have said, seems ruled by the notion of choice imprisoning the self in a formula—this metaphysic, in *les Faux Monnayeurs*, seems to come to a stop just before it becomes conscious of itself, just before the stage of affirmations. I don't mean by this that

Gide should have explained his ideas to us or sought to prove a thesis; that is an error of which his artistic sense was incapable; I mean that his vision of the world does not impose itself in his novel the way his earlier vision had emerged with such supple energy in his *récits*. That Gide exhibits a certain coquetry in letting his novel proceed in a dubitative mode is more than likely; but such discretion, such attenuating suggestions risk evaporating altogether. The fault may be the reader's, yet by playing so cunningly with him, is not the novelist in danger of betraying the meaning of his work itself for the sake of a surface approval?

"It is appropriate," Gide says in the *Journal des Faux Monnayeurs*, "quite unlike Meredith or James, to let the reader get the advantage over me, to deal with him in such a way as to allow him to think that he is more intelligent than the author, more moral, more perspicacious, and that he is discovering many things in the characters and many truths in the course of the narrative despite the author and, so to speak, without the author's knowing it."

A metaphysic is constituted by a group of assertions. Gide's appears instead to consist of a series of questions. This, moreover, is why he unsettles us. Actually he affords us less a new world than the necessity of remaking our own. He offers us less a vision of the universe than the persuasion to destroy the old one. "What would I like this novel to be?" he says in his *Journal*, "A crossroads, a rendezvous of problems."

These questions the author asks, leaving us free to answer them as we see fit, nonetheless conceal certain secret answers. Gide's metaphysic is an insinuating one, and one must be able to detect its clues. The reader recalls that beneath Renan's apparent skepticism lies a powerfully entrenched positivism. Similarly, beneath Gide's restlessness are hidden well-tried convictions. Since they are paradoxical, and since he intends us to

accept them (being himself extremely resistant to paradoxes), Gide attempts to seduce us and to suggest what
at first glance might offend us. He wants the seed cast
within us to sprout. A curious position for a novelist. It is
really a moralist's attitude, but camouflaged. Gide's is
not Bourget's ponderous *roman à thèse,* nor Huxley's
novel steeped in ideology, but, in fact, the critical novel.

Criticism is not so much expressed as tendentiously
inserted in the relations among the characters and in the
play of events. Destroying prejudices, awakening emotions, suggesting a new social and moral state—this
seems to be Gide's prescription for the novel, and we
see how it prevails in the work by what must be
called, strange as it may seem, Gide's moralizing side
(though he severely confines it within the limits of the
work of art). Further, we see how the social and psychological vision of the world constituted by the Gidean
criticism of our civilization's values (which would be
aesthetically sterile if it were content with being purely
negative, but which aims, on the contrary, at fecundity
because it explicitly, though discreetly, constitutes a
new set of values) permits the novelist all the same to
achieve an interpretative and individual delineation of
the real world. If Gide's *les Faux Monnayeurs* seems to
be above all a critical essay, it nonetheless conceals in its
substructure a very firm intellectual metaphysic—that is,
the indispensable basis for any novel worth the name.
But in Gide this basis is very difficult to see.

Gide has been careful to place his metaphysic only in
the implications of the work, in the resonance it wakens
in our consciousness. *Les Faux Monnayeurs* is a work
the author has singularly dominated, enveloped, and
isolated from himself.

Gide has done this by accompanying the problems
with quite practical suggestions that are equivalent to
answers, to *advice.* The double play of implicit satire
and disguised praise, or else the author's declared sym-

pathies and antipathies for his characters, the skillful
dosage of approval and reproach he administers as he
metes out an impartial justice to these beings suggest
that *les Faux Monnayeurs* is another *sotie*. There is an
echo of *Prométhée* in Edouard's dialogue with Bernard
about the role of ideas that live at men's expense, and
Bernard's resolute character frequently reminds us of
Lafcadio's spirit of initiative: he is a Lafcadio who will
come out all right. The critique of human action in all
its forms extends, with greater scope, Gide's first ironic
work, and shows us, in the riper *Faux Monnayeurs*,
something like the *Paludes* of a fifty-year-old man.

Les Faux Monnayeurs can be made to reveal an entire critique of man and of institutions: family, marriage,
education, religion. The condemnations would be counterbalanced and ultimately complemented by secret rec-
ommendations. Indeed, our entire tradition would be
shaken by them; an outlined philosophy of novelty, of
progress, would be involved too. But Gide, who refuses
to be taken in, is well aware that even the spirit of revolt
is subject to ankylosis, and in his *Journal des Faux Monnayeurs* he expresses a profound notion, that of a great
novelist indeed, when he resolves, if he is to write a second novel, to show better than he has done in *les Faux
Monnayeurs* that "many acts of one generation find their
explanation in the generation that follows . . . the way
one generation, after having criticized and reproached
the conjugal gestures and attitudes, for instance, of its
predecessor, finds itself obliged to repeat virtually the
same ones."

The most surprising commendation to be discerned in
les Faux Monnayeurs, though one close to Gide's heart,
for he devoted many pages of *Si le Grain ne meurt . . .*
and the entire argument of *Corydon* to it, is that of
pederasty. Here Gide's talent and his sense of understatement serve him admirably. One can say, even
though there is not one moment of ambiguity in *les*

Faux Monnayeurs, there is still not one word that shocks the reader in Edouard's affairs or in Robert de Passavant's brief *amour* with Olivier. Many readers will have been completely hoodwinked. Gide's intention has been to "normalize" the erotic relations between persons of the male sex within the novel, and Edouard's conversations with Olivier—his initial annoyance, his delight at the end—incontestably renew the dialogue of lovers with a freshness that makes us forget entirely the scabrous side of the subject. Pauline's conversation with Edouard concerning Olivier, tendentious as it is, manages, by the power of art, we might say—but is it not rather by the power of conviction?—to appear both natural and plausible. Gide's sincerity has been all the more unobtrusive for being so complete and of such disarming frankness.

We see how in Gide the insinuation of doubt and anxiety prepares the way for rebellion and reform. His vision of the world is above all a condemnation, with as much bearing on the individual as on society, and is naturally completed by a therapeutic quite vague in its expression but distinct in its basic assumptions. Whatever his conception of it, reality interests him less in itself than for its possibilities of transformation, its future. One might suppose that a true novelist would be less of a pedagogue and a reformer. Whatever the case, if we wish to discern the principle axes of the Gidean speculation concerning the world, it seems to me that out of the host of problems raised by *les Faux Monnayeurs* we must concern ourselves with the following three:

1) *The value of evil.* Gide manifests a certain complacency toward evil, and he has been reproached for the maliciousness, the cruelty of his book. I think this is an error; if one looks carefully, one finds kindness in it instead, though obviously under a somewhat aggressive guise, as is sometimes the case with truly active charity. Gide's indulgence of evil is no doubt the artist's demonic attraction he has described, but it is still more

the conviction that evil is a force, a force not to be found in apathy and resignation, a force that can become a factor of progress. Still, the virtue of evil must be adjusted and controlled (and this is what is effected in the case of Bernard, whose disturbing early peccadilloes are utterly indulged by Edouard and give way to an irreproachable generosity). Gide does not take sides with evil, but he watches for an opportunity to reform it.

2) *The destiny of men.* Throughout the book Gide is extremely attentive to what life does with individuals, or rather what individuals do with life. It must be admitted that almost all of them ruin it, and that it almost always spoils them. Consider the deplorable end of most of the characters in *les Faux Monnayeurs.* Bernard wins the author's predilection because he does not aim at any particular goal; like Gide's characteristic heroes, he attempts to navigate in the open sea and become himself. But the weak will do better to stay where they are. And there is a fine gallery of them in the book. One might catalogue the characters in *les Faux Monnayeurs* as a function of their bearing in confronting life.

3) *Real and apparent values.* This is the very symbol of *les Faux Monnayeurs,* obvious in cases of false values, like Passavant or old Azaïs, but which extends to others like Lady Griffith and applies more subtly, in more or less measured doses, to most of the characters, even to Edouard, for any action which exceeds its intention (Edouard's amiability), any words which exceed their thought (Olivier's boastfulness), any feeling which exceeds its conviction (Douviers' jealousy), any kind of hypocrisy, introduces counterfeit coin into the commerce of men; and we are all, in some respect, counterfeiters. Gide has even given us the caricature of his demonetizing project: Strouvilhou's exaggerated scheme

to ruin true values. Strouvilhou effects a devaluation, whereas Passavant is content to produce inflation.

The general effect of these views seems to testify to a great pessimism, yet nothing of the kind is true; under this severe appearance Gide's *élan* maintains a latent yet controlling optimism, for which his love of youth and fascination with the future are, in the novel itself, a sure guarantee. But the disequilibrium between whatever consternation the book seems to present—particularly in the accumulation of disasters at the end—and the secret youthfulness behind its inspiration may, indeed, deceive the reader; from this irritating brew, one must manage to concoct a tonic.

We shall be quite surprised, in other respects—apart from one or two paradoxes for which Gide is unlikely to win many adherents—to find at the basis of this critique a eulogy of good sense. This is what the author claims for himself as opposed to his heroes—for the sympathy he does not withhold, especially from those most different from himself, never keeps him from judging them: "What is missing in each of my heroes, whom I have carved from my own flesh, is that drop of good sense that keeps me from carrying their follies as far as they do."

Reflection reveals that criticism—or the implicit metaphysic which nourishes it—has determined the structure and the composition of *les Faux Monnayeurs*. Nor would it be difficult to demonstrate that this structure is the ultimate expression of one of Gide's earliest tendencies.

There is a curious passage in *la Prisonnière* where Proust remarks, apropos of the composer Vinteuil, "Perhaps it is this unknown, individual quality no other composer had ever revealed . . . which is the most authentic proof of genius, much more than the content of the work itself," and, applying the notion to literature: "The great literary creators have never written more than a single work, or rather have merely refracted, through various mediums, the same beauty which they bring into the world." And he seeks this characteristic in images that reveal their author's secret: in Stendhal, it is a "certain feeling of altitude" which is linked "to the life of the spirit; the high place where Julian Sorel is confined, the tower on top of which Fabrice is jailed, the steeple where the Abbé Blanès studies astrology and from which Fabrice has such a splendid view."

I propose to apply this profound intuition of Proust's to Gide's work. By doing so, we discover an attitude, or rather a certain spiritual image, which frequently strikes us in his work. It is not simply a certain duplication of the self, although this too plays a great role in Gide, who makes the individual an observer of himself —what Benjamin Constant, whose admirable *Adolphe*, by its pitiless clarity and its preoccupation with truth in delineation, reminds us of Gide's *récits*, called: "That portion of ourselves which is so to speak the spectator of the other." It is much more the reduplication of the object *within itself*.

Everyone knows those bottles on the label of which is printed a picture of that same bottle in miniature, so that the observer can lose himself in infinity if this image is pursued further. Whence a tendency to false complication, but at the same time a gain in inner resonance. Though Gide conceived this imaginative schema early in his career, it continued to be functional. In 1893 he notes: "I like discovering in a work of art . . . transposed to the scale of the characters, the very subject of that work. Nothing illuminates it better and establishes more surely all the proportions of the whole. Thus in certain paintings by Memling or Quentin Metsys, a tiny dark convex mirror reflects the interior of the room where the scene painted occurs. Similarly in Velásquez' 'Meninas' (though in a different way). Finally, in literature, in *Hamlet*'s play within the play, and in many other dramas. In *Wilhelm Meister*, the marionette scenes or the parties at the château. In *The Fall of the House of Usher*, the passage Roderick is reading, etc. None of these examples is entirely fair. What would be much more so, what would say better what it was I wanted in my *Cahiers*, in my *Narcisse* and in my *Tentative*, is the comparison with that method in heraldry which consists of putting a second blazon in the center of the first, *en abyme*."

How many times Gide will be tempted by composition *en abyme!* The reader will recall Ménalque's playing, though more harshly, in *l'Immoraliste* and *les Nourritures*, the very game of Michel or of the young hedonist. He will recall the hero of *Paludes* writing *Paludes*, just as the hero of *les Faux Monnayeurs* is writing *les Faux Monnayeurs* and, in a parodic mode, the bourgeois novelist of *les Caves du Vatican* supposes he can imagine an inconsistent hero whose model Lafcadio has furnished him. In the works where this repetition of the subject does not give the composition its form, we can at least find frequent traces of this attitude: Prométhée's lecture sums up, in a sense, the entire book . . . I suspect one could even discern in certain of Gide's sentences the stamp of this spontaneous method of his mind, that genius for reprise which gives his thought a kind of double awareness. And if he does not establish it within the work, he will sometimes recall it by a sign (in *le Retour de l'enfant prodigue*, is not the kneeling figure of the donor a vestige of this need for a double investiture?), or else he will suggest it to the attentive reader by a host of passages from his *Journal*, where he manifests toward each of his books a curious concern to situate it in the ensemble of his work and in the harmony of his diverse intentions.

Each individual work of Gide's within the whole

oeuvre, each part of Gide which has expressed itself in a work in relation to the entire concert of Gide's personality, plays this role of blazon within blazon. The young Gide's imperious need to *represent* has been delegated to all his works, each of which distinguishes itself from the others and yet symbolizes, by its harmonics or the complements which it implies or suggests, the totality of a thought whose complexity intends each fragment to bear its sign. It is somewhat true of Gide's artistic creation as of Leibnitz' world, that each monad is representative of it and repeats it in its own fashion. What else is that fondness for intimate journals, manifested not only in Gide's life but in a number of his characters—Alissa, the pastor of *la Symphonie pastorale*, the heroine of *l'École des Femmes*—but proof of this need for reduplication of the object, to gain a better scrutiny of it of course, but above all to transpose it to a higher level. So that if, finally, it is critical curiosity which initiates the doubling, it is really an aesthetic aspiration which is its effective force. This creative will is so powerful in Gide—perhaps the more so for being in conflict with a relative indigence of imagination—that it has somehow shifted its object within itself, not content to create a work (so arduously with regard to matter, so easily with regard to form), but compelling him to set within this work still another image of his desire. As *les Nourritures* is a kind of poem filled with poems, so his novel must comprehend the idea of the novel. It is surprising that in his plays Gide has not devised, like Rotrou in his *Saint-Genest* or Shakespeare in *Hamlet*, a play within a play, a stage on the stage, with a relation between the two—for, after all, it is indeed this double structure with the kind of relationship it affords which gives *les Faux Monnayeurs* its characteristic physiognomy.

We have noted Gide's predilection for indirect presentation of character in the *récit*. We might say that it is the novel as a whole that he approaches indirectly. He finds it profoundly repugnant to proceed, like the realists, by direct imitation or by reproduction. Bernard, apropos of Edouard's project, declares: "A good novel is written more naïvely than that. First of all, you have to believe in the story you're telling . . . and tell it quite simply." This opinion, which is perhaps that of common sense, is not at all that of an artist. But perhaps the great novelist is not essentially an artist; indeed it appears that in a Balzac, a Dickens, a Dostoevsky, or even a Proust, many purely aesthetic preoccupations have often been relegated to the background or sometimes even vanished completely. "Too much an artist to be a novelist" will be the objection to Gide. And the case of artist-novelists like Meredith or James or even Flaubert may perhaps apply this counterproof, that the perfection they introduced into the genre was at the expense of power. A classicism of the novel— as one might admire it in Flaubert, for instance—involves an art of sacrifices, which elsewhere (in poetry, in the drama) affords only advantages, but which in this kind of fiction that competes with life results in an impoverishment.

The novel is the genre which by nature repudiates purity. In the *Journal des Faux Monnayeurs* Gide writes: "Purge the novel of all the elements which do not specifically belong to the novel . . . as for this pure novel, no one . . . has written it . . ." and he adds, after various developments: "putting all that in Edouard's mouth . . . would permit me to add that I do not agree with him in every detail; . . . I doubt if a novel purer than Mérimée's *La double Méprise* could be imagined." The choice of this latter example sufficiently testifies that the pure novel would be the skeletal novel. Gide has stated elsewhere that by the pure novel he meant the refusal to make use of what could be expressed by better means: painting, the cinema, even the phonograph—but this opposes only the realism that unimaginatively attempts to reproduce nature and merely reaffirms the necessity of the arbitrary in artistic recreation; Gide does not mean that the novelist's universe must be drained of the material world and reduced to psychological life. Gide avoids descriptions, portraits, and neglects particularizing his heroes physically: this is a preference, but one that cannot be made into a law.

A certain tendency to schematization in developments is therefore added to the internal complication of the plot of *les Faux Monnayeurs*. This is what gives the work that contradictory aspect of richness and dryness. Actually we find here the same quest for clarity, an art of drawing, of etching, which appears in the composition itself, whose entanglement is due only to the interlacing of two series: the basic narration of facts and the analysis of the attempt to integrate them into a fiction. Gide explains in the *Journal des Faux Monnayeurs:* "Strictly speaking, the book has no one center around which my efforts converge; it is around two points, as in an ellipse, that these efforts are polarized. On the one hand, the event, the fact, the external datum; on the other, the very effort of the novelist to make a book out of it all. And that is the chief subject, the new focus which throws the narrative off center and turns it toward the imaginative. In short, I see this notebook in which I am writing the history of the book itself put whole into the book, forming its principal interest, for the greater irritation of the reader."

We thus discover the shiftiness for which we reproach the author: "the novelist's effort to make a book out of it all" has constantly tended to become "this notebook in which I am writing the history of the book itself"; whereas the subject, for us, would have consisted in interlacing with the narrated reality not the account of the novelist's failures to make a novel out of that reality, but the novel itself—however different—which reality would have suggested to him.

If *les Faux Monnayeurs* is the novel of the novel, it is also the novel of the novelist. In it one learns how to write a novel, and also how not to write a novel. A phrase from the *Journal*, dated 1893, might serve as an epigraph to the story of Edouard at grips with his work: "I wanted to show, in this *Tentative amoureuse*, the book's influence on the person writing it, and during this very act of writing." Like the writer of *Paludes*, Edouard multiplies the points of view concerning his project. Here is how Gide, in the *Journal des Faux Monnayeurs*, judges this attitude: "Each time Edouard is called upon to explain the plan of his novel, he speaks of it in a different way. In short, he is bluffing; he is fundamentally afraid he will never be able to finish it." Gide has insisted on Edouard's incapacity to finish his book. He is even more severe toward him than the uncoached reader would be, for at last, at the moment of great joy Olivier gives him, Edouard, his imagination inflamed, glimpses the whole of his book, and in one sitting he writes the first thirty pages of *les Faux Monnayeurs* with the same ease as Gide. We are therefore somewhat surprised at the condemnation his creator levels at him: "Furthermore, as far as this pure novel is concerned, he will never manage to write it." Gide gives us the reasons for this failure, but not in *les Faux Monnayeurs*, only in the *Journal des Faux Monnayeurs*: "I must be careful to respect in Edouard everything that makes him unable to write his book. He understands many things, but is constantly in pursuit of himself through everything and everyone. True devotion is almost impossible for him. He is an amateur, a *raté*. A character all the harder to establish since I am giving him a good deal of myself; I have to step back and put him at some distance from myself in order to see him properly." An extremely interesting passage that shows

ANDRÉ GIDE

how Gide insists on distinguishing himself from a character we might too easily identify with him. It must
be said that the other characters in the novel also seem
to think that Edouard will not write his book, and that
he himself appears to doubt as much for a moment, but
then one wonders if this failure does not run counter to
the novel's chief intention: the novelist's effort to make
a novel out of reality. It is true that we will not read
Edouard's *Faux Monnayeurs,* and this is perhaps on account of his defection, but in that case his failure seems
to be chiefly Gide's.

Whatever the case, Edouard's preoccupations provide the substance of a charming comedy situated, as
we should expect, in the very center of the book
(chapter three of the second part), and whose verve
is dazzling. It is the conversation in which he explains
to Sophroniska, Laura, and Bernard what *les Faux
Monnayeurs* will be and concerning which he notes in
his *Journal:* "I said nothing but asininities."

The reader will perhaps recall that I remarked apropos of Gide's *récits* that by putting them together one
might make a novel out of them. And by analyzing *les
Faux Monnayeurs* in a certain way, anatomizing the
book and separating the destinies mingled in it, one
might obtain a certain number of independent *récits.*
There would be—aside from the novel of the novel as we
have just seen—Edouard's amours, the story of Laura
and Douviers, the wrecking of Vincent by a femme fa-
tale (Lady Griffith), the old age of La Pérouse, the story
of Boris . . . The defect of some of these, perhaps, is
that they are so easily detachable (the entire story of La
Pérouse is told in a series of visits made by Edouard to
his old piano teacher, and these moving conversations
are among the most beautiful pages in the book). I do
not think that a true novel allows itself to be dissected
in this way. Of course Gide has proliferated connec-

tions among these various plots. But he has had some
difficulty doing so. He has made a great effort to relate
his characters. Edouard declares that he sees his own
as "orphans." As for the links between their destinies, I
am afraid that they are occasionally quite artificial.
There are certainly preparations which lack any veri-
similitude. Why does little Boris, sent after his cure to
the Vedel boarding school, fall back into the old habits
so deleterious to his health? Because one of his schoolmates, Ghéridanisol, shows him again the text of the
"talisman" attached to these practices and which Sophroniska had had such difficulty getting him to abandon
during his cure in Switzerland. Ghéridanisol, who has
obscure designs, gets this talisman from his cousin
Strouvilhou. Yet who will believe that the doctor, who
knows the psychoanalytic importance of this parchment, has let it out of her hands so readily? "I have
asked her," Edouard notes, "to show me this famous
talisman. She tells me that she no longer has it, that
she gave it to someone who was interested in Boris and
who had asked her for it as a souvenir. 'A certain Monsieur Strouvilhou, whom I met here some time before
your arrival.'" I also suggest as quite contestable the
incident of the lost cloakroom ticket without which
Bernard could not steal Edouard's suitcase, read his
journal, and thereby intervene in his life and Laura's.
It is quite surprising, too, that it should be precisely at
Saas Fée that Bernard gets hold of a counterfeit coin
which will permit him to effect a brilliant flank attack
in the discussion of the novel.

However far a novelist may be from realism, it is inevitable that his creation should borrow much from his
times and his personal experience. And Gide himself
had indicated, in various places, a good share of the
sources of his novel: the gang in the Luxembourg (from
the *Journal de Rouen* and *Le Figaro* of September

1906), the affair of the anarchist counterfeiters in 1907, the provoked suicide of young Nény, a student at the Lycée Blaise-Pascal in Clermont-Ferrand (1909), which inspired Boris' tragic death, the letter from Ch. B. on suicide and happiness which is the starting-point of Olivier's false suicide, Gide's encounter with a student from the Lycée Henri-IV stealing a book from a book-stall (May 2, 1921), which happened just in time to establish the beginning of little Georges' corruption, and a number of details noted as the circumstances occurred, like the fat lady who never finished her sentences, a *tic* Gide attributed to his pastor's wife. Lady Griffith's story about the wreck of the *Bourgogne* includes authentic details. Without elaborating this search for sources which, as Gide says, transforms certain academic criticism into a kind of detective work, one can compare Laura's story with Gide's allusions in his *Journal* (January 11, 1923) to the "drama" that calls him to E——'s side, particularly since he connects it with several pages of Edouard's *Journal* concerning the interpretation of events. "This exclamation: 'A proper religious education would have kept her from doing that' might be said in a tone of regret, of reproach, as well as of approval, and would signify either 'What luck!' 'How fortunate that . . . ! !' or 'What a shame!'"

But it is his youth in particular which furnished Gide a rich subject matter. It matters little that he tells us, in the *Journal des Faux Monnayeurs:* "The best parts of my book are those of pure invention. If I spoiled the portrait of old La Pérouse, it is because I brought it too close to reality; I neither knew how nor was able to lose sight of my model. The account of that first visit should be done over. La Pérouse will not come to life and I will really see him only when he has completely replaced his original. Nothing so far has given me so much trouble. The difficulty is to invent when your memory holds you back." "Have completely reworked

this chapter which I think is now quite good." Yet the
scenes with La Pérouse are unanimously considered the
best in the book—and I think it is because they are
most heavily ballasted with reality. Gide has written
movingly, in *Si le Grain ne meurt* . . . and in his *Journal*, about his old piano teacher. Indeed the visits to
La Pérouse are almost too perfect—as polished as the
famous scene of Uzès Protestant hospitality in *Si le
Grain ne meurt* . . . Connoisseurs of the future will
not look for Gide here, any more than they seek Flaubert in anthology pieces like the "Mercenaries' Banquet" or the scene of the farm exhibition, but turn to
more secret, less obviously shellacked pages. The pages
on La Pérouse are Gide's *récit de Théramène*. That
Gide has been embarrassed by the proximity of his
models does not mean that he has failed to take advantage of his familiarity with them. This is what gives
such full and true resonance to the evocation of *milieux*
he has managed to resuscitate, without any physical description *à la* Balzac, but by a purely moral reconstruction, as in the extraordinary atmosphere of the Azaïs
boarding school, where the meager and futile virtues of
puritanism mask a ferment of vices, deviations, and
hypocrisies. We note the lively accuracy of the conversations between students or schoolboys which at one
end touch the second-rate *avant-garde* literary circles
so brilliantly reconstituted in the *Argonautes* banquet,
and at the other the underworld which we glimpse
through several chinks in the narrative and which Judge
Profitandieu will have to deal with.

In a page of the *Journal des Faux Monnayeurs*, Gide
offers sympathy as the key to his work, but it is a
sympathy aroused especially by what differs from himself: "It is certainly easier for me to make a character
speak than to express myself *in propria persona;* especially when the character I am creating differs most
from me." This remark helps to explain the coldness of

Edouard's character. Gide has obviously given him a good deal of himself. We find, in Gide's work or in his *Journal,* traces of a number of remarks he has put in his hero's mouth. I shall limit myself to one example: Edouard advises Olivier, who writes poetry, to let himself be guided by the words, and himself comments on this advice in his *Journal;* we find this idea, with a quite different, and far richer, development, expressed with regard to Chopin, who let himself be guided by the notes, in the opusculum entitled *Caractères.* But Gide has put himself in all his characters. The biologist Vincent's remark on the development of terminal buds to the detriment of the rest derives from a note of Gide's in his *Journal,* where he observes from his salon window the birds pecking at the new buds in the garden. When we have a good critical edition of *les Faux Monnayeurs,* the abundance of texts to be compared will give the notes a considerable importance and utility, and the work's meaning will be noticeably deepened thereby. We shall see that *les Faux Monnayeurs* is Gide's most completely representative work, the *summa* of his thought, at least until he explicitly turns to social problems.

A character like Armand, much less important than Edouard, is nonetheless one of the most intense Gide has created. Reality had come to his assistance somewhat with the recollection of a certain Armand B—— whom he had known and already sketched in *Si le Grain ne meurt . . .* but whom he must have endowed with the experience of his days of discouragement, impotence, or disgust. To nourish on oneself a character who is *not* oneself appears to be the attitude of the novelist who wants to maintain the life of imaginary beings—without, however, incurring the reproach of never describing anyone but himself. But, as in the unborn child, it is not easy to distinguish what is his own from what he inherits from his mother. "I have little difficulty understanding the formation of an imaginary character, and from what self-rejection it is made," Gide says energetically, apropos of Passavant and of Vincent, but the phrase is particularly instructive applied to Passavant; this is the character whom Gide most detests; in him he castigates the opposite of his own nature and consequently, perhaps, a trace of that nature as well. Otherwise he would feel only indifference toward him. But one must also not forget that Passavant represents an exasperating species of false artists who live only for immediate success. *Les Faux Monnayeurs* is not a *roman à clef,* but one might inscribe several names, or one name, more or less plausibly above Passavant's countenance.

Le Journal des Faux Monnayeurs affords us a wealth of precious information as to the way in which Gide conceives of the invention of his characters. Edouard, in a fragment which has not gone into the novel, confides his embarrassment to Lafcadio; he sees each of his heroes as "an orphan, an only son, a bachelor, and childless." He is hard put to furnish them with families and social situations. This reflects Gide's attitude, when he writes in his own *Journal* of the "enormous effort" he must make "to bring his characters to life and endow them with real relationships." It is important to interpret these remarks on his characters properly, for they are more explicit than the text of the novel itself. Lady Griffith is a character who "should remain somewhat outside the book. She has no moral existence, nor even, strictly speaking, any personality . . ." "Bernard: his character still uncertain. At the beginning, completely insubordinate. Becomes motivated, defined and limited throughout the book, thanks to his love affairs. Each love, each adoration involves a devotion, a dedication. He can be in despair over this at first, but soon realizes that it is only by limiting his field of action that he can define it clearly.

"Olivier: his character gradually distorted. He commits actions profoundly contrary to his nature and tastes, out of spite and violence. An abominable disgust with himself is the result. The progressive blunting of his personality—his brother Vincent is the same (stress the defeat of his virtue at the moment when he begins to win at gambling). I have not been able to indicate this clearly enough.

"Vincent and Olivier have quite fine and noble instincts and plunge into life with a lofty vision of what they must do—but they have weak characters and let themselves be deflected. Bernard, on the contrary, reacts against each influence and fights back. —Misdeal: Edouard should have adopted Olivier, it is Olivier whom he loved."

Gide actually questions himself as to the future of his characters, at least of those who have a future. About Bernard he wonders, "Will he be able to rise to the point of accepting, assuming the contradictions of his too-rich nature?" And the reader will recall the entire chapter at the end of the second part devoted to a review of his heroes and their destiny.

Gide attempts to live with his characters, to separate them from himself in such a way as to receive unexpected impressions from them, as from strangers. He is astonished, for instance, to find Profitandieu more interesting than he thought and abruptly decides to "redraw him altogether."

But perhaps what most illuminates Gide's relations with his characters is a letter to Charles Du Bos, reprinted in the miscellany *Divers*, where he contrasts Dostoevsky with Henry James: "The secret of the great novelist lies not in his control of situations, but rather in the multiplicity of his inner possibilities." He must be "in connivance" with his heroes. This sense of complicity is perhaps the basis of Gide's entire aesthetic. I would complete it with his capacity for detachment.

Ultimately there is always this same mixture of sympathy and clear-sighted intelligence with an eternal human curiosity.

In order to introduce us to a character's state of mind, Gide observes a dramatist's principle: seek "the direct expression . . . some phrase . . . directly revealing his inner state—rather than describing that state." He reduces the amount of psychological analysis in favor of dramatic expression. His salutary doctrine is also a precautionary one: "Be careful to keep a character talking only to the person to whom he is speaking." "Never discuss ideas save as a function of temperaments and characters." It is also a dramatist's notion that influences him, at the beginning of the third part, "to bring each of his characters downstage in turn and give him the place of honor for a moment." The reader will have noticed the considerable amount of room taken up by dialogue in *les Faux Monnayeurs*. This abundance is opposed to the extreme scarcity of descriptions. The success of these dialogues is at least equal—perhaps even superior, by their naturalness and vitality—to that of the *récits*. It is because all of Gide's dialogues are *heard*. A crucial page of the *Journal des Faux Monnayeurs* details Gide's aesthetic on this point—we might call Gide an acoustic novelist, as opposed to optical novelists like the Goncourts: "The bad novelist constructs his characters; he directs them and makes them talk. The true novelist listens to them and watches them act; he eavesdrops on them before he knows them, and it is from what he overhears that he gradually understands who they are . . . I perceive the least inflections of their voices with the utmost clarity."

Alongside this variety and veracity of conversation in his characters, Gide's own style in *les Faux Monnayeurs* is utterly severe. He has aimed at the greatest simplicity. The style, he notes in the *Journal des Faux Mon-*

nayeurs in March 1924, "must offer no surface interest, no 'modeling.' Everything must be said in the flattest manner, which will make the prestidigitators say: what do you find to admire in that?" And Gide's own *Journal*, as early as 1921: "*currente calamo . . .* that is how this book must be written." It has even been rumored that Gide wanted to write *les Faux Monnayeurs* badly. I scarcely need say that he has not succeeded. He has succeeded only in freeing himself from a certain formal coquetry, a certain preciosity which still persisted in his works. Written in a tone less *sustained* than *Si le Grain ne meurt . . . , les Faux Monnayeurs* is the simplest in style of Gide's works of imagination. He will later carry this style, in *Oedipe* for example, to the point of dryness.

But if the narrative that connects the dialogues is of a refreshing ease and rapidity, we must consider separately the author's asides. For despite the advice of Roger Martin du Gard and contrary to the lesson of Flaubert, Gide often comments on his heroes' actions or thought. It is the manner of Stendhal. It seems to me that these reflections—and even as early as *les Caves*—are rather affected and less effective than Gide's reserve or the suggestions he is so skillful at inserting between the lines, in the spaces between paragraphs, in the margins of the text. As important as what Gide tells us about his characters is what he does *not* say. Gide has introduced into the novel, already expressive and developed as a genre, the spirit of litotes, an understatement more proper to poetry and sometimes to tragedy. He confides in the reader in order to extend the indications of the text in his mind: "It is no use explaining throughout the book what the careful reader has understood; that is to insult him." The entire book must ultimately produce an analogous effect: "Once my book is finished, I draw the line and leave it up to the reader to perform the operation; addition, subtraction, it matters little; I don't believe it is my responsibility. So much the worse for the lazy reader: I want others. To disturb, that is my role."

The entire clandestine side of *les Faux Monnayeurs* has thus been treated tacitly. Whereas Proust described homosexuality in two ways, only one of which was open: directly in characters like Charlus, by transposition when he converted young men into *jeunes filles en fleurs*, Gide has completely parenthesized the affairs of Edouard or of Passavant with Olivier.

Edouard's dawning interest in Caloub is a marvel of an evasive conclusion. Even as early as *les Caves*, the conclusion remained in suspense. The *récits*, on the contrary, come to explicit ends. No doubt Gide sees in this an essential difference between the novel and the tale: the tale ends as an episode whose closed outline is inscribed once and for all in our experience, while the novel, like life itself, does not end. "Could be continued" is what we are expressly told of *les Faux Monnayeurs*.

The strongest ambition which tempted Gide in writing *les Faux Monnayeurs* was the one that has haunted all great novelists: the return to the epic. "Why conceal it from myself: what tempts me is the epic genre. . . . Until now the novel in every country has always clung to reality." And there is in *les Faux Monnayeurs* an occasional striving for the epic tone. It has not been a happy one. "*Les Faux Monnayeurs*, or the Temptation of the Epic," Gide would have said in the days of his little treatises.

He has tried to introduce, from the book's beginning, a fantastic and supernatural element, to make the Jardin du Luxembourg into "a place as legendary as Shakespeare's Forest of Arden." We are far from the mark. Despite the ambitions of Lucien Bercail, Bernard's young poet friend who proposes to take the Luxembourg for the subject of one of his poems, Gide's Lux-

embourg is less mythological than that of Anatole
France.

Gide has also tried to give the devil a role in his
novel. But too often the demon seems merely a manner
of speaking; when Bernard, for example, is impelled by
curiosity to read his mother's correspondence, it is impossible to regard his temptation as an epic personifica-
tion of Satan. It is especially in Vincent's story that the
devil is called in to the rescue; he deceives Vincent,
makes him hand his brother over to Passavant, and
finally possesses him to the point where Vincent, gone
mad, takes himself for the devil. We cannot believe as
much. In the appendix to the *Journal des Faux Monnayeurs* Gide gives us a strange and sophistic *Identification du démon,* a draft of which, in this same *Journal,*
he announced under the title of a *Traité de la non-
existence du diable.* "The more one denies him, the
more reality one gives him . . . Could well become the
central subject of the entire book, that is, the invisible
point around which everything would gravitate . . .
Success in the worst, and deterioration of the most exquisite qualities," and farther on: "Why do you fear
me? You know perfectly well I 'don't exist' . . . this very
important phrase, one of the keystones of the book."
Finally he would like "one character [the devil] to
circulate incognito throughout the entire book, his reality growing stronger the less he was believed in." We
see the importance Gide attached to this introduction
of the demon into his book. He has utterly failed at it.
The entire demoniac aspect (so successful in *Saül*) is inadequate in *les Faux Monnayeurs.* It should either have
been suppressed (bringing the book closer to a modern
conception of life) or else presented more openly (as a
Catholic novelist might have done), but not insinuated
so timidly; we can grant that it was quite difficult to
proceed as directly as Milton.

When Gide has Bernard meet an angel (we didn't
know Bernard believed in angels) and wrestle with him

all night long, we have the impression of *veneer* as indisputably as in Chateaubriand's supernatural scenes in *Les Natchez*.

Nothing is supernatural save when it is real, or considered as such. That is why we readily accept mystical little Bronja's seeing angels, or old and despairing La Pérouse's imagining God as a torturer; but then we are no longer in the epic, we are in the psychological novel.

The only epic tendencies which one might consider with a certain tolerance occur in several passages of a special tone, where a certain poetic freedom functions, thanks to which the author, the poet, surveys events from on high, passes from one place to another, utilizes chronological coincidences and hastens the march of time: "It is the hour when Laura, after having wept and groaned for a long time in her wretched hotel room is about to fall asleep. On the deck of the ship taking him back to France, Edouard, at the first gleam of dawn, rereads the letter he has received from her, a plaintive letter in which she begs him to help her. Already the gentle shore of his native land is in sight, but through the fog it takes an experienced eye to discern it. Not a cloud in the sky, where God's countenance will smile. The eyelid of the reddening horizon is already rising. How hot it will be in Paris! It is time to get back to Bernard. Here he is, waking up in Olivier's bed." These amusing passages are really not much more than trifles and not even particularly well attuned to the acuity of the novel's tone. It is not enough to turn one's back on realism to assume the epic tone. Gide has a critical mentality, not an epic one.

If there were an unreal character to whom one might be tempted to grant poetic dignity in *les Faux Monnayeurs*, it would be one comparable to the Comic Spirit that circulates in Meredith's novels—it would be, indeed, the Critical Spirit; but this delegate of the author's would be quite anti-epic in temperament; it is, indeed, the personal enemy of the supernatural, and if it understands poetry, it has nothing poetic about it. Besides, it too would be only a personified metaphor.

At first Gide wanted to make *les Faux Monnayeurs* a *summa* of his experience, but in the course of events he was obliged to reduce an ambition that would have strained the most flexible of artistic genres. Early in 1921 he writes in the *Journal des Faux Monnayeurs:* "In order to write this book properly, I must convince myself that it is the only novel and the last book I shall write. I want to pour everything into it without reservation." But in his own *Journal,* at the end of the same year: "My book will not succeed until I can get rid of the conviction that it is my last, that I shall write no others. I shall find it easier to suppress parasitical elements if I have confidence that I can put them elsewhere. In the material heaped up before me, there is enough to nourish half a dozen novels." The artist, who knows the art of sacrifices, has won out. The book still remains very full. Let us not complain that *les Faux Monnayeurs* is too rich a book, and let us confess that it is not an overloaded one. There are, on the contrary, few novels which, though of similar complexity, have such ease of manner. One can get lost in it, but one circulates easily throughout. The control of the elements set in motion is perfect, perhaps too perfect. The characters do not escape their creator, and the events do not carry him away in spite of himself. On the contrary, one is rather tempted to reproach *les Faux Monnayeurs* for its sobriety. Gide is so apprehensive of excess, so eager to leave us hungry for more that too often we should like a little more development, a little more analysis, a little more transition. I know this is precisely the contrary of what Gide desired, and it is certainly quite gratifying to see him leaving it up to the reader to imagine what he does not tell, to understand what he

merely sketches, to divine what he suggests, and to link
discontinuities or extend latent intentions . . . It is an
agreeable exercise for the mind, a stimulant for its
sloth. But one may wonder if this mental gymnastic
constitutes one of the pleasures of the novel. I am afraid
that the interest we take in it, though of a reassuring
alacrity, diverts to this technique of comprehension a
pleasure which should rather focus on the work's essence. And for this reason, though Gide's art is extremely engaging, I suspect that his characters and
their vicissitudes, with perhaps two or three exceptions,
touch us much less. There is a disequilibrium in interest which would be less prejudicial were it reversed;
if characters and events were closer to our hearts, we
would more readily excuse any clumsiness of technique
or even lack of zest in the presentation, or subtlety in
critical illumination.

In *Un esprit non prévenu*, Gide expresses his confidence in the fate reserved for his major work: "They
persist in calling *les Faux Monnayeurs* a failure. The
same thing was said at first of *l'Education sentimentale*
and *The Possessed* . . . In ten or twenty years, it will
be admitted that what my book is reproached for today
are its rarest qualities." Of course *les Faux Monnayeurs*
is not a failure. Of course its qualities are of the rarest.
But even so, it is perhaps not a novel—neither a pure
novel, if there is such a thing, nor above all a completed novel. It is a magnificent *récit*, encumbered with
a novelized aesthetic and insidiously contaminated by a
tendentious ideology; it is still a *sotie*, but of dimensions
and importance superior to that other pseudo-novel:
les Caves du Vatican, whose survival appears equally
certain.

What can we say about the comparison with the two
works whose precedent Gide invokes? *The Possessed?*
Les Faux Monnayeurs has indeed been called Gide's

Possessed. But we must admit that it does not work the same spell upon us which we cannot escape in reading the great Russian's masterpiece. No doubt Gide does not aim at such an effect, but this is also because he cannot attain it.

As for *l'Education sentimentale*, it was long regarded as a failure; that was a mistake, but not an absurd one; it was an error of narrow-mindedness resulting from the fact that the nature of the subject which justified this eccentric and protracted composition had not been understood. Of course Gide could easily turn this argument against us. But we have explicitly not reproached him for having invented a new perspective and having conceived an architecture in relation to it. We have reproached him for not having kept the promises his intention implied. Where do we find the transformation, which he announced, from real facts to imagined narrative, the metamorphosis effected by the novelist? Long as *les Faux Monnayeurs* is, it is still too short; missing from it is that novel of *les Faux Monnayeurs* which Edouard was supposed to write, or at least sizable fragments of that novel. He has given us only the latter's *Journal*, and he has used the latter either to record his ideas on the novel (it is Edouard's *Journal des Faux Monnayeurs*, different from Gide's), or to narrate some of the real events out of which Gide's novel is made—which directly contradicts Gide's initial intention; Edouard's *Journal* should not have encroached upon the narrative of reality, and part of the book's ambiguity is due to this unfortunate encroachment. On the other hand, what the work should have given us (those passages of Edouard's novel in which reality would have been transposed, and whose interesting comparison with the original facts presented elsewhere would have been the reader's delightful responsibility) Gide deprives us of altogether. One can scarcely make an exception for the fragment which Edouard uses to warn the straying Georges, and which is only a draft he finds unsatisfactory. All we can divine of such a process is found *outside* Gide's frame: we can compare with *les Faux Monnayeurs* those events which Gide borrowed from newspapers of the period or from his personal life, but these are merely fragments which do not afford the constant confrontation of nature and the writer's life with the novel's alchemy by which he transmutes them into a work of art. I submit that Gide himself has performed this transmutation; consequently that part of his work which is pure *récit* is admirable (as beautiful as in his perfect tales); but he has concealed, not spoiled but spirited away the second of his intentions which, according to him, was to be the principal one, for he has not given us the novel Edouard dreams of writing. He has escaped by a defeat, leading us to understand that Edouard was incapable of writing it. But then Edouard is no longer a novelist, or at least no longer that novelist who justified the interest Gide took in him and who gave *les Faux Monnayeurs* its true meaning. It mattered little that the reality from which Edouard started in order to compose his novel was in fact, a false reality already invented by Gide, for a painting is painted only by painting its model too, as in those works that show an artist in a studio perpetuating on canvas the features of a woman supposedly alive, but whom we see, in the frame, beside an easel holding her portrait. Gide's defeat consists precisely in painting beside the model an easel with its back to the spectator; even though he may show us the painter, brush in hand, he is cheating by not showing us what this painter can do.

More than *The Possessed* or *l'Education sentimentale*, *les Faux Monnayeurs* suggests one of those considerable works in which posterity prefers to seek the complexity of a great writer; works which, like *Wilhelm Meister*, failing by both excess and default, have not assumed the perfect continuity and movement of a masterpiece characteristic of a great genre. Like Goethe's thought, all proportions observed, Gide's is rich enough not to suffer from having occasionally overflowed the conditions of a classical art of which, fundamentally, it still remains a tributary.

A CHRONOLOGICAL LIST OF WORKS BY GIDE WHICH ARE DISCUSSED, MENTIONED, OR CITED IN THE TEXT. CONVENIENT EDITIONS OF GIDE'S WORKS IN TRANSLATION ARE GIVEN IN PARENTHESES.

1889–1949   *Journal*   (*Gide Journals*, Vol. I (1889–1924), Vol. II (1924–1949) edited by Justin O'Brien, Vintage Books, 1956)

1891   *les Cahiers d'André Walter*

1891   *le Traité du Narcisse*

1892   *les Poésies d'André Walter*

1893   *le Voyage d'Urien*   (*Urien's Travels*, in *New Directions 14*, 1952)

1893   *la Tentative amoureuse*

1893–1938   *Correspondance: Francis Jammes et André Gide*

1895   *Paludes*   (in *Marshlands* and *Prometheus Misbound*, New York, in *New Directions*, 1953)

1897   *les Nourritures terrestres*   (*Fruits of the Earth*, Alfred A. Knopf, Inc., 1949)

1899   *El Hadj ou le Traité du faux prophète*

1899   *Philoctète ou le Traité des trois morales*   (*Philoctetes*, in *My Theater*, Alfred A. Knopf, Inc.)

1899   *le Prométhée mal enchaîné*   (in *Marshlands* and *Prometheus Misbound*, New York, in *New Directions*, 1953)

1901   *le Roi Candaule*   (*King Candaules*, in *My Theater*, Alfred A. Knopf, Inc., 1952)

1902   *l'Immoraliste*   (*The Immoralist*, Vintage Books, 1954)

1903   *Prétextes*   (*Pretexts*, Meridian Books, 1959)

1903   *Saül* (*Saul*, in *My Theater*, Alfred A. Knopf, Inc., 1952)

1906   *Amyntas*

1907   *le Retour de l'enfant prodigue* (*The Return of the Prodigal Son*, Bantam Books, 1960)

1909   *la Porte étroite* (*Strait is the Gate*, Vintage Books, 1956)

1911   *Isabelle* ("Isabelle", in *Two Symphonies*, Alfred A. Knopf, Inc., 1949)

1912   *Bethsabé*

1914   *les Caves du Vatican* (*Lafcadio's Adventures*, Vintage Books, 1960)

1919   *la Symphonie pastorale* (*The Pastoral Symphony* in *Two Symphonies*, Alfred A. Knopf, Inc., 1949)

1923   *Dostoevsky* (*Dostoevsky*, in *New Directions*, 1949)

1924   *Corydon* (*Corydon*, Noonday Press, 1961)

1926   *les Faux Monnayeurs* (*The Counterfeiters* and *Journal of the Counterfeiters*, Alfred A. Knopf, Inc., 1951)

1926   *le Journal des Faux Monnayeurs* (in *The Counterfeiters* and *Journal of the Counterfeiters*, Alfred A. Knopf, Inc., 1951)

1926   *Si le Grain ne meurt . . .* (*If It Die*, Vintage Books, 1961)

1929   *Un Esprit non prévenu*

1929   *l'École des Femmes*, 1930 *Robert*, 1936 *Geneviève* (*The School for Wives, Robert* [and] *Geneviève*, Alfred A. Knopf, 1950)

1930   *l'Affaire Redureau*

1931   *Oedipe* (*Oedipus*, in *Two Legends*, Vintage Books, 1958)

1931   *Divers*

1934   *Perséphone* (*Persephone*, in *My Theater*, Alfred A. Knopf, Inc., 1952)

1935 *les Nouvelles Nourritures* (in *Fruits of the Earth*, Alfred A. Knopf, Inc., 1949)
1942 *le Treizième Arbre*
1949 *Robert ou l'Intérêt général*